199

A Passion for Narrative

A GUIDE FOR WRITING FICTION

A Passion for Narrative

A Guide for
Writing Fiction

Jack Hodgins

St. Martin's Press
New York

Library of Congress Cataloging-in-Publication Data

Hodgins, Jack.
A passion for narrative / Jack Hodgins.
p.   cm.
ISBN 0-312-11042-1
1. Fiction—Technique.   I. Title.
PN3355.H56   1994
808.3—dc20   94-712   CIP

First published in Canada by McClelland & Stewart Inc.

First U.S. Edition: May 1994
10 9 8 7 6 5 4 3 2 1

Contents

To Earle Birney and Jack Cameron,
with gratitude for their passionate dedication
to both teaching and literature

A Passion for Narrative
A GUIDE FOR WRITING FICTION

The Natural Storyteller: An Introduction

꼱

There are three points of view from which a writer can be considered: he may be considered as a storyteller, as a teacher, and as an enchanter. A major writer combines these three – storyteller, teacher, enchanter – but it is the enchanter in him that predominates and makes him a major writer.

To the storyteller we turn for entertainment, for mental excitement of the simplest kind, for emotional participation, for the pleasure of travelling in some remote region in space or time. A slightly different though not necessarily higher mind looks for the teacher in the writer. Propagandist, moralist, prophet – this is the rising sequence. We may go to the teacher not only for moral education but also for direct knowledge, for simple facts.... Finally, and above all, a great writer is always a great enchanter, and it is here that we come to the really exciting part, when we try to grasp the individual magic of his genius and to study the style, the imagery, the pattern of his novels or poems.

(Vladimir Nabokov, *Lectures on Literature*)

"Flames surrounded us – remember that? Smoke, and howling wind! I never felt such heat. You had to keep something wet against your mouth just to breathe."

"Fire come roaring down off Constitution Hill and across the top of the timber, right through all them farms up Howard Road –"

"Cows went crazy. Stampeded!"

"Horses had better sense, they found a swamp and stood in it right through the night."

Sometimes we could hear with an ear to a knothole in the attic bedroom wall. Sometimes we had to creep out and sit at the top of the stairs. Gradually, we slid down, one step at a time, to listen in the shadow of the landing. The family had gathered in the living room – my mother and father, my father's brothers and their wives, my father's sisters and their husbands. This could be any occasion – Christmas, a funeral, an ordinary Saturday night. Sooner or later they would start to remember, would tell one another stories they already knew. How two brothers blew up the schoolyard privy and almost got themselves expelled. How the Old Man ran away from Ontario and met Ma as he was fleeing west through Nebraska. How the worst forest fire in the history of Vancouver Island came down off the mountains and surrounded the stump ranch and threatened to wipe the whole family off the face of the earth.

"You think the Old Man woulda let us run for our lives? He put us to work on the roof."

"Some of us down the well. Dipping gunny sacks in the water. Somebody ran them up to you others on the roof. Who was it?"

"Then that poor Clifford boy died."

"We didn't know that then!"

"We didn't know at the time but we knew afterwards. He was on his way up the lane, running for help. Cut off when the wind changed."

"Who remembers dawn? The barn was all smouldering rafters –"

"The worst was, you could see the burnt bodies of the cattle lying around. Deer too. It looked like some kind of smoking hell. I sat down on the roof and cried."

"We all did."

"We did not. Old Man would've booted our backsides. We had to get down and start cleaning up. That old son-of-a-gun didn't know anything but *work!*"

This was the sort of thing I listened to: uncles and aunts reliving their shared childhood. They told the stories to themselves – no other audience was needed. Tale after tale went by, but came back to go by again. The fire roared, the Old Man shouted orders, once again Granny Hodgins saved her canary. (This house did not go up in flames, but three others had been struck by lightning and burned to the ground. She'd escaped every time, running outside with her canary held high in its cage.)

Eventually my brother and I would creep upstairs to bed. Under the blankets, with the aid of a flashlight, I drew pictures of flames and smoke and terrified cattle dying, figures beating out sparks on a roof, a frightened boy fleeing for his life down a country road.

"I don't think we're going to make it!" cried one of the figures.

The Old Man roared: "Work harder, you useless bums, or I'll take the boots to ya!"

The balloons of talk grew larger than the awkward figures who spoke them. Narrative broke free and spilled down the page, took up pages of its own, filled in the details no one had ever mentioned – I imagined them, I had seen the place and run my hands over the blackened stumps, I had almost begun to believe I'd been there myself. I drew, wrote, dreamed – creating for myself a place in a story from which I had been excluded.

I suppose I've been doing something like that ever since: remembering other people's stories, living in other people's skins, spinning out of words the magic of a fictional universe.

"What an astonishing world this is!" those relatives' voices imply, when I remember them. "It's amazing we're still alive!" Behind all the near tragedies, real tragedies, epic struggles, and community celebrations that got out of hand, I hear the constant undercurrent of their laughter. Always, beneath the retroactive horror and relief and amazement, there was the comic wonder and almost uncontainable joy experienced in the very act of telling. It didn't matter that the others had heard it before. You told it because you'd found a way of putting it into words. You told it because this was a way of saying: *Aren't we poor humans something!*

That I drew as well as wrote the stories was perfectly natural – the comic strips were my first literature. When it came time to start school, the promise held out was that I would be taught how to read. If that was the case, I believed that school was quite unnecessary. I already knew how to read – or so I told my parents. In the attic of our farmhouse, I'd discovered stack after stack of coloured weekend comics left behind by a former owner and I'd spent many afternoons poring over them. *The Katzenjammer Kids, Mutt and Jeff, Popeye.* By staring long enough, I eventually figured out what the characters must be saying to one another in order to make some sense of their actions. Why go to school when I'd already learned how to read?

My parents soon set me straight. "Those funnies aren't in English! The people who lived here had them sent from Finland! What good will reading Finnish be to you?"

I hadn't learned to read the language I spoke. What I'd learned to read instead was facial expressions, body language, and action. As it turned out, these would be useful skills for the writer of fiction one day, but they didn't help me avoid going to school.

Once school had taught me to read English, I read whatever I could get my hands on – which eventually would be just about everything from *Tobacco Road* to *Scaramouche* and the novels of Zane Grey. I had my favourites: *Toby Tyler*, *Big Red*, *The Savage Gentleman*, *The Bridge of San Luis Rey*, *The Red Pony*. (I read *The Red Pony* under the covers by flashlight. This one was passed around the schoolyard, the country kids' idea of a dirty book. Nobody told us it was literature.) Books were forms of magic, once you could read them. From the moment I'd learned to read, I wanted to be one of those people who put magic between the covers!

In high school, the young English teacher who had introduced us to the poetry of Robert Frost and the essays of Roderick Haig-Brown persuaded the school board to buy five copies of *The Old Man and the Sea* for the school library. Then – perhaps he wasn't sure we'd make use of them otherwise – he read one of those copies aloud. Sometime during that reading – which he strung out over several days, as I recall – a longing that had been with me all my life suddenly took on sharper focus: I would devote my life to the writing of serious fiction.

Wanting is not the same as doing. I was nearly thirty years old – with several rejected stories and novels behind me and dozens of rejection slips that encouraged me to keep on trying – before it occurred to me that, since I couldn't count on finding in the larger world the sort of willing audience my aunts and uncles enjoyed in one another, there must be certain secrets I ought to learn if I wanted my stories to be read. I didn't know that other would-be writers put in apprenticeships; I thought (in my isolation and insecurity) that if publishers weren't falling all over themselves to publish you by your twenty-fifth birthday you just didn't have what it took – you ought to quit fooling yourself, do something sensible with your life.

Still, the dream deserved a little more effort – just in case. I read the very few books on writing I could find in the local library, and carefully reread a number of stories by writers I most admired, trying to figure out how they had achieved their effect. I don't remember now what I learned from the exercise, but the next story I wrote was accepted by a literary magazine, and stories thereafter began to find editors who liked them.

Perhaps the most important result of that time spent in search of the fiction writer's secrets was the realization of just how important it was that I learn to do this well: the passion for writing stories was so powerful in me that if I didn't learn what I needed to learn I would be doomed to write bad stories for the rest of my life.

This book tries to set out some of the things I have subsequently begun to understand – with no small measure of hard work, but with joy and gratitude as well. In the years of working with young writers who possess a similar passion for the narrative act, I have been forced to find ways of communicating something of what I have learned. By publishing these pages I realize that I will not be able to follow along explaining myself, and that I will find it impossible to communicate any change of opinion. On the other hand, I may no longer receive so many letters from former students saying, "Do you still have a copy of that handout you gave us back in 1982?"

There were plenty of reasons to avoid doing this book. I have always been aware, for instance, that many successful writers believe (and loudly proclaim) that "writing cannot be taught," and of course I agree with them if they mean that "writing superbly cannot be learned by following instructions." Years of working with students have shown me, however, that teaching can be thought of as the process of arranging things so that learning can happen. And writers can be helped to become better. This cannot be accomplished so effectively between the covers of a book as it can in discussions between teacher and student, especially when they are armed with the specific successes and failures of particular stories to talk about. Nevertheless, something of the process can be approximated.

With every new story the writer is once again a beginner, faced with the task of having to learn all over again how to write. Knowing this does not bolster the sort of confidence needed for advising others. Furthermore, I'm all too conscious of how wide is the gap between my own fiction and my initial and continuing hopes for it. I know I will go on changing my mind, I will go on learning and discovering new things about the mysterious business of writing fiction, and will curse myself for not having learned them in time to include them within these pages. I will drive my editor crazy with additions and deletions right up until he screams "Stop! We've already gone to the printers!" and then I will still go on muttering to myself and making notes and wishing that I could have another chance.

None of these reasons seems to have deterred me, however. Perhaps this is because of the pleasure I have had in working with dedicated young writers for more than twenty years, in watching their writing improve from story to story and from draft to draft, and in receiving letters and copies of their books in later years. Or, perhaps it is simply that my own passion for all aspects of narrative makes it impossible for me to keep my thoughts to myself.

What to Expect of This Book

• You'll find no chapter telling you why you should take up the practice of writing fiction. That is because there are already plenty of people writing fiction and I don't want to be blamed if you discover that no one will publish yours. If you aren't already passionately eager to write fiction, you probably shouldn't read any further. It's going to be a lot of work.

• Even though I would be the first to acknowledge that every story arrives in its own way, and that every writer approaches material in a different manner, the chapters of this book have been organized in a fashion that may imply a recommended sequence. *Some* kind of order had to be imposed or you would be wading through chaos. If I knew of a way to discuss all these matters at the same time without causing confusion, I would have done so.

• Some passages may sound as though I am prescribing. Consider that I'm only talking to myself, thinking out loud. None of these thoughts suggests rules, or even a consistent philosophical position. This is neither "How *I* write" nor "How *you* should write" but "Some thoughts about necessary skills if you want to write."

• A sequence of writing exercises is included at the end of Chapters 2 through 10. Don't just read them and think, "A person should try this sometime." They are meant to be *done*. Anyone can sit around and think about writing. Real writers write. People who seriously want to learn how to write don't just read books about it, they practise. These exercises are an opportunity for you to practise in an organized manner.

• I have tried to put aside personal taste and write what follows in a manner that will make it of some interest and use to fiction writers of all types. Whether you are inclined to realism, minimalism, fantasy, science fiction, or metafictional postmodern deconstructionism, as a beginning writer trying to find a way into your own stories you can benefit from a careful examination of these materials – even if you may one day find some of them to be no longer of any real interest to you.

• That I have not included a discussion of critical theory or literary ideology is not meant to suggest these are of little interest or value to the fiction writer. Besides being familiar with superior works of fiction, the writer should also become aware of ways in which contemporary writer-critics are exploring the relationship between writer and reader. There is little point in shopping for a theory to "adopt" for the sake of fashion or comradeship, however. I believe the only theory worth having is the one you work out for yourself in a manner that is consistent with the way you see the world – even if, in the process, your view of the world may be altered. But this is not the business of a book devoted mainly to an exploration of skills.

• You won't be surprised to see that the book includes plenty of examples, but you may be surprised to see that some of them are by writers unknown to you. This doesn't mean that I'm suggesting you turn to second-rate writers for your models. Some years ago the large publishers in the United States and Great Britain carved the English-speaking world in two, ensuring that Canadian bookstores would be filled with American books and that Australian and New Zealand bookshops would be filled with British books – virtually guaranteeing that Canadian, Australian, and New Zealand readers would have little access to the books written by the writers in one another's country. Some writers have crossed this invisible border, of course, but many books by some wonderful writers have been confined to less than half the English-speaking world. My hope is that some of these quoted passages will not only serve as specific models within the book's context but will also excite your interest enough to send you chasing off after books by writers who interest you. Brief notes on the authors are provided at the back of the book to help you find them.

A Word about the Format

The fragmentary appearance of these pages is deliberate. I haven't tried and simply failed to write a fluidly continuous text that would be a relaxing and interesting "good read." Such books can be inspirational but not necessarily useful. The format (with its stops and starts, its lists and columns, its challenges and exercises) is intended to encourage a certain approach and to imply certain premises:

1. that there is no beginning, end, or proper sequence for the act of writing fiction, or for learning to write it
2. that there is no such thing as complete knowledge about writing fiction, nor a complete explanation about any aspect of it
3. that the content of this book is intended to be just barely full enough to give you plenty to think about, but not so full as to do your thinking for you
4. that the book is intended to be revisited through any of its many doors as often as it serves your purposes, and
5. that learning to write fiction is not a matter of accumulating knowledge or skills in some sequentially developmental way but of *preparing yourself to build a new writer out of yourself and out of your relationship to new material every time you prepare for a new story or novel.*

A Final Premise: The Natural Storyteller and the Maker of Artifice

Like most other people, writers carry a network of tensions within them. The fiction writer, I believe, experiences a constant tension between "the natural storyteller" and "the maker of artifice," to borrow a phrase used by critic Joseph W. Reed, Jr, in his study of William Faulkner's techniques.

On the one hand, there is the love for narration – an interest in characters, a delight in surprises, a taste for crises, a joy in discovering and revealing what happens next. This may be thought of as the novelist's reservoir, in which we may find:

- anecdotes
- snatches of dialogue
- moments of crisis
- haunting images
- bits and pieces of character
- causes and effects
- interesting places
- archetypal figures
- an urge to capture people's complete attention and rivet them with "and then . . ."

This reservoir is the combined result of imagination, experience, memory, and love of "story."

On the other hand, the writer is aware of fiction as art, and of the writer's necessity to become a maker of artifice. This requires the acquisition of skills for:

- ordering events
- calculating and creating effects
- choosing the most effective point of view
- knowing when and how to begin, when and how to end

- managing the reader's changing relationship with and understanding of characters
- turning language to a desired effect

These skills can be discovered from the careful study of writers one
admires, from an effort to understand the new needs peculiar to
each new story, and from constant practice and experimentation.

Some student writers claim to be all "natural storyteller." They
say this so you will believe that they are born geniuses. Sometimes,
of course, they may be right. Except in inspired cases, however, most
of the results are noticeably difficult to read, betraying a disregard
(if not contempt) for the reader. When they fail, these writers are
puzzled that the reader did not feel the same as they did about the
narrative. They don't understand or care that it is up to them to *create* the story's effect upon its readers.

Some student writers appear to be all learned technique. When a
great deal of learned technique is brought to bear upon a paucity of
deeply felt material, the result is often a story that feels manufactured. It may have "nothing wrong with it" but it often rings hollow,
seems to be about nothing important, and makes the reader think
"So what?" or "I don't think that story was worth the writing."

What you learn here about narrative technique remains merely
theoretical unless you are also learning how to dip into that all-
important reservoir for those elements that make up your material,
elements that make you feel passionate about telling a story.

The beginning writer who thinks that it is necessary to learn everything discussed in this book before beginning a story may find that
writing a story has become impossible – too much to know, too
many models to live up to, too many things to keep in mind all at
once! To avoid the paralysis of the self-conscious centipede, I will
suggest here what I will emphasize later – that although a casual
reading through the book may serve to give you ideas for stories and

provoke an excitement about ways in which the stories may be told, a closer look will be more useful during the rewriting of your stories, when the editor in you (tied up and muzzled during first drafts) can be set loose.

> The only way, I think, to learn to write short stories is to write them, and then to try to discover what you have done. The time to think of technique is when you've actually got the story in front of you.
>
> (Flannery O'Connor, "Writing Short Stories," in *Mystery and Manners*)

Getting Started:
Finding Stories Meant for You

૪ઌ

But the wide creative vision, though no fragment of human experience can appear wholly empty to it, yet seeks by instinct those subjects in which some phase of our common plight stands forth dramatically and typically, subjects which, in themselves, are a kind of summary or foreshortening of life's dispersed and inconclusive occurrences.

. . . But whatever the central episode or situation chosen by the novelist, his tale will be about only just so much of it as he reacts to. A gold mine is worth nothing unless the owner has the machinery for extracting the ore, and each subject must be considered first in itself, and next in relation to the novelist's power of extracting from it what it contains.

(Edith Wharton, *The Writing of Fiction*)

Recognizing Good Story Material When You See It

What is this world if not an organism that lives by the endless interweaving of stories? From the fiction writer's point of view, the world is constantly offering up material rich in story potential. Overheard conversations, anecdotes told by friends, someone observed on the street, ideas suggested by the mood of a place, memories of people who have touched our lives, newspaper accounts of conflicts between the champions of opposing ideals – our days are filled with these possibilities. It is important, however, to recognize promising material when it appears – especially those story ideas that are suited to our particular tastes and capabilities.

Sometimes just about everything a good story needs can be represented, in miniature, in a simple newspaper account. Consider the following news item.

DEATH ENCOUNTERS COUPLE LOOKING FOR FLYING SAUCER
GRAND MARAIS, Minn. (AP) – Drawn by messages from "some higher power," Gerald Flach and Laverne Landis drove last month from St. Paul, Minn., to the snowy, frozen wilderness of northeastern Minnesota to wait for a flying saucer, authorities say. For more than four weeks they waited in their snowbound compact car, eating only vitamins and drinking water from nearby Loon Lake.

On Monday, a motorist found Flach, 38, an electrician from West St. Paul, semiconscious on Gunflint Trail, 65 kilometres northwest of Grand Marais. Rescue squad members found Landis, 48, dead in the front seat of the car a few hundred metres off the main road. An autopsy determined she died from a combination of hypothermia, dehydration and starvation. Flach, described by friends as having becoming obsessed with UFOs in recent months, was taken to Cook County North Shore Hospital in Grand Marais, where he remained Thursday.

"Flach said he had been receiving messages through Ms Landis from some higher power," Redfield said. "The most recent message directed them to go to the end of the Gunflint Trail and await further messages. These people kind of believed in flying saucers."

Here is enough for a fiction writer's imagination to create any number of stories. The account gives you intriguing characters whose motives you might want to explore. It suggests the opportunity for these characters to have conflicting emotions about what they are going through. It offers a setting that becomes an actor in the drama. It offers a glimpse into an approach to reality that could be imagined causing conflict within a larger community. It leaves certain questions unanswered, so that the writer's imagination can continue the story. It allows for a variety of approaches – to one writer this might be an opportunity for a serious psychological study of two personalities under pressure, while to another it might be the beginning of a science fiction adventure (perhaps the woman was indeed taken away in the saucer but left her body behind). Another writer might find comic potential in it.

The basic elements of the story allow for varying degrees of conflict. For instance, one writer might be interested only in the internal struggle experienced by the character who has terrible private doubts about this venture. Another may wish to expand that struggle to a conflict between the individuals – one wants to turn back, one wants to stay. A third writer may wish to expand that struggle even further to include a split community, some of whom believe this couple's reports and support their effort, and some of whom would try to stop them from making the rendezvous. And of course it is also possible to see that struggle between two groups as a metaphorical struggle between values, or ideals. Interesting conflicts often have this sort of potential for expansion.

Recognizing good story potential in an anecdote or a news item is not the same as recognizing the story elements that should find their fictional life in your hands rather than in someone else's.

Examine the following account for elements with potential for a good story. Keeping in mind Edith Wharton's warning quoted at the beginning of this chapter, consider which elements within it attract you most strongly. Can you imagine alterations to this particular "gold mine" that would allow you to consider it one for which you have the necessary power for "extracting its ore"? Spend some time thinking about this, since you will later be invited to write passages suggested by this account.

MINER'S LATEST CLAIM BACKFIRES

FIREWEED, B.C. – A down-on-his-luck miner was thwarted by his lover's respect for the law in what police describe as a case of broken dreams and broken hearts.

The miner, Curt Milligan, 25, works a private claim near his isolated cabin north of the little mountain town of Nugget. On Friday morning he rode his motorbike down out of the hills and crossed the rain-swollen Borderline River on a hand-rope raft. He then walked into Nugget (pop 1700) and robbed the Royal Bank of $30,000.

"I thought he was joking," said witness Miriam Marsden, a local florist who was in the bank at the time. "But then I saw his knife."

"I had no intention of taking a hostage," Milligan said in a statement to the court. "But something got into me. Maybe it was the witnesses – I didn't want them calling the police until I was safely across the river, so I took Mrs Lindstrom along."

Milligan and his hostage, bank manager Jane Lindstrom, 52, did not get safely across the river, however. The raft rope broke when they were in midstream, and they were washed several kilometres down river. They finally came to a stop against the river bank not far from the farm owned by the parents of Milligan's fiancée, Lily Cates, 22. Milligan and Lindstrom, who had been slightly injured, found their way to the farmhouse where Cates, a clerk at the local assayer's office, helped to bandage the bank manager's arm.

"He told me what he'd done," Ms Cates told the court. "He said he'd done it for me, to buy nice things, but I told him it was wrong, he had to turn himself in. At first he wouldn't believe me. So Mrs Lindstrom and I grabbed him to take the knife away."

Milligan fought back, breaking two chairs and smashing dishes, but the two women overwhelmed him and tied him up with rope. "I'm not very strong myself," said Cates, "but Mrs Lindstrom is a big woman."

In provincial court this Monday, Milligan was sentenced to three years for armed robbery and two years concurrent for abduction. In passing sentence, Judge W. Chalmers noted that although the money was fully recovered, he wished to make this case an example to others.

"Things have been going bad for me lately," Milligan later told reporters. "I can't believe things went this far. All I wanted was enough money to buy a few things to cheer myself up, so the place would be nice enough for Lily to marry me. She keeps putting me off. But I didn't intend to let things get out of hand, I didn't mean for things to go so far. I feel terrible about it."

When asked if the engagement was off, Lily Cates refused to comment.

Why Writers Write

Wright Morris suggests that when he sits down to write a new novel he is setting out to discover how the world is doing out there. Walker Percy claims to know already how the world is doing: not very well. Something has gone wrong, he suggests, and it is the novelist's job to act as a diagnostic physician and find out what the problem is.

Anne Tyler says, "I write because I want more than one life; I insist on a wider selection. It's greed, plain and simple." John Updike says, "There has to be an irritation that makes you want to cry out. All fiction is, in a funny way, protest fiction."

> *With me it has something to do with the fight against death, the feeling that we lose everything every day, and writing is a way of convincing yourself perhaps that you're doing something about this. . . . There's that feeling about the – I was talking about the external world, the sights and sounds and smells – I can't stand to let go without some effort at this, at capturing them in words, and of course I don't see why one has to do that. You can experience things directly without feeling that you have to do that, but I suppose I just experience things finally when I do get them into words.*

(Alice Munro, in *Eleven Canadian Novelists*)

Recently, a class of fiction students at the University of Victoria discussed their reasons for wanting to write fiction. Some proclaimed a love of story, some a love of words. One young woman confessed that she had really wanted to be an inventor but when an invention failed to gain acceptance for a science fair about the same time as a teacher falsely accused her of plagiarizing the first story she'd ever written, she decided to give up one kind of inventing for another.

For the man who sat beside her, however, story writing was a way of handling fear – fear of what he would be doing if he wasn't writing. Five years earlier, he said, he hadn't been able to write a complete sentence; nor did he care. He didn't read. Racing forms, spread sheets, and sporting journals mattered. Losing was his big fear – he was frightened of being a loser. In prison he had had time to think about this – banned from his beloved racetrack for life, exiled from the country of his choice, and aware of a twenty-year sentence hanging over his head, he started to read. Then he started to write. He won a prison writing contest. Then he was aware that prisoners lying in all the other cells were reading his story. Something magic, he said, had happened. Writing for him had taken on some of the same sort of excitement as he'd experienced while watching a horse in his care cross the finish line.

Some writers credit the admiration or envy inspired by specific published works. Many remember a teacher who exposed them to the world of books. One student spoke first of his kindergarten teacher, "a big woman, whose wide corduroy skirt enveloped the tiny seat she perched on like some great amoeba. She opened a book, raising her eyes to quiet the morning, and started to read." For him, writing was a way to "recover the feeling of each morning sitting down upon the carpet when Mrs Ellis opened her book." He explained further in writing. "The final book on the reading list of what was probably to be my last literature course before I ventured down the path of silicon chips or busted organs was *The Poorhouse Fair* [by John Updike]. More than anything else, the novel frightened me. After all the pages and pages of titillation and distraction I had turned over the years, I realized that this was what writing can be, what writing can do. It revealed that we live in a world of missed connections, of reaching out from our solitude for an intimacy that will at last justify the painful stretching of the reach, though never quite grasping it. All the characters in the novel . . . were so strikingly real in their struggles, so frustratingly proud and ultimately alone. Yet despite all their missed connections, their solitude is somehow transcended in the end for the reader, for me, *in* me, by Updike's frightening ability to pull them together in this one slim book. I knew that this was the way back to those mornings around Mrs Ellis's knees – that I would have to struggle for the connections as Updike had, as we all must, and perhaps fail as magnificently as his characters will every time the book is opened" (David Leach).

> *[Writing] is simply a way of life before all other ways, a way to observe the world and to move through life, among human beings, and to record it all above all and to shape it, to give it sense, and to express something of myself in it. Writing is something I cannot imagine living without, nor scarcely would want to.*
>
> (William Goyen, in *The Writer's Chapbook*)

How Stories Announce Themselves

I think of my writer's reservoir – all memory and imagination and hoarded experience – as a kind of private aquarium whose thick waters teem with a wondrous population of unusual creatures, all constantly in motion:

- memories of personal experiences
- aspects of people recalled or encountered
- anecdotes told by friends and acquaintances
- overheard contests of wills
- stories and novels read and admired
- snatches of dialogue
- haunting images recalled
- places that continue to fascinate
- archetypal figures that haunt
- feared anticipated scenarios
- dreams
- events read about in newspapers and magazines

Swimming past, circling, and swimming past again, they contemplate my presence like malevolent sharks, or cheerful porpoises, or comical blowfish, while they anticipate the moment they will swim to the surface and throw themselves into my world. When they do, as often as not it will be for the purpose of nudging a story into life. Anything might do it; a story can begin with anything, however small, so long as it fascinates or worries or puzzles me enough:

- a person, a group of people
- an event
- an idea
- a place
- a voice heard, remembered, or imagined
- a metaphor

Any of these might stimulate the imagination into story, but often a single element, a single nudge may not be enough by itself. *Why is this person hanging around, just standing there with her suitcase? Why isn't she doing something?* Sooner or later a second element will present itself – equally puzzling at first – which may eventually be seen to have some connection to the first. *Ah! This tiny village at the end of the road – whose rickety buildings cling to the edge of the land, above the sea, suggesting desperation to me when I first saw it years ago – is where this woman has come to. She doesn't know anyone. She has just stepped down from a bus. She has run to the end of the world.* In my experience, the moment of recognizing connections amongst a number of potential ideas is the moment where some kind of explosion occurs, where fuzzy characters come clear and a story begins to take on life.

It is not so for everyone. I've talked to writers who keep a file of newspaper clippings and daily go looking in it for story ideas, putting this clipping next to that one. I've talked to writers who speak of dipping into the well of memory, almost as though hypnotized, and coming up with the lumber to build a story. (And why should a well not store lumber?) And I have talked with writers who stare at the ceiling, or out the window, until an idea presents itself, and to others who sit and write words and word combinations until the words themselves start telling, and to others who pit voice and point of view against a narrative situation until they find a workable combination. I suppose I have done all of these things myself, at one time or another, to tempt those creatures to the surface. For most writers, whatever the exercise that precedes the story, there comes the moment when the initiating impulse – whether it be character or events or ideas – has triggered a fluttering throb of excitement somewhere in the diaphragm that will not subside – increases rather – until the story has been lived through, written through, dreamed through to its end. At least some of that excitement comes from the urgent desire to see what manner of creature this thing will insist on becoming.

> The thing which prompts you to sit down and write must be something which haunts you.
> (Janet Frame, in *In the Same Room*)

Is There Anything We Must or Must Not Write About?

Some writers insist that you have no right to tell stories from a point of view that is not your own, that if you are a woman you have no business writing stories about men, and vice versa, that if you are white you have no business writing stories about people whose skin is not white. (There are some who would suggest that if you are both white and a male you have no business writing anything at all – your predecessors have hogged the stage for too long.)

Margaret Atwood has addressed this situation in her introduction to *Best American Short Stories 1989*.

> Not only does [this view] condemn as thieves and imposters such writers as George Eliot, James Joyce, Emily Brontë, and William Faulkner . . . it is also inhibiting to the imagination in a fundamental way. It's only a short step from saying we can't write from the point of view of an "other" to saying we can't read that way either, and from there to the

position that no one can really understand anyone else, so we might as
well stop trying. . . . Surely the delight and the wonder come not from
who tells the story but from what the story tells, and how.

(Margaret Atwood, Introduction to *Best American Short Stories*
1989)

Some will tell you that you have an obligation to lend your writing talent to some worthy Cause – to make us all furious about the destruction of the rainforests, to fill us with indignation about the treatment of the Inuit of the eastern Arctic, to urge us to raise an army and free the prisoners of some South American country. These are honourable goals, worthy of a novelist's attention – and certainly writers must write about matters they care deeply about – but fiction that is dedicated primarily to convincing the reader of the rightness of a single point of view is too often more interested in persuasion than in truth.

The Australian novelist Shirley Hazzard and the Canadian novelist Gabrielle Roy have both recorded their response to those who demand the dedication of fiction to a political agenda.

Philistinism used to dress itself up as patriotism. Now, I suppose, it
seeks some other form of self-righteousness. It would be madness to
reject the highest products of humanism – of genius, of civilisation itself
– because, in going beyond the confines of prejudice, they cannot be
made to serve some theory. I feel that art wastes its breath when it con-
tends with such arguments, which don't stem from thought or princi-
ple, but from envy, self-dramatisation, ill will, ignorance. Art that
addresses itself to some objective other than truth in human affairs
ceases to be truthful. Whoever is concerned for the wise conduct of the
world, must first want the truth.

(Shirley Hazzard, interviewed in *Island,* issue 50)

Engagement is a very important démarche d'esprit, *but one must*
understand what engagement is. If it's a political engagement, all very

well – at certain times, perhaps, in history – but it's a very dangerous one, because it can obscure your view and lead you to a false testimony. The main engagement of the writer is towards truthfulness; therefore he must keep his mind and his judgement free. Each time he can be engaged only with all the facts, and in all truthfulness, and after having seen everything all around him.

(Gabrielle Roy, in *Conversations with Canadian Novelists 2*)

While these questions are worth our consideration, we should be very careful about accepting someone else's notion of what we ought to be doing with our time and talent. Are some areas of human interest more important than others, more worthy of our attention? Was Jane Austen wasting her time writing novels of family life, romance, and the social expectations of her day rather than sending her characters off into the midst of the wars or political intrigues that were then convulsing Napoleon's Europe?

Rather than wonder if she ought to throw a war or a revolution into her next book, Helen Garner says,

What I know about is domesticity, about marriage and families and children, so that's what I write about and therefore a lot of my events take place in people's houses. Anyway, I was feeling particularly bad about this one day, I was walking along the street thinking, "My God, my scope, it's so small, it's so small," and I looked in the window of a print shop and they had that Van Gogh picture of the inside of his bedroom. I stood there and looked at it and I thought, "That's a wonderful painting and everyone knows it's a wonderful painting, and what is it? It's only got a chair and a bed. It's a painting of somebody's bedroom, their own bedroom." I found that very encouraging. There's no way you can know if your own work's important, you do it because you like it and it's the only thing that makes you happy.

(Helen Garner, in *Yacker*)

How Do Writers Write?

As I begin writing a novel I have a general idea of what the story is going
to be. I have some trajectories in mind, that is, the chronology of the
action. One character starts here and finishes there, for example. I have
this kind of information about the characters, a general outline of the
story. But I never respect this outline, this plan. I need some general
scheme, but I know that I will change it in many ways. What I enjoy in
writing a novel is to discover the possibilities of a story.
(Mario Vargas Llosa, *A Writer's Reality*)

Writers who insist on working from a plan will often admit, with
Vargas Llosa, that it is necessary to be prepared to alter the plan or
even to abandon it. John Braine suggests a scheme for arriving at
such a plan: begin by writing a simple five-hundred-word synopsis,
the briefest of guides to a story line, before attempting the first draft.
In writing the first draft, he suggests (evoking Hemingway) that
nothing matters but to finish it. Never go back, never revise. When
the first draft is finished, he suggests reducing it to a summary, a
condensed version of the story, of no more than two thousand
words. "The best method is to write the summary of the novel again
and again until you've got a credible story" (John Braine, *Writing a*
Novel). Even then, he suggests reducing that refined summary to a
synopsis before beginning a second draft. The purpose of all this
reducing and rewriting of the condensed version is to ensure that in
subsequent drafts you are working with a story line that has already
been tested for weaknesses, inconsistencies, gaps in logic, and
impossibilities.

Getting Started

Many writers find getting started the hardest part. By "getting started" they sometimes mean beginning a new project. Margaret Laurence said that she came into a book with incredible difficulty. "I do everything possible not to begin until it becomes absolutely impossible to evade any longer, that is, the torture of writing becomes less than the torture of not writing" (Margaret Laurence, in *Eleven Canadian Novelists*).

Often, just beginning a new day's writing is as difficult as beginning a new project. Interviews with writers are filled with catalogues of stalling techniques (washing dishes, sharpening pencils, staring at the phone and willing it to ring) and with devices to overcome the horror or fear of the blank page (stopping work in the middle of a sentence so that it's necessary to finish that sentence the next day, rereading and revising yesterday's work, pretending that it isn't "real" writing but only "making notes"). All writers seem to agree that it is important to be at the desk, or at least in the right room, ready to go. Mordecai Richler says that there are some days when he finds it impossible to begin, yet he will spend his four hours in his office anyway. "I may read magazines, I may do a crossword puzzle or check all the baseball averages or get some work done; there are days when it goes and days when it doesn't go. But I think I have to go every day in order to earn the good days" (Mordecai Richler, in *Eleven Canadian Novelists*).

The difficulty in beginning may be caused by simple laziness, a fear of discovering that the story will not continue revealing itself as it did yesterday, an uncertainty about the decision to follow one possible story direction rather than another (options diminishing), or a crippling sense of one's own terrible responsibility not to disappoint, to be *good*.

Approaches to beginning a story will be dealt with in a later chapter. Difficulty with just beginning a day's writing may be lessened by eliminating any sense of obligation to be writing something to be proud of. Until you have completed a first draft of a story or novel, you have no responsibility but to entertain yourself, explore your material, and follow your characters around. Yet, beginning prematurely even what you think of as a "first draft" may also be intimidating.

Often it is a good idea to resist starting on a first draft of a story so long as you have nothing more than "an idea" or "a character." Instead, I suggest you write "pieces" – bits of description, snatches of dialogue, notes on ideas, and so on. Do this until one of the pieces catches fire and you can't bear not to keep going, or else until staring at all these pieces causes an explosion of insight, some new understanding that comes from the connections amongst them, giving you a richer sense of what you're up to.

Eventually, amongst those bits and pieces, there will be some half-imagined people beginning to take on life. They may be totally invented, they may be imitations of real people you've observed, they may be people manufactured out of bits and pieces collected in your notebook. One of them, or some of them, will start to haunt you. Puzzle you. Intrigue you. "What makes *him* tick?" "Why do I keep thinking about *her*? Where did she come from anyway?" Since writing will include both *discovering* these people for yourself and *revealing* them to your reader, it may be a good idea to hold off writing anything except more bits and pieces until you stumble upon something that jolts you – frightens you, alarms you, startles you, delights you, makes you laugh. "Okay, now *you're* someone I'm going to *pursue!*"

For some, this may be the time to pause, to let those characters walk around in the imagination, to visit locations that may be associated with the settings of the story, to do whatever research might be necessary so that you know as much as your characters about their jobs, their interests, their neighbourhood.

Once a story idea or a cast of characters has seized her attention, demanding to be written, Janette Turner Hospital spends considerable time doing research appropriate to the material. Her way to research, she says,

> is to do a lot of riding in trains and a lot of walking and talking to people. Absorbing sounds and dialogue. Getting into some quite amazing conversations with Sydney cabbies – they're great. It may involve, as it did with Borderline, reading a lot of material, quite frequently newspapers in libraries, but often the current journals and magazines. But, as I said, for Borderline I spent a lot of time walking around Central Square trying to capture the feeling I wanted. I think I absorb a novel through my nerve ends. I absorb the feel of the grit under my feet, of a city's smells. . . . I also have a very intense full-time-thinking period, which I consider work on the novel. Three or four months I suppose, of bringing my characters into being.

> (Janette Turner Hospital, in Yacker 2)

THE FIRST DRAFT

Write the first draft for no one but yourself. Write to find out what you're writing about. Think of this as just a way of nailing the story down so that it can't get away. No eyes but yours will see it. Writing the first draft should be fun (you're telling yourself a story, after all) and surprising (you're making a journey, where people will reveal things you hadn't anticipated) and free (you can change your mind or change direction as often as you want so long as you feel you're getting somewhere that might pay off).

When you look back at what you've done, it will be as though you have just completed ploughing a field. What will be interesting (and important) now is to discover what – besides predictable soil – you've unearthed along the way.

Walk over the field and have a good look at the surprises. What rocks and broken bottles and mammoth bones came to the surface without your permission? Don't be too quick to throw them away.

(Don't be too quick to make them welcome either.) This is your chance to discover that your material has more to offer than you'd suspected. If you're a writer who doesn't want a story to do anything more or less than you'd decided ahead of time, you'll throw them all out and brush the dirt from your hands and gaze with pride at your perfectly ploughed field. If you're a writer who suspects that a million unfathomable reasons lie behind your choice of a particular piece of material to write about, you may also suspect that the material contains more than first appears. Stare. Stare. Flannery O'Connor said it takes a certain kind of stupidity to be a good fiction writer – the kind of stupidity that requires you to stare at something before you begin to understand it. This means staring not only at the world out there but at the lumps and bumps and glittery things that surface during the writing of your own work. Assume there is a secret story hidden within the story you thought you were writing, then search for its clues, think what the clues might mean; have enough respect for both the material and the process to believe there's more going on here than you have consciously done. A good story, honestly written, will have a life of its own, like the natural terrain, and before going through and tossing out everything that wasn't consciously intended, the writer ought to take a good close look at everything. That donkey jawbone or that broken bottle may come in handy yet. They may even be clues to help you understand what you're up to. Potential is what you're looking for here – what does this story want to become?

> We need stories. We can't identify ourselves without them. We're always telling ourselves stories about who we are: that's what history is, what the idea of nation or an individual is. The purpose of fiction is to help us answer the question we must constantly be asking ourselves: who do we think we are and what do we think we're doing?
>
> (Robert Stone, in *The Writer's Chapbook*)

Reprise: How Do You Recognize the Material You Ought to Be Writing About?

This list ignores the fact that you may presently be writing whatever stories happen to suggest themselves, simply in order to learn the skills you'll need for writing those future stories about which you will then answer "yes" to the following questions.

1. Is there something about the story that only you can offer?
2. Is there something about it that excites you in some way beyond easy explanation?
3. Is there something about it that seems dangerous? ("If I don't do this right I could ruin a good story idea.")
4. Is there something about it that seems to suggest it is larger than you think, that you will have to select rather than add?
5. Is there a sense that this story already exists somewhere just waiting to be told – or do you think you're going to have to make it all up and hammer and nail it together?
6. Is there something about it that makes you wish someone else had already written it because you know it's the kind of story *you* would like to read?
7. Is there something about it that seems appropriate to your nature, your voice, your way of looking at the world?
8. Has it presented itself to you in a manner that suggests that hidden riches await you once you start exploring?
9. Are you beginning to see natural and exciting *connections* between this bare story idea and several other images, people, places, or ideas you can hardly wait to write about?
10. Would you rather be writing this story than reading a book by your favourite writer? Do you think this story deserves to be written as effectively as your favourite writer writes?

Finding the Stories Meant for You: A Beginning

A. "Free-fall" a page of "automatic writing" to follow each of these opening phrases:

1. The most frightening person in my childhood was . . .
2. If I were prime minister . . .
3. Whenever I find myself in a pensive mood I remember . . .
4. Place? I'll give you "place". The most affecting place in my life is . . .
5. Was I anxious to grow up?
6. If I ever get a chance to avenge myself upon X . . .
7. Another letter from the Emperor! . . .
8. Hey? Don't ask me nothin'! Like, hey, man – what do I know about . . .
9. The person I wish I could bring back is . . .
10. School, school, school, I wonder if . . .

B. Which of the above came most easily? Look these over. Which surprises you? Which has thrown up the most vivid images or moments? Which has produced the most effective tone? Where – in any of these – can you spot the *hint* of a story idea, however small? Circle them. Put each of these circled phrases or ideas at the centre of a blank page and spend a little time jotting around it any images, ideas, people, places, smells, or sounds that come to mind. Circle these words and search amongst them for connections. Without pausing to think, or to let the editor in you have any say, write a passage growing out of any group of connected phrases or sentences. (A similar approach, called "clustering," is suggested in Gabriele Rico's *Writing the Natural Way.*)

C.1. Make a list of all the jobs you have some familiarity with – your parents' careers, your weekend jobs while in high school, your summer jobs while at university, your own careers in the "workforce."

2. Examine this list closely and circle those jobs you feel you know more about than you suspect the general reader does.

3. Examine the list of circled jobs carefully. In each case stare hard enough to discover what metaphors might be implied by the work. For instance, somebody who fixes pot-holes in roads might be thought of as "making life go smoother for other people." You should be able to do better than that.

4. Choose one job that seems to have the most potential and begin creating a character who does this work.

5. Write a passage – a page or so – in which you show your character thinking about his or her role while doing a job of work. Write it in such a way that you plant the metaphor in your reader's thoughts without explicitly stating it.

6. Do this same thing with other careers.

D. Later you will be asked to take a close look at places that have strongly influenced your imagination. For now, select a favourite (or most feared) geographical spot which played a role of some importance in your childhood – a river bank, an attic, a neighbour's slaughter house. Write words and phrases that evoke the smell of the place, the textures, the sounds, the images. Write sentences that use these words to *suggest* (rather than report) how you felt about that place. Write a full paragraph or more in which you show yourself entering that place. Then add the arrival of the person who would see the place most differently. How has this person's presence changed the language? In a second passage, write about this place from that other person's point of view.

───────────────

RECOMMENDED FURTHER READING
ON WRITERS' PURPOSES AND APPROACHES

Three Genres, Stephen Minot. Chapter 13
Ways of Seeing, John Berger
Text Book, Scholes, Comley & Ulmer. Part 3
The Eye of the Story, Eudora Welty. Part II, "Words into Fiction"
The Writing Book, Kate Grenville. Chapter 2
If You Want to Write, Brenda Ueland
Lectures on Literature, Vladimir Nabokov
Afterwords, Thomas McCormack (ed)
The Writing Life, Annie Dillard
The Uses of Literature, Italo Calvino
Six Memos, Italo Calvino
Don Quixote, Carlos Fuentes
The Art of the Novel, Milan Kundera
The Writer and Her Work, Janet Sternburg (ed)
The Novel Today, Malcolm Bradbury (ed)
"Moral Fiction," John Gardner (*Hudson Review*)
"The Diagnostic Novel," Walker Percy (*Harper's*)
"The Reason for Stories," Robert Stone (*Harper's*)
"Stalking the Billion-Footed Beast," Tom Wolfe (*Harper's*)
"Goodness Knows Nothing of Beauty," William Gass (*Harper's*)
"The Literature of Replenishment," John Barth (*Harper's*)
About Fiction, Wright Morris
The Narrative Voice, John Metcalf (ed)
Sixteen By Twelve, John Metcalf (ed)
Writers Revealed, R. Hartell (ed)

One Good Sentence After Another

෯෧

Stephen Spender has described the qualities of literary composition as (a) inspiration, (b) memory, (c) concentration, (d) faith, and (e) song. Inspiration is the moment of conception of the vague structure and form that the story or novel will later take on in specific ways. Memory includes all the singular details that the writer can bring to the work from the well of his own consciousness – the sensations, the images, the characters, and the events that will serve the original concept. Concentration is the means of bringing the awareness to the surface and applying it to the work. If it is complete, concentration will control such matters as tone and point of view, maintaining a consistency that will give the work much of its unity. Faith is the attitude that the writer must, at all cost, maintain in relation to his material and to his gifts as a writer. Song is the expert use of language, not merely in the sense of correct usage, but in the sense that language is the means by which a certain music is created, a sound in the ears as well as logic for the mind. It is meter, it is rhythm, it is emphasis, it is even gesture.

(Ray B. West, Jr, *The Art of Writing Fiction*)

Some Thoughts on Writing Good Prose

It seems to me very important to be able to get at the exact tone or texture of how things are. I can't really claim that it is linked to any kind of a religious feeling about the world, and yet that might come closest to describing it.

(Alice Munro, in *Eleven Canadian Novelists*)

My task which I am trying to achieve is, by the power of the written word, to make you hear, to make you feel – it is, before all, to make you see.

(Joseph Conrad, "The Creative Process")

When students at the University of Victoria asked a visiting publisher what was the most important quality publishers looked for in manuscripts, the guest suggested that publishers look for some evidence that the writer can actually write well – that is, use the English language skilfully. Other matters would depend upon it.

When the same students asked Irish novelist and short story writer John McGahern how to write good fiction, McGahern replied that you first write one good sentence, and then you must write another good sentence to follow it.

That it is necessary to write good sentences comes as a surprise to all too many young writers. So much energy goes into learning the skills necessary for the various aspects of story writing – plot construction, character development, point of view, and so on – that it's possible to forget that those skills don't matter very much if you don't know how to express what you want to say in readable prose. Of course, you don't want to be satisfied with merely "readable" or "adequate" prose, either. A good deal of the pleasure of writing comes from the joyful wielding of the power you are granted once you have more than adequate control of your words, sentences, and paragraphs. That power comes from an awareness of the potential in words – their meanings, their sounds, their connotations; in the various effects that can be created when certain words are put together; in the amazing transformations that are possible in a sentence, through varying the rhythm, the order, or the length.

The previous chapter encouraged you to write your early drafts with unselfconscious abandon. Despite appearances, this chapter has not set out to contradict that advice by implying that you should be an accomplished prose stylist before learning the various techniques involved in developing a narrative. Placed much later in the book, this chapter might have suggested that good writing is something you "apply" to your narrative afterwards. Learning to write well is a part of the entire process, and my intention here is only to alert you to its importance. The simple fact of the matter is that the more facility you have with prose the more effectively you can create characters, unfold a plot, and establish a point of view.

I haven't got very much sympathy with people who say "This is a wonderful story, even though it's poorly written, because it's dealing with this important topic or that important issue." If the story is not working on the page, if the story is not successful in terms of the words chosen and the imagery used, then I'm afraid it's a failure as far as I'm concerned.

(Owen Marshall, in In the Same Room)

The following passages are from the opening pages of two very different novels. In each example, it can be seen that the writer pays careful attention to his prose. Words are chosen for their sounds, for their literal meanings, and for their connotations. Attention is paid to rhythm, and its effect; to repeated sounds, and their consequences. Metaphors are used. The results are very different from one another. Read them carefully, several times, and see if you can tell what makes the difference. (Don't read them quickly in your haste to get on to the "useful tips." The most useful thing a writer can do is read successful writers closely and examine how they achieve their effect.)

A cart drove between the two big stringybarks and stopped. These were the dominant trees in that part of the bush, rising above the involved scrub with the simplicity of true grandeur. So the cart stopped, grazing the hairy side of a tree, and the horse, shaggy and stolid as the tree, sighed and took root.

The man who sat in the cart got down. He rubbed his hands together, because already it was cold, a curdle of cold cloud in a pale sky, and copper in the west. On the air you could smell the frost. As the man rubbed his hands, the friction of cold skin intensified the coldness of the air and the solitude of that place. Birds looked from twigs, and the eyes of animals were drawn to what was happening. The man lifting a bundle from a cart. A dog lifting his leg on an ant-hill. The lip drooping on the sweaty horse.

(Patrick White, *The Tree of Man*)

Johannes Kepler, asleep in his ruff, has dreamed the solution to the cosmic mystery. He holds it cupped in his mind as in his hands he would a precious something of unearthly frailty and splendour. O do not wake! But he will. Mistress Barbara, with a grain of grim satisfaction, shook him by his ill-shod foot, and at once the fabulous egg burst, leaving only a bit of glair and a few coordinates of broken shell.

And 0.00429.

He was cramped and cold, with a vile gum of sleep in his mouth. Opening an eye he spied his wife reaching for his dangling foot again, and dealt her a tiny kick to the knuckles. She looked at him, and under that fat flushed look he winced and made elaborate business with the brim of his borrowed hat. The child Regina, his stepdaughter, primly perched beside her mother, took in this little skirmish with her accustomed mild gaze. Young Tyge Brahe appeared then, leaning down from on high into the carriage window, a pale moist melanochroid, lean of limb, limp of paw, with a sly eye.

"We are arrived, sir," he said, smirking. That *sir*. Kepler, wiping his mouth discreetly on his sleeve, alighted on quaking legs from the carriage.

(John Banville, *Kepler*)

In the Patrick White passage, a pioneer moves himself onto a block of land and prepares to make his home. The horse, which already has something in common with the stringybark tree, "takes root." The dog does what dogs do when they wish to stake out their territory. The man, of course, intends to stake out his territory as well; he will also "take root" if he can. But it is not so easy for him. Note the hostility that surrounds him: animals watch, the word "cold" appears four times, the very alliteration seems unfriendly. But the prose itself suggests he will eventually succeed – it plods. The man is such a stranger here that he doesn't even yet have a name, but he will ploddingly do what he has to do, and maybe – by becoming dominant himself – will achieve something like the simple grandeur of that dominant tree.

John Banville's prose does not plod. It rocks and swings us, as a carriage might. Sounds make our ears perk up: "Opening an eye he spied his wife . . ." This writing wants to be read aloud. The narrator even blurts to his long-ago protagonist: "O do not wake!" But unfortunately, the protagonist belongs to history and the modern writer cannot keep him asleep with a simple warning. Even if you did not know who Kepler was, it is likely that you would feel the story to be happening a long time ago. The writing has the weight and richness of history in it, a measured and almost threatening tone that makes it easy to understand why Kepler, when he alights from his carriage, is quaking. Who would not quake, to be welcomed by one "lean of limb, limp of paw, with a sly eye"?

It is fairly safe to suggest that both these writers are *aware* of the power of words and sentences and know how to use this power to create a desired effect. This is not to suggest that every reader will respond with equal admiration to both of these passages. This, too, is a reminder of the importance of knowing the effect of your prose. As many writers have suggested, the beginning passages of a story teach us how to read it. They also tell us whether we want to read it. As Wright Morris has written, "The writing says to the reader, 'Look, this is for you,' or says it is not" (*On Fiction*). Wright, a masterful stylist, knows that his writing style does not appeal to everyone, but has such confidence in the effects he produces that he trusts the work to let the potential readers know right away what they are in for.

Perhaps it is necessary for the writer to fall in love with words. "I love words," writes Audrey Thomas. "I love the way they suddenly surprise you; I love the way *everyone*, high or low, uses them to paint pictures – that is to say metaphorically.

> . . . *Words, words, words . . . I can't leave them alone; I am obsessed. I move through the city watching for signs with letters missing ("Beef live with onions" advertises a cheap café near Granville and Broadway, "ELF SERVE" says a gas station out on Hastings) and I am always on the lookout for messages within words: can you see the harm in pharmacy, the dent in accident, the over in lover? In short, I play.*
>
> (Audrey Thomas, "Basmati Rice," in *Canadian Literature*)

It should not be assumed from the passages by White and Banville that all writers who take special care with words and sentences write prose that draws attention to itself. The ordinary reader is likely to pass through the following paragraph by Mavis Gallant without being conscious at all of the writing. The prose tends to be transparent, so that the content speaks directly to the reader without awareness of style. Yet the reader interested in how things are done will notice that Gallant has paid as much attention to her choice of words, the selection of details, the rhythms of her phrases, and the arrangement of her sentences as White and Banville.

On a bright morning in June I arrived in Montreal, where I'd been born, from New York, where I had been living and going to school. My luggage was a small suitcase and an Edwardian picnic hamper – a preposterous piece of baggage my father had brought from England some twenty years before; it had been with me since childhood, when his death turned my life into a helpless migration. In my purse was a birth certificate and five American dollars, my total fortune, the parting gift of a Canadian actress in New York, who had taken me to see *Mayerling* before I got on the train. She was kind and good and terribly hard up, and she had no idea that apart from some loose change I had nothing more. The birth certificate, which testified I was Linnet Muir, daughter of Angus and of Charlotte, was my right of passage. I did not own a passport and possibly never had seen one. In those days there was almost no such thing as a "Canadian". You were Canadian-born, and a British subject, too, and you had a third label with no consular reality, like the racial tag that on Soviet passports will make a German of someone who has never been to Germany. In Canada you were also whatever your father happened to be, which in my case was English. He was half Scot, but English by birth, by mother, by instinct. I did not feel a scrap British or English, but I was not an American either. In American schools I had refused to salute the flag. My denial of that curiously Fascist-looking celebration, with the right arm stuck straight out, and my silence when the others intoned the trusting ". . . and justice for all" had never been thought offensive, only stubborn. Americans then were accustomed to gratitude from foreigners but did not demand it; they quite innocently could not imagine any country fit to live in except their own. If I could not recognize it, too bad for me. Besides, I was not a refugee – just someone from the backwoods. "You got schools in Canada?" I had been asked. "You got radios?" And once, from a teacher, "What do they major in up there? Basket-weaving?"

(Mavis Gallant, "In Youth Is Pleasure," in *Home Truths*)

Gallant insists that style is not something that is added to the prose afterwards, "like a charming and universal slip-cover." Such a writer is likely to be determinedly aware of the effects created by words chosen, of the responses of readers to sentence rhythms, and of the differences that can be made by varying arrangements. In the paragraph above, for instance, we construct from the vocabulary and the sentence patterns an image of the young woman who is narrating. We sense the state of her emotions and notice a rather rambling approach to giving information. There is a discernible difference between her own use of language ("Americans then were accustomed to gratitude from foreigners but did not demand it") and that of the American students she quotes ("You got radios?"). The alliteration in "a preposterous piece of baggage" is not too noticeable and yet helps to make the piece of baggage more embarrassingly unusual than, say, "a ridiculous piece of baggage" might have done. Notice, even, how the Americans' questions are arranged so that they rise to something very like the punch line in a joke. There is no question that with "Basket-weaving?" the paragraph must end.

In *Ana Historic*, Daphne Marlatt does not intend that the writing be invisible; she intends that the writing be given at least as much attention as her story. In fact, the manner in which words and sentences and even punctuation are handled reflects the novel's central interest.

> what is she editing out and for whom? besides herself? it is herself there though she writes "the" eye and not "my." objective: out there and real (possibly) to others. she is thinking about those possible others leaning over her shoulder as she writes. or does she strive only to capture in words a real she feels beyond her? those enormous Trees with their capital letter, a colour no word can convey. i lean over her shoulder as she tries, as she doubts: why write at all? why not leave the place as wordless as she finds it? because there is "into –" what? frightening preposition. into the unspoken urge of a body insisting itself in the words.
>
> (Daphne Marlatt, *Ana Historic*)

Weak Writing

There is an infinite number of ways in which writing can be weak, or clumsy, or awkward, or ungrammatical, or confusing. Phyllis Naylor lists a few of them:

> *Possibly you were tired and lapsed into clichés without realizing it; or you used trite or hackneyed situations and phrases. Maybe you changed viewpoint, and instead of looking outward from your character's eyes, you find that you were writing about him instead.*
>
> *Did you use stilted dialogue or pet words that jar, or include a particular word too many times on a page, use too many adjectives or adverbs, or overuse dialect? Your writing might have fallen flat because it is grammatically too correct, your English so precise that it doesn't bend at all and your characters seem stiff. Perhaps the speech idiom of your protagonist does not match his thought idiom. Your transitions might be jerky.*
>
> (Phyllis Naylor, *The Craft of Writing a Novel*)

This is only the beginning – and even this small list of problems may be enough to scare you off trying at all. But, like other aspects of writing fiction discussed in this book, the business of making your prose as effective as it can be must not become such a concern during a first draft as to intimidate you. Keep in mind that most of the best prose you've read is almost certainly the result of much rewriting.

Show, Don't Tell?

Probably no slogan is used so often in writing workshops as "Show, don't tell!" What it suggests is that good writing communicates by working through the reader's five senses. To "show" is to make the reader see, hear, smell, feel, and even taste the story. To "tell," on the other hand, is to ask the reader to trust your conclusions without giving the evidence, and to hope that a secondhand version of events, dealing in abstractions and generalizations, will do.

Writing is illusion-making. We may believe (at least temporarily) what we're shown, but we only half believe what we're told. "Show, don't tell" is a notion that seems so right that it exerts the kind of tyranny which invites resistance. And indeed, there are occasions when it seems the rule should be, if not ignored, at least challenged. To insist, too literally, upon *showing* everything, could lock you into the writing of endless detailed scenes, when sometimes much of a scene can be summarized in fast narrative – *telling*. And occasionally it may be desirable to create the effect of distance in the narrating voice – the wise old narrator in a fairy-tale, for instance – whose effect is dependent upon the creation of a yarn-spinning tone.

Even so, since it is desirable within summary narrative to keep the story as specific and concrete as possible so that the reader can see what is happening, I suppose that even when you think *telling* seems preferable to *showing*, it is the selection of concrete details that makes the telling work. The prose that seems to be telling successfully is either doing a whole lot of effective showing along the way or has cast a spell over the reader with a smokescreen of language so skilfully used that the very texture of the language itself has become a satisfyingly sensual substitute for showing.

Types of Prose in Fiction

Almost all fiction is made up of a combination of four basic types of prose writing: exposition, narrative, scene, and half scene. Each of these serves a different purpose.

Consider the examples below.

1. EXPOSITION

Easily six feet tall, she carried a hundred and eighty pounds on her generous frame without prompting speculation as to what she had against girdles. She could touch the floor effortlessly with the flat of her palms and pack an eighty pound sack of chicken feed on her shoulder. She dyed her hair auburn in defiance of local mores, and never went to town to play bridge, whist, or canasta without wearing a hat and getting dressed to the teeth. Grandma loved card games of all varieties and considered anyone who didn't a mental defective.

(Guy Vanderhaeghe, "The Watcher")

Passages of exposition give the reader information needed for understanding the rest of the story. This may be description of a place or person, information about background, or necessary data on a situation.

2. NARRATIVE

For five whole glaring days they worked away like this, too tired and stiff at night to want to go anywhere but to bed. They had all the hay won except the final meadow when the weather broke. The girls

never thought they would lift their faces to the rain in gratitude.
They watched it waste the meadows for the whole day.

(John McGahern, *Amongst Women*)

In much fiction, fast narrative or summary narrative is confined to
passages where it is necessary to move from one scene to another
(through time and/or space) without getting bogged down in
details. Telling much of the story in this fashion could cause the
reader to feel it's going by too fast, and is unsatisfactory and shallow.
It's difficult to get involved in this kind of writing if it continues for
long, though a few writers have used it brilliantly in narrating epic
stories.

3. SCENE

In about five minutes they came back to me, the girl drinking a
bottle of orange pop.

"This is Adelaide," George said. "Adelaide, Adeline. Sweet Adeline. I'm going to call her Sweet A, Sweet A."

Adelaide sucked at her straw, paying not much attention.

"She hasn't got a date," George said. "You haven't got a date have
you, honey?"

Adelaide shook her head very slightly.

"Doesn't hear half what you say to her," George said. "Adelaide,
Sweet A, have you got any friends? Have you got any nice, young little
girl friend to go out with Dickie? You and me and her and Dickie?"

"Depends," said Adelaide. "Where do you want to go?"

"Anywhere you say. Go for a drive. Drive up to Owen Sound,
maybe."

"You got a car?"

"Yeah, yeah, we got a car. C'mon, you must have some nice little
friend for Dickie." He put his arm around this girl, spreading his fingers over her blouse. "C'mon out and I'll show you the car."

(Alice Munro, "Thanks for the Ride")

It is in the scene that the reader is invited to participate. People are seen close up. Conflict is dramatized. Plot is moved forward by the decisions made. We don't need to see everything in a scene but we expect to see it clearly. It is noticeable that much fiction is built primarily of scenes.

4. HALF SCENE

In recent years he has suffered greatly from savage and inexplicable pains of the back. At first he took it to be some consequence of whaling: damage done in the long hours alert with harpoon, often in wild weather, the sea always jarring. Once he rode eighty-six miles to the nearest physician, who failed to find anything organically wrong. The pain has come and gone, near crippling, crushing him to the ground as if under rocks and old iron. Now he understands these cruel symptoms to have been the weight of Marie Louise's grief. The pain is gone, quite gone: he knows it will never return.

"Yes," he informs Marie Louise. "Of course we're staying here with you. Where else could I go?"

She weeps for all of two days.

Luke digs and plants a large garden for his parents, fetches and carries, and effects repairs to Lovelock House where he can. The condition of the tower, however, defeats him; he forbids the children to climb it, and tries to persuade Herman to at least use it less. His wife Tui, no longer as shy as the songbird for which she was named, likewise helps in the house where she can, sweeping and laundering, though she finds it impossible to ease Marie Louise from the kitchen; that kingdom, for the moment, cannot be claimed.

(Maurice Shadbolt, *The Lovelock Version*)

While we are moving quickly through fast narrative sequences, the half scene is the occasional pause, which picks up essential snatches of conversation or close-up action. The approach is often used in histories, where several events over months or years are narrated rapidly, pausing for important landmark exchanges between historical figures involved.

But how do you know when the material deserves a scene and when it should be rushed through in narrative? How do you know how much exposition is necessary? Sometimes you won't know until you've written your first or second draft and discovered what kind of story you have on your hands. You will probably build scenes around the most important encounters that contribute to plot movement and character revelation. You will probably use summary narrative or half scenes when it is important for us to know about certain actions or events over a period of time but not important for us to be there "in person", so to speak, for the details. And you will probably have to experiment with exposition to discover just how many or how few of the details of place, people, and action you feel we need to witness for ourselves in order to get the effect you want.

Writing the Successful Scene

A writer who has chosen to devote a full scene to an encounter must have decided it is important that we see these people up close at this time, and that the exchange between (or amongst) them will be of some importance. We will learn more about the characters. We will sense the plot moving forward, perhaps even changing direction.

We will witness, quite often, an exchange that has the dynamics of a competition. Each character comes into the scene wanting something of the other. Power shifts from one side to the other, and sometimes back. However subtly it is handled, somebody wins, somebody loses – for now.

So that we will be involved and not merely looking on, the author will often show us tell-tale gestures, draw our attention to appearances, and make certain we notice important elements in the setting.

It is probably a good idea to pause, before writing a scene, and ask yourself what each character is bringing to the situation (especially emotions and intentions), what each character feels about the other, what details of the setting are worth selecting. It is a good idea, as well, to consider whether this is a scene that needs to be recorded in detail, or whether it should be moved through quickly.

Of course you may not be able to answer the questions before you write the scene, but by pausing to ask them you are putting yourself in a position where you'll recognize the important elements of your scene as they surface during writing, and will then be able to rewrite it more effectively.

In the following fragment from a scene in Peter Carey's *The Tax Inspector,* one person (Maria, a tax inspector who has come to do an audit on a family business) is outside in the rain wanting in, while the other (Cathy, a member of the family with reason to avoid close scrutiny of the books) is inside determined to keep her out. A third person in the background has her own agenda. Notice how the author delivers the dialogue like a competition, with each person determined to stop the other person from getting what she wants. It is, like many strong scenes, a power struggle.

Rain drummed on the iron roof, spilled out of gutters, splashed out on to the landing around Maria's feet. There was a noise like furniture falling over. The woman in cowboy boots turned her head and shouted back into the room behind her: "It's not Mortimer ... It ... is ... *not* Mort." She turned back to Maria and blew out some air and raised her eyebrows. "Sorry," she said. She scrutinized the I. D. card again. When she had read the front she opened it up and read the authorization. When she looked up her face had changed.

"Look," she said, coming out into the rain, and partly closing the door behind her. Maria held out her umbrella.

"Jack," the old woman called.

"Look, Mrs Catchprice is very sick."

"Jack..."

"I'm Cathy McPherson. I'm her daughter."

"Jack, Mort, help me."

Cathy McPherson turned and flung the door wide open. Maria had a view of a dog's bowl, of a 2-metre-high stack of yellowing newspapers.

"It's not Jack," shrieked Cathy McPherson. "Look, look. Can you see? You stupid old woman. It's the bloody Tax Department."

Maria could smell something sweet and alcoholic on Cathy McPherson's breath. She could see the texture of her skin, which was not as good as it had looked through the flyscreen. She thought: if I was forty-five and I could afford boots like those, I'd be saving money for a facelift.

"This is ugly," Cathy McPherson said. "I know it's ugly. I'm sorry. You really have to talk to her?"

"I have an appointment with her for ten o'clock."

(Peter Carey, *The Tax Inspector*)

Improving Your Prose

Asking the following questions about a passage of your writing might help you to understand how it may be improved. This is not to suggest that "doing" all these things will automatically make your prose better. Know the effect you want, then experiment.

1. Have you chosen specific and concrete words throughout, aware of their sounds and rhythms and connotations as well as all their dictionary meanings?
2. Have you chosen words that are honest – that is, specific, direct, unadorned, plain?
3. Have you used only words necessary for the effect you want?
4. Have you chosen language that appeals to more than just one or two of the five senses?
5. Have you chosen "energy" words, in particular verbs that *move* the prose?
6. Have you conveyed your (or your character's) feelings indirectly?
7. Do your sentences imply some depth of meaning for the reader who is sensitive to subtext and implication?
8. Have you varied the lengths and patterns of sentences, experimenting with the effects of following long sentences with a short sentence, or following short sentences with a long sentence?
9. Have general ideas been supported by examples?
10. Have you considered arranging things in ascending order of importance, of saving the best for the last?
11. Have you used comparison, contrast, metaphor, or analogy to sharpen meaning?
12. Are transitions between sentences and paragraphs smooth or abrupt – depending upon which creates the more appropriate effect?

13. Do sentences move in coherent order, according to time, or space, or ideas, or logic?
14. Have you considered arranging parallel ideas in parallel structure?
15. Have you experimented with emphasis by changing position, order, or proportion?
16. Have you experimented with emphasis by changing rhythm and cadence?
17. Have you considered sound or colour or choice of details to achieve tone?
18. Have you remained aware of the point of view, or angle of vision?
19. Have you experimented with the effect of repeating similar strong beginnings for a series of sentences, or similar strong endings?
20. Have you used sharp unusual images or original turns of phrase?
21. Does everything strive for clarity?

Coherence in Paragraphs

The sentences in a coherent paragraph are arranged in an organized pattern – a logical order (which could be chronological, spatial, causal). The sentences in a coherent paragraph are related and connected to one another in some way – by consistency in point of view (person, tense, number), by repetition of grammatical structure (parallel), by repetition of key words or ideas, and/or by transitional words or phrases.

Examples of transitional words and phrases:

1. for *addition*: again, and, besides, and then, equally important, finally, further, furthermore, in addition, last, first, lastly, likewise, next, secondly, thirdly, too . . .
2. for *contrast*: and yet, at the same time, although true, but, for all that, however, in contrast, nevertheless, on the contrary, on the other hand, still, in spite of . . .
3. for *comparison*: likewise, in a like manner, in the same way, similarly . . .
4. for *summary*: in brief, on the whole, to sum up, in conclusion, to conclude . . .
5. for *special features or examples*: for example, for instance, indeed, in fact, in other words, that is, in particular . . .
6. for *result*: accordingly, consequently, therefore, thus, truly, as a result, then . . .
7. for *passage of time*: afterwards, at length, until, immediately, in the meantime, meanwhile, soon, at last, after a short time, while, thereafter, temporarily, presently, shortly, lately, since . . .
8. for *concession*: of course, after all, naturally, I admit, although this may be true . . .

For a more complete list of transition words and phrases consult the writer's handbook on your desk.

_____

A Sampling

The following passages are obviously different in intent but have been written by writers equally interested in "getting it right." Examine them closely, and consider the words, the sounds, the rhythms, the sentence structure, the paragraph patterns, and their influence upon the total effect. Also, listen with your inner ear as you read, and try to describe the difference in "voices" you hear telling each passage.

> Ara went to the door. She threw the water from the basin into the dust. She watched the water roll in balls on the ground. Roll and divide and spin.
>
> The old lady had disappeared.
>
> Ara put on a straw hat. She tied it with a bootlace under the chin. She wiped the top of the table with her apron which she threw behind a pile of papers in the corner. She went to the fence and leaned against the rails.
>
> If a man lost the road in the land around William Potter's, he couldn't find his way by keeping to the creek bottom for the creek flowed this way and that at the land's whim. The earth fell away in hills and clefts as if it had been dropped carelessly wrinkled on the bare floor of the world.
>
> Even God's eye could not spy out the men lost here already, Ara thought. He had looked mercifully on the people of Nineveh though they did not know their right hand and their left. But there were not enough people here to attract his attention. The cattle were scrub cattle. The men lay like sift in the cracks of the earth.
>
> (Sheila Watson, *The Double Hook*)

He lived – in his job and during these evening walks – in a silence, with noise and conversation all around him. To be understood, his reactions had to exaggerate themselves. The family idiot. A stroke victim. "Paderick," the shopkeepers would call him as he handed them money and a list of foods Hana had written out in Macedonian, accepting whatever they gave him. He felt himself expand into an innocent. Every true thing he learned about character he learned at this time in his life. Once, when they were at the Teck Cinema watching a Chaplin film he found himself laughing out loud, joining the others in their laughter. And he caught someone's eye, the body bending forward to look at him, who had the same realization – that this mutual laughter was conversation.

(Michael Ondaatje, *In the Skin of a Lion*)

With her enormous circular sunglasses, she looked like some fabled aphid, striped hugely with scarf and brilliantly white in the morning. She could see no movement anywhere in the port and this, too, was strange, for some glint or glitter should have shown itself. From the bridge came the tick-tick of the radio and a giant hump of moving back as Brinkman worried the controls and gadgetry Miss Paradise never troubled to understand but could use as source of male-adulating ahs. Cars, engines, even cameras, were articles of faith for her that she accepted round-eyed and gazed at phoney-innocent, a pulsating mass of wonder when salesmen spieled or male friends adjusted. It had not worked with Captain Brinkman who chose that moment to stare at her rudely, she felt, through the protective glass he kept between himself and the passengers. In defense she linked arms with her friend who was tottering a little in her way-out north-of-Capricorn footwear and feeling the effects of the heat already. Together they tumtittitummed a *nil desperandum* back along the deck.

(Thea Astley, *A Boat Load of Home Folk*)

Construct a gibbet. Use a tree, a tree is just the thing. One with a smooth tall trunk well-rooted in the ground, with a high strong branch at the right angle. Loop over it a rope, and there you have a gibbet for a Hanged Man. Not a pretty thing for a garden, you say, but you'd be wrong. For the Hanged Man dangles gallantly by one foot and turning upside down observes the world. Its powers cannot harm him, he sees it clearly and afresh, all new. He is an individual. And he has a halo round his head.

(Marion Halligan, "The Hanged Man in the Garden")

Heavens, she thought.

Withdrawing to her stateroom to supervise Dawson at the last minute packing. And eyeing closer her tired hand behind which, out of focus, were white pilasters and the pink *putti* of the room.

Knock knock.

Mr Macintyre, said Dawson.

Minnie rose.

Mr Macintyre, she said. How odd.

His old eyes watering on her waistband.

Miss Lomax, said Mr Macintyre.

Perhaps you had best be seated.

Minnie sat.

I am the bearer, Miss Lomax, of sad tidings.

Minnie raised her eyes. Screwing them up.

Papa? she said.

Macintyre nodded.

Minnie frowned.

(Stevan Eldred-Grigg, "When Bawds and Whores Do Churches Build")

Improving Your Prose

She entered the room. She stood just inside the door for a while. She saw someone she recognized. He waved at her over the heads of the standing crowd. She began to make her way towards him. Firemen were having a convention downtown tonight. A man blocked her way. He asked if they had been introduced. She ignored him. He grasped her arm. She felt herself beginning to lose consciousness. She fled from the room.

I hope you understand why this is a very bad paragraph. Nouns are vague, and general. Verbs are weak and ordinary. All sentences are of the same type, of similar length, with the same subject-verb pattern. No cause-and-effect relationships are drawn to our attention. In fact, one sentence is not related to the others at all. The sentences fail to reflect any mood or create any feeling in the reader except boredom.

As a result, the paragraph lacks unity and coherence. Its prose jerks along, without any narrative drive. We can't see anything, or use any of the other senses either. We don't learn anything about the people or understand what is going on.

Try to improve the paragraph according to the following suggestions:

1. Give it unity – by pruning or by making connections.
2. Strengthen the vocabulary throughout, by substituting more specific nouns and more colourful verbs first; then, only where useful, by adding adjectives or adverbs or other kinds of modifiers.
3. Vary the types and lengths of sentences.
4. Give it coherence by using transition devices.
5. Improve the rhythm by joining sentences, or by creating subordinate clauses and/or modifying phrases, or by beginning some sentences with introductory and/or connecting phrases.
6. Decide how your character feels, choose the details that support that feeling, and make the sentence structure or rhythm appropriate.

Writing Small Stories

These short exercises will give you an opportunity to experiment with your prose.

A. Write a one-page biography of one of the words listed below. After doing research, tell the entertaining history of this word from its beginning (in whatever language and country) to its present life in your region of the world. Include its travels, its marriages, its divorces, and the personality changes it has undergone during its life.

delicious	catastrophe	sketch
atrocity	anxiety	draw
masquerade	spinster	cougar
head	chauvinism	environment
augment	clarity	charity
integrity		

B. Write a one-page summary of a building's process of construction, revealing indirectly the story of the people building it or the story of the people for whom it is being built. Consider whether architectural features can be used metaphorically to help tell the story.

C. In one or two pages, write a week's worth of daily "accounts" for a small business, making it your task to imply the story of the person keeping the accounts during that week.

D. Write a one-page story which begins "Nothing of real importance happened that day" and then reveal through the thoughts or actions of a character during a day's sequence of unimportant events that something important *did* happen internally.

Limbering Up with Milligan's Folly: Prose

The "Miner's Latest Claim Backfires" news clipping will recur throughout this book as the subject of a series of writing assignments. The intention is not that you necessarily work your way through a first draft of a story but that you accumulate materials that will make a first draft possible. While making decisions for any assignment, don't be intimidated by a suspicion that you will be tied to those decisions in later assignments. You must feel free at every point to alter any previous decision where a better one has occurred. Despite the accumulating nature of this series of assignments, you will not be locked into an organized sequence, but will be experimenting anew at every stage even while using what's helpful from previous assignments.

Go back and carefully reread the "Lonely Miner" clipping at the beginning of Chapter 2.

A. Imagine that Milligan and Lindstrom have just scrambled ashore and have figured out between them where they are and what they must do next. Write a paragraph of summary narrative to act as a bridge between this scene and the scene in which they are inside the house with Milligan's fiancée, Lily Cates.

B. Imagine that Milligan has just stepped off the raft and is about to cross the street to enter the bank. Write a paragraph describing what he sees, in a manner that reflects his mood. Write a paragraph that give us information about Milligan, from the point of view of Mrs Marsden, who is inside the bank and sees him looking towards her.

C. Write a scene on the raft, chronicling the dialogue and action between Milligan and Lindstrom as the raft pulls away from the town side of the river.

D. Imagine that Milligan and Lindstrom are on that raft, which is running down river out of control. Write a passage of summary narrative in which you show their movement down the river, pausing to record only the briefest necessities of dialogue between them as they go.

RECOMMENDED FURTHER READING ON GOOD WRITING

Three Genres, Stephen Minot. Chapters 12, 20 & 23
Writing Fiction, R.V. Cassill. Chapters 3, 8 & 9
Literature: Structure, Sound, and Sense, Laurence Perrine.
    Chapters 1, 2 & 4
Living by Fiction, Annie Dillard. Part II, Chapter 7
The Rhetoric of Fiction, Wayne Booth. Part I.vi
A Reader's Guide to Literary Terms, Beckson & Ganz
The Writer's Craft, John Hersey (ed)
The Canadian Writer's Handbook, Messenger & De Bruyn (eds)
Writing in General and the Short Story in Particular, Rust Hills
The Art of Fiction, John Gardner. Part I, Chapter 2; Part II,
    Chapter 6
Webster's Word Histories
Modern English Usage, Fowler
The Elements of Style, Strunk & White

Setting: "A Plausible Abode"

৯৯

No place is a place until things that have happened in it are remembered in history, ballads, yarns, legends, or monuments. Fictions serve as well as facts. Rip Van Winkle, though a fiction, enriches the Catskills. Real-life Mississippi spreads across unmarked boundaries into Yoknapatawpha County.

(Wallace Stegner, *Where the Bluebird Sings to the Lemonade Springs*)

The Importance of Place

Besides furnishing a plausible abode for the novel's world of feeling, place has a good deal to do with making the characters real, that is, themselves, and keeping them so.
(Eudora Welty, *The Eye of the Story*)

"I hear this fella last week, he went and burned his own house down, with his wife and kids inside."
"Naw – I can't believe anyone'd do a thing like that."
"It was Bernie Baxter's cousin did it, over in Bixton."
"Oh, Bixton! Them people over there are all a little crazy."

Perhaps the first job of the fiction writer is to convince the reader to believe in the world of the story – at least temporarily. If the task is to convince the reader that the tale you are about to tell *really happened*, the most readily available and convincing argument seems to be: *It really happened because it happened in the town of X.* If it happened in a town called X then how could we doubt that it happened at all? Joseph Conrad considered this important enough to spend several pages establishing the town of Sulaco and the Republic of Costaguana at the beginning of *Nostromo*. He knew that if we were

72

going to believe the sort of thing that was about to happen in this story then we had better be first convinced that the place exists.

Few modern writers risk devoting so much space to the job. Do modern readers take less convincing than Conrad's original readers, or have modern writers simply learned to be sneakier, aware that today's readers may have got used to changing the channel?

Although some writers consider place to have little to do with the matter, most will eventually admit, however grudgingly, that we might be more appropriately affected by this death-bed scene if we knew whether it was taking place in a public hospital room, a damp prison dungeon, or a stifling war-zone tent. Unless, of course, the very absence of a setting is the point: that a death-bed scene is one of those things for which place and circumstances are largely irrelevant – dying is dying and loss is loss, and the rest of the world doesn't matter.

If fiction depends for its life on place, so does the fiction writer. David Malouf writes that he is interested in "how the elements of a place and our inner lives cross and illuminate one another, how we interpret space, and in so doing make our first maps of reality, how we mythologize spaces and through that mythology (a good deal of it inherited) find our way into a culture" ("A First Place: The Mapping of a World").

To an audience in Sydney, where he was about to read from *12 Edmondstone Street*, Malouf made the following comments:

If you grow up in the kind of wooden house that I grew up in, and if your first sense of space is that house and the way its rooms are laid out, and if your first sense of dimensions is developed there, then that really is your first reading of the world and you go on to apply that to whatever else you look at. In one part of my mind every city is a city of hills like

Brisbane: where you go up and down and where, when you get to the top of the street, you see something new. . . . An Adelaide friend tells me that he grew up thinking cities were flat. He really did think that if you looked down a street you ought to be able to see all the way to the end of it. . . . I can't believe that we are not deeply determined by such factors. The lecture I am about to read a bit of, was an attempt to argue how I might have been determined, uniquely, by Brisbane. And I wanted, at the end of that piece, to ask my hearers to go away and think about the place they came from, and the house they lived in, and ask themselves what their initiation into reality was in their first house – not just through the shape of it, the architecture of it, but the objects that were in it, the kind of mythology and history it contained, and the way all of these factors lead us out into the world, so that our first apprehension of culture – both Australian culture and a larger culture than that imme-diate *world – might come through the particular objects in that house.*
(David Malouf, in *Writers in Action*)

The tourist may look at a place and think "What does it do? What is it like? How much does it please me?" but the fiction writer must look at a place and think "What does it suggest? What does it mean to me? What does it mean to my characters?"

A passage that takes full advantage of a setting occurs in a scene in Shirley Hazzard's *The Transit of Venus* where she locates a meeting between two people (one of them about to give information that will destroy the life of the other) in Harrod's rug department, "which had the space and solemnity of a cathedral," and where "thick rolled strips of carpet stood or lay like the fallen drums of col-umns in a temple." One character's inner world of sacred hope is then devastated before our eyes.

To follow this model too seriously is to risk disaster, but the hint is worth consideration: since you're in the business of weaving a spell, of creating a world, you may as well enrol the help of every element, including setting, in the task. Consider whether the settings of your story offer, through metaphor, some significant comment upon the various scenes.

In attempting to explain the symbiotic relationship that exists between her writing and the landscape, New Zealander Keri Hulme suggests that it may have begun when, as a very short-sighted child, she had to *feel* things to figure out what they were.

> *I think it was that physical contact and awareness of the shape of the land as much as anything. Added to that, there was the way people still do, but used to talk much more, about pieces of land as though they were still inhabited by a person, the person they were named after or because of an incident that had occurred there, whether it was a bloody little massacre like the old men's battle at Moeraki or simply the rock line known as Paeko. There was a magic of words attached to pieces of land and this is one of the things that I found curious, when, for instance, at school we started reading "nature poetry" and none of it was the way I saw it or heard it or felt it. It was a very different land altogether.*
>
> (Keri Hulme, in *In the Same Room*)

You and the Map: A Warning

In many parts of the world it is still possible that you may be one of the first writers in the community to publish fiction, or even the first in your region. This means that you have been blessed with a piece of the world that is virginal, fictionally speaking, and that you haven't a James Joyce looking over your shoulder, reminding you that he has already done it better.

Unfortunately, the people of your place may assume that you've made it your task to "put this place on the map." By that, they mean that you will tell the world "what it's like here." It is assumed, of course, that you will tell only the good things. "You'll speak for the rest of us."

As if it isn't already dangerous enough to be a fiction writer! Someone is bound to recognize that beat-up old Ford pickup in your story and claim that you're taking liberties. But this could be even worse. "Dear Novelist, I was born in the same valley as you and haven't been back for twenty years, but when I read your books I feel myself carried back . . ." You may get to like this sort of thing. You may be tempted to believe that you actually *have* become the voice of your place. You may begin to believe that it is your main job as a fiction writer to "get the place right."

If this happens, you're in trouble. It is presumptuous to think that you have somehow been elected to speak for a place and its inhabitants. If your intention really *is* only to "get the place right" you may have missed your calling – you probably should be writing history or geography and sociology books, not fiction. Furthermore, you would be trying to do something impossible. Is there just one truth about a place, agreed upon by everyone who lives there? There is only one person's vision of it, another's experience of it, another's intentions for it . . . And amongst them, your own. Formed, perhaps, from a lifetime of extraordinary observation, but nevertheless your own.

As a fiction writer, you are obliged to pay attention to place, I think, and to its effect upon its inhabitants, and to the metaphors it offers your interest in the human story. You may already be aware that much of the most powerfully universal fiction has been, para-doxically, concerned with the minute details of some tiny corner of the world. But whether you happen to be the first or one amongst many to write fiction out of your region, it is probably a good idea to think of place, however unique and powerful, as one more element to be employed in the service of your fiction – rather than to con-sider your fiction as a voice employed by the place. To dedicate your fiction to the service of place is to invite your employers to tell you how to do it, and worse, to risk forgetting what other, larger things fiction can do.

Setting and Style

If landscape can be seen as contributing to the characters, the actions, and even the meaning in a fiction, you might want to consider the extent to which a particular landscape, or landscapes (including that first house), may have affected you. Was Larry McMurtry's spare, lean horizontal style influenced by a childhood in Texas? (He insists that it was.) Would the novels of Patrick White have been less sprawling, his sentences shorter, his casts smaller, his plots less complex, if he were writing about tiny, crowded Holland, say, instead of vast Australia? (In a 1977 speech, he said, "I believe that geography . . . is what makes us.") Janette Turner Hospital has said, "I think they are the two dominant influences on my prose: The King James Version of the Bible and the Queensland rainforest. The principle of beauty in a rainforest is in the lavishness, the baroque, and it is true of the King James English too" (*Writers in Action*).

I once complained to a writer friend that every time I start a new story my goal is to write it in fast, tight, clean, clear prose – *The Old Man and The Sea*; *The Bridge of San Luis Rey* – but that once I get into the job, prose springs up all around me like a jungle: new people get into the act, the story becomes more complex and mysterious than I'd anticipated, all of the world seems to want to be part of the action. Less puzzled by this than I, my friend suggested that things could not be otherwise. "You were born and raised in a temperate rainforest. You have a rainforest brain – fecund and complex as a jungle. Don't fight it. So long as you're writing *about* the Vancouver Island world, this is not only inevitable but appropriate."

Describing or Constructing?

If the writer thinks of the process of writing as "discovering" setting (that is, discovering its most salient features, discovering its meaning) in the same way as it is "discovering" the secrets of its characters, perhaps it is wise to think that the writer's task is not to "describe" a place – real or invented – but to "construct" it.

If someone describes Venice for us, Venice remains several thousand kilometres away, and still unreachable, however pungent its canals are made to seem, however elaborate its buildings, however much our friend insists that the place is sinking into the sea. We might as well go off and find a picture book, pore over the coloured photos. Or endure an evening of amateur slides. If someone were to go to the trouble of constructing Venice for us, on the other hand, that would be another matter.

What's the difference? The constructed Venice may not be the original one – where strangers we've never met are at this moment tromping across the Bridge of Sighs and scattering pigeons in St Mark's Square – but it will be one we can see, smell, reach out and touch. Better still, it will be one we can have real feelings about. (That other Venice gave us only feelings about the returned tourist: "How long will this go on?") The visitor back from Dorchester will rave about the old buildings, complain about the rain, show you a photo of the buildings that Hardy used for Henchard's house. We nod, and smile, and yawn, and perhaps decide that one day we really ought to go there. When Hardy constructs his own version of Dorchester, however, and calls it Casterbridge, he knows enough to select the details that matter and erect them with suitable prose in a manner that encourages us to see the compact little box of a city, square and old, a sudden contained cluster in a green and rolling rural landscape – an architect's view of a mathematical figure, rectangles dissected by lines.

The temptation to nail down every detail of a real place may be powerful. The temptation to wax eloquent and enthusiastic about its charms or horrors may be more powerful still. But you are neither a landscape painter nor a representative for the Chamber of Commerce. You are a writer of fiction, which means that you are in charge of inventing a world, of constructing it out of a carefully selected handful of details, of finding meaning in that world, and of convincing your reader that your story is so tied to this place that if the characters took up their plot and hauled themselves off to Monte Carlo the story would not be the story any more.

> *The impression produced by a landscape, a street or a house should always, to the novelist, be an event in the history of a soul, and the use of the "descriptive passage," and its style, should be determined by the fact that it must depict only what the intelligence concerned would have noticed, and always in terms within the register of that intelligence.*
>
> (Edith Wharton, *The Writing of Fiction*)

Various Roles Setting Might Play in a Story

1. NEGLIGIBLE

Some writers wish their fictions to happen in a world without unique features – the generic big city, an average desert. This may be intended to suggest the writer's view: that settings do not affect character or action as much as others insist, perhaps, or that the reader should be permitted to supply his own experience of setting to the story, or that the world of today has so reduced the importance of immediate setting (making us all inhabitants, say, of the no-place television world) that there is little point in taking up space on the page with setting.

Unfortunately, the absence of any discernible setting also may reflect a belief on the part of an insecure writer that the piece of the world in which she lives may be uninteresting to readers in cultural centres (where books are published, bought, and sold to the movies). "If I set it in 'a noisy metropolis' they may think it's New York – automatically making it more interesting than if they think it's Edmonton, the only city I've seen." This seldom works. Characters who live in nowhere have been deprived of specific cultural and physical surroundings, which affect our lives every day.

The characters in the story by the committed believer in setting's irrelevance, on the other hand, will live in a world where the absence of specific cultural and physical factors is made to *be* their cultural and physical world.

2. STAGE SET ONLY (NEEDED SCENERY)

Having established *where* and *when* a story happens, and having drawn our attention to the important features of setting, some writers are then content to let the story play itself out without much more attention to place. After mentioning a location in the opening paragraph – "a small town north of Christchurch" – this writer may also give us information about life in that town, and then make sure we always see a few of the most important elements of the setting for each scene, but give that setting no major role to play, or any real importance in the minds of the characters. It is enough, this writer implies in this particular story, simply to know where we are.

3. LOCAL COLOUR

Occasionally a writer will go to so much trouble to draw attention to aspects unique to the setting that the entire story is flavoured. The implication is that this story could not possibly have happened anywhere else. The intention is to create an unforgettable impression of a location. The result is sometimes effective and entertaining, but it can also be absurd. Here the writer does not allow setting to take its place amongst the various important factors that contribute to the authenticity of a story, but is attempting to entertain with local features for their own sake. The setting is invited to go through its bag of tricks for the people.

This is a risky business. Phonetically spelled dialogue that is intended to suggest local dialect can be annoying, and very difficult to read. (It will also be "heard" in different ways by people in different parts of the globe. If dialect is important, paying attention to rhythms is safer than putting the reader through a lot of phonetic spelling.) Too many observed oddities of place can distract the reader from the story. "Colourful" local characters lounging around in the background, or behaving in a stereotypically eccentric manner, could possibly be insulting to a racial or cultural group. Too often, an extreme reliance upon local colour can result in writing that reads like cartoons.

If these comments sound discouraging, they are intended to discourage only excess. The unusual setting, closely observed and sharply reported, can be one of the factors that make a story both enjoyable and memorable.

Bret Harte's "The Outcasts of Poker Flat" tells a good story, but also gives a great deal of attention to colourful details of life in a mining town of the Old West. W.O. Mitchell's *Who Has Seen the Wind* opens with four paragraphs of description of the setting, beginning with the words: "Here was the least common denominator of nature, the skeleton requirements simply, of land and sky – Saskatchewan prairie." Part of the appeal to the reader lies in the degree to which the novel depicts life in small-town Saskatchewan. But it is clear at the same time that Mitchell is more interested in his characters and the way characters and setting affect one another in this prairie town of "some eighteen hundred souls."

4. ATMOSPHERE

The following passage illustrates how a skilled writer may use setting to create atmosphere. A successful passage will not only make it clear what a character is feeling but will also make the reader feel much the same. Here, at a remote logging camp, the boy Jerome has just witnessed his mother's death, and is being stalked by the killer.

Nothing moved in the clearing. The long cookhouse with the two metal pipes that served as chimneys stood silent, its sloping roof whitened by the moon, its walls dark, its windows glittering like gun metal. He heard the sigh and gurgle of the river as it poured among the tree trunks along the flooded banks, but there was no sound of men and no light in any of the bunkhouses. He could not see the bunkhouse which was still occupied, but if there had been lights in it he would have seen their glimmer through the trees.

With the instinct of an animal Jerome got up and changed his position, slinking through the shadows among the stumps at the edge of the forest-fringe to a place he knew about thirty feet away. He found it, a depression in the ground about ten feet from the edge of the moonlight, and lay down and scooped pine needles over himself to conceal the whiteness of his shirt and skin. Lying flat with his chin in his hands and his elbows in the needles, he stared at the kitchen door and listened to the pounding of his heart.

(Hugh MacLennan, *The Watch That Ends the Night*)

5. CONTRIBUTOR TO ACTION, AFFECTING CHARACTER

Your characters take on clearer and more forceful reality if they have a cultural and geographical and historical context. Roch Carrier's novels *La Guerre, Yes Sir* and *Garden of Earthly Delights* gain much of their impact from the extent to which the characters' attitudes and behaviour have been influenced by the realities of their lives in a tiny Quebec village of some decades ago. Henry Lawson's story "The Drover's Wife" examines the life of a woman left to look after her children in a primitive two-room cabin in the flat, bare, hot world of the Australian outback. A single episode in which she protects her children from a poisonous snake that has invaded the house tells us everything we need to know about her and her life. Presumably, Mordecai Richler's Duddy Kravitz would have been quite another sort of person if he'd been brought up in a city other than Montreal, or even a few blocks west within the same city.

6. A MAJOR CHARACTER IN THE DRAMA

In some stories, the central struggle experienced by the protagonist
is with the environment – a rising flood, a fire in the attic, a snow
storm that makes communication impossible. The setting, then,
has become the main antagonist. In other stories, the protagonist
may depend upon some aspect of setting to support him in his quest
– the giant pumpkin that wins a prize, the farm that wins the heart
of the mail-order bride.

In Sinclair Ross's short story "One's a Heifer" a Saskatchewan
farm boy during a Great Depression winter sets out on horseback
across the frozen landscape to bring back two stray calves, and is
certain he sees them disappearing into the dilapidated barn of an
unsettlingly eccentric bachelor with "a strange wavering look in his
eyes." The man, named Vickers, denies the calves are in the barn and
goes to great lengths to prevent the boy from entering a locked stall.
Clearly he is hiding something. Night falls and the boy is far from
home. Wanting to catch the farmer asleep and sneak out to liberate
his calves, he stays the night. But the old bachelor does not sleep;
instead he makes the boy a kind of prisoner to his talk, rambling on
about a young housekeeper who came to him from a large family of
people he thought of as stupid, a young woman he sent away again
and again for her incompetence, though she kept coming back. In
the morning, when the man has once again prevented the boy from
getting inside the locked part of the barn, the boy rides home to discover that the calves came home soon after he'd left the day before.
Both the boy and the reader are left with the question: What or who
was hidden inside that barn?

In this story, it is difficult to imagine any of the elements of setting removed without significantly altering the story – if it hadn't
been sub-zero weather, for instance, or if it hadn't been the Canadian prairies where farms are so far apart, if it hadn't been for the
Great Depression when farmers were so desperately poor, if that
barn had not contained a stall that could be locked off from the rest,

or if the boy had not travelled too far to get home before dark. While the story's *situation* had been set up by circumstances before the story had even begun, the development of the story's *plot* is largely determined by its setting. Even the boy's courage and tenacity can be seen as qualities strengthened by the place and time in which he lived.

7. METAPHOR, SOMETIMES A POWERFUL CENTRAL SYMBOL

When we read the first page of Randolph Stow's *Tourmaline*, there is little question that he is introducing the setting in a manner that suggests it will have some importance to the story that follows.

> It is not the same country at five in the afternoon. That is the hardest time, when all the heat of the day rises, and every pebble glares, wounding the eyes, shortening the breath; the time when the practice of living is hardest to defend, and nothing seems easier than to cease, to become a stone, hot and still. At five in the afternoon there is one colour only, and that is brick-red, burning. After sunset, the blue dusk and later the stars. The sky is the garden of Tourmaline.
>
> To describe the town, I must begin with the sun. The sun is close here. If you look at Tourmaline, shade your eyes. It is a town of corrugated iron, and in the heat the corrugations shimmer.
>
> (Randolph Stow, *Tourmaline*)

This landscape is "blunt and red and barren, littered with the fragments of broken mountains, flat, waterless." It is clear the setting has already cast a spell that will affect the entire action of the novel. Here the landscape suggests not only the important specifics of place that the story's characters must live with but also a sort of overriding emblem of the harshness of life itself, at least as Stow sees it, for people who live there.

Stephen Crane's "The Bride Comes to Yellow Sky" is a superb example of a story where setting plays a major role. Since it takes place in a town in the Old West – that is, the Old West of the United

States – we may expect a great deal of local colour. In fact, the writer goes to considerable trouble to make us believe in the place. Gradually, though we recognize stereotypes, we begin to realize that the setting plays a central role in the drama. The setting is under siege. When the sheriff returns from the East with a wife, everything changes. A wild gunman is "disarmed" by the surprise. The rules have changed. Once the East has come West, the West is no longer the West!

Time

It seems to me that in the concept of narrative resides the radical future of the novel. To do away with narrative is utter nonsense: the novel uniquely confronts the human experience of time and space. Narrative is more significant than meaning.

(Robert Kroetsch, "Towards an Essay: My Upstate New York Journals," in *The Lovely Treachery of Words*)

Consider how important in stories are such words as "then" and "afterwards," "once" and "soon" and "later." Time words. Stories exist in time – are trapped in time – and yet use time to shape themselves to a desired end.

Whether or not your story mentions the time of day or the time of year, you should know them, for they can affect the behaviour of your characters and will certainly affect how the landscape is seen.

The short story may be thought of as "an art of snapshots" (Alice Munro) or "a flash of fireflies" (Nadine Gordimer). Both metaphors suggest that the short story, however much time may pass between beginning and end, offers the reader an unsustained glimpse, a sharp insight into a moment of human life – sometimes several. The emphasis is on sharpness, brilliance, the wise selection of telling details, the surprise, the caught-out, the strangely absent, and the ominous hint of a future, rather than upon the shifting, the changing, the unfolding, the accumulating, the entanglement in networks of events, which is more often of interest to the novel.

The novel, in fact, takes time as one of its subjects. Time passes, slowly or quickly; time exerts pressure, imposes urgency; time promises and then withholds the promise; time gradually sees people change, or change one another; time waits, to spring surprises, or leads down mysterious trails to disappointment. Time allows itself to be apportioned into equal chapters, or to be unrolled in a single, breathless, and endless song, or to be coiled back again and again on itself to confront its own past, to be speeded up or to stop for a while, or to be compressed to a narrow wedge deep as thought. The novelist can mould time into any shape imaginable, but cannot escape it. In a novel, time can play a role as large as place, assuming the force and complexity of a character.

> Instead of fairy immunity to change, there is the vulnerability of human imperfection caught up in human emotion, and so there is growth, there is crisis, there is fulfillment, there is decay. . . . Suspense is a necessity in a novel because it is a main condition of our existence. Suspense is known only to mortals, and its agent and messenger is time.
>
> (Eudora Welty, *The Eye of the Story*)

Of course there is more than one time going on in a story. There is the passage of time from the first episode to the last in the world of the story's characters – from the disastrous Saturday night party to the boating accident three weeks later. There is the passing of time for the story's *telling,* its own pace, pauses and surges, moving the reader inevitably from the first page to the last, often with increasing speed towards the end. There is the manipulating of the character's actual time to the *shape* of the telling, with its reversals to revisit the past, its flashforwards to glimpse the future, its pauses for thought, its races through less-important moments or years, and its leaps across the empty spaces of time that are altogether unimportant. And of course there is the other unseen but implied story of all that happened to the story's writer during the time spent fashioning it. It is enough to make you wish the topic had never been brought up – but it must be brought up for the storyteller, and it must be thought about, with respect to the role that time plays in each and every story written.

The Importance of Staring

Stare at your setting until you discover what it has to offer you. Recently a student showed me a story in which a family sits talking on the front porch. Gradually as we read we become aware that they share a terrible family secret. The writer tried to suggest the threat of this secret by planting a hundred-foot fish in a lake not far from the house. This seemed like a fairly good idea, except that the lake was not related to the story in any other way. Any discerning reader would guess that the lake had been dug and filled and populated by the writer herself, eager to support her story with a symbol. In conversation, one of us referred to the fact that the family was "sitting on this horrible secret." It seemed to me that the writer's instincts had already supplied her with everything she needed; she simply hadn't taken full advantage of it. These people spend the whole story sitting not only upon their secret but also upon their front porch. We thought for a while about porches. What do porches have to offer a story about a family struggling with a terrible secret? What might you find under the porch? What objects of the past may be under there, chewed by dogs and coated in dust? The next draft of that story had eliminated the artificial lake and its imported fish. Without wearing neon signs (that lake had seemed ringed with signs saying "SYMBOL OVER HERE, FOLKS!") the porch itself had become the metaphorical dividing line between past and present, seen and hidden.

Some Questions to Ask about Setting in Your Story

1. Are you seeing originally? Or are there passages where you have relied on the way someone else has reported seeing the world? Have you depended upon television or a movie for your vision?

2. Have you helped your reader to respond to your setting with more senses than just sight? What about the sounds, of the city at night, for example? What about the texture of things touched? What about the smell rising from that swamp of croaking frogs?

3. Have you taken advantage of setting in your attempts to make a character seem real? This may mean using the setting in a metaphorical manner, but it may also mean showing how the character reacts to an environment, or acts upon it.

4. Have you considered aspects of your protagonist's setting beyond physical environment? Have you considered social milieu, for instance? Peer groups, and their pressures? Standards upheld by the community? The values held important by a family?

5. Does the time period in which the story takes place affect either the action or the characters? If so, have you taken care that the reader knows when the story is taking place?

6. Could you explain to a reader why setting is *essential* to your story? (That includes the absence of a specified setting as well.)

7. In *Technique in Fiction,* Macauley and Lanning consider various roles that place can take in a story: place as character, place as destiny, place as narrative element, place as period, place as backdrop. Have you considered whether any of these possibilities would enrich your story?

8. If you have become a landscape painter at any point in your story, consider how much of this is necessary. Consider, too, whether you took advantage of every opportunity to *use* the painted landscape – selecting the details the observing character would notice, arranging them in an order that reflects the observing character's state of mind and angle of vision. Has your story come to a dead stop while we admire the scenery, or have you found a way of keeping the narrative flowing through and past it? Have you merely described these bits of the world so that the reader may see and enjoy them, as you have, or have you constructed them, out of the materials of world and memory and imagination, precisely in order to add their unique and irreplaceable nature to the story?

9. To what extent is the passage of time important to the story? Have you considered the time of day and the time of year and their effect upon places and people? Have you avoided drawing attention to easy associations (young love in spring)? Is it always clear to the reader when significant time has passed? Are transitions clear?

Evoking "Place"

For each of these passages that introduce setting, consider how the writer has used the sounds and shapes of words as well as their meanings, the rhythms of sentences, figures of speech, angle of vision, and tone. In each case, consider what feelings, ideas, and even stories are suggested by the passage. Can you tell how important the setting must be in each case? Do you detect any hints that suggest the role the setting might play? Is there any indication that the writer is aware of metaphorical possibilities in the setting?

To birds of the more soaring kind Casterbridge must have appeared on this fine evening as a mosaic-work of subdued reds, browns, greys, and crystals, held together by a rectangular frame of deep green. To the level eye of humanity it stood as an indistinct mass behind a dense stockade of limes and chestnuts, set in the midst of miles of rotund down and concave field. The mass became gradually dissected by the vision into towers, gables, chimneys, and casements, the highest glazings shining bleared and bloodshot with the coppery fire they caught from the belt of sunlit cloud in the west.

(Thomas Hardy, *The Mayor of Casterbridge*)

Our house had never been painted. The wood grew silver-grey, decorated with swirls of weatherworn grain. I think it never truly had an outside. The verandah all round (the style you still see in Queensland) made it like a house whose walls had been taken down, if you know what I mean. You looked straight in to the skeleton, among rooms and open doors, with, often enough, the family sprawled or squatting on the verandah in the spaces between the posts which held up its flimsy iron roof.

(Rodney Hall, *Captivity Captive*)

He lived in an old-style prairie house, two storeys high, narrow, with a steep peaked roof. It had two front doors, one above the other. The first door was at ground level, but the second door was directly above it and opened out from his bedroom. There were no stairs, no balcony, from this second exit, just a flat clapboard wall and a door that opened into thin air. When asked about it, my mother said that it was his door to heaven, and the day Alec died, he'd step through it into God's hands. Alec said it was there because the local carpenter, when hired to build a two-storey house, used the same floor plans for both levels and didn't have enough brains to leave the door out.

(W.D. Valgardson, "The Man Who Was Always Running Out of Toilet Paper")

The birds. To the tag end of trillions of years of decay and growth come the birds: bellbirds, lyrebirds, lorikeets, parakeets. Shadow and rotting sweetnesses lure them. On their wings is such a weight of color that they float dazed on the green air, slowly losing height, drifting down to where Charade sits crushing the mosses and ferns. Oh, she gasps. Oh.

She is five, perhaps six years old, rapt, knees hugged up under her chin. The fallen tree trunk behind her back, given over to creepers, is collapsing softly, and along its jellied spine where a flock of new saplings has a toehold – there is walnut, silky oak, mahogany – the jostling and clamoring for light is constant and silent and deadly earnest. If she sits still long enough, the philodendron will loop itself around her ankles, and kingfishers will nest in her hair.

(Janette Turner Hospital, *Charades*)

I crossed the little brick bridge beyond the plum tree, pausing to look at the eel-haunted creek where my younger children and my children's children swam. Meg had slipped some crusts into my pocket for the eels but with my burned hand I could not take them out. I do not know why I enjoy calling these creatures up from their deeps. Slimy and snake-like, they drive themselves through the water like thoughts better not admitted. Do I still have evil passions? No! I have conquered. My ideal was Wordsworth's, plain living and high thinking, and all I have ever known of lust or rage or envy or greed I have plucked from my heart and put from me and the very place where they had their life I have burned in the cleansing flame. It is not pride that speaks.

(Maurice Gee, *Plumb*)

The train went by. An acrid smell of smoke filled the streets, and a cloud of soot hovered between the sky and the roofs of the buildings. As the soot fell toward the ground, the church steeple emerged without a base, like a spectral arrow in the clouds. The clock appeared next, its illuminated face breaking through puffs of steam. Little by little the whole church stood out, a tall edifice in the Jesuit style. In the center of the garden a Sacred Heart opened arms wide to receive the last particles of soot.

(Gabrielle Roy, *The Tin Flute*, trans. by Hannah Josephson)

Now I've reached the place where I used to get off the streetcar, stepping into the curbside mounds of January slush, into the grating wind that cut up from the lake between the flat-roofed dowdy buildings that were for us the closest thing to urbanity. But this part of the city is no longer flat, dowdy, shabby-genteel. Tubular neon in cursive script decorates the restored brick facades, and there's a lot of brass trim, a lot of real estate, a lot of money. Up ahead there are huge oblong towers, all of glass, lit up, like enormous gravestones of cold light. Frozen assets.

(Margaret Atwood, *Cat's Eye*)

Activities for Finding and Exploring Your Place

Before searching for those skills that will help you handle setting in your current story, spend some time with the following activities, which are designed to help you discover the settings that already matter to you, and to find ways of responding to them. Out of these exercises may come any number of stories you may not have discovered otherwise.

1. Reread the passage by David Malouf early in the chapter. Do some thinking about your first house. Attempt, in a few pages, to reconstruct the house as you discovered it. Consider shape, peculiar architectural elements, objects that were in it, the kind of mythology and history it contained, its secrets. Finally, suggest how your

familiarity with this house and your exploration of it may have influenced the way you see the world.

2. Write a few pages in which you reconstruct the world immediately outside your childhood house. Bring its objects to vivid life for the reader who hasn't been there. Explore what different aspects of this world meant to you then, or mean to you now. As with the previous assignment, consider how this "first" world may have influenced the way you see the larger world you've encountered since; perhaps imagine how it may influence the way you see even the larger world you haven't yet encountered.

3. List the places where you have spent enough time that you have more than a tourist's understanding and feeling for them. (Be more specific than, say, "Argentina," if in fact you spent three years living on "a cattle station in the pampas region of Argentina.") Consider which of these places still have meaning in your life. Why? Can you select specific buildings, landscapes, times, or images that represent whatever it is in a place that means something to you? How many of these places have actually had a definite influence upon the sort of person you are today? Write a short passage in which your intention is to make a specific setting leap to life for your reader. Move in close to a setting that is as specific as possible (e.g., the gauchos' quarters on that pampas ranch) and attempt to render it vividly to the senses even as you use it subtly to suggest the meaning you find in it.

4. Begin a special notebook in which you will write your personal mythology. (Keen and Valley-Fox's *Your Mythic Journey* is a book that should be of interest to fiction writers in search of their own material.) Recollect and record the stories your childhood community told itself by way of explaining its existence in the world ("How we snuck down to Grantham in the middle of the night with horses

and dragged the little church up to here." "How we met at the General Store to see how many had survived the forest fire"), the stories your family told itself about its place in the world and the place of different members within the family ("Uncle George got his hands on all the money, and spent it all on some floozy in San Francisco – that's why we're all so poor." "Mother smuggled her jewellery out of Russia inside cans of vegetables, but lost them when the boat went down in the Bering Strait"), and the stories that you have accumulated to account for all that has happened to you in your life ("I knew it was time to leave home – and never go back – the day my grandmother discovered I'd been sneaking rings and brooches from her jewellery case and giving them to Emily Marsden"). This is not a brief one-time assignment, but one that could go on through the rest of your life.

> *To remain vibrant throughout a lifetime we must always be inventing ourselves, weaving new themes into our life-narratives, remembering our past, re-visioning our future, reauthorizing the myth by which we live.*
> (Sam Keen and Anne Valley-Fox, *Your Mythic Journey*)

5. Reread the news clipping "Death Encounters Couple Looking for Flying Saucer", early in Chapter 2, and consider the roles setting might play in a story based on that event. Certain conclusions can be drawn from the fact that the woman died of hypothermia, as well as starvation and dehydration. Snow and wilderness are mentioned. Think of ways in which the snow, the wilderness, and the isolated road are appropriate contributors to the story. Write a paragraph from the point of view of either person as they drive up this lonely road towards the meeting place. Fill the observed landscape with excitement, hope, anticipation, or anxiety. Write a second passage from the same person's point of view, looking out through the window, say, a week after parking at the meeting place.

Project upon the observed landscape the person's feelings at this time.

6. Write a paragraph in which you describe a person passing through a specific location – say, the main street of a small town – and write each sentence so that while it is about the person and the person's actions, you have slipped in the necessary elements of the location in subordinate and apparently incidental positions only. Your goal: to leave your readers with a sharp and memorable impression of a location they can't remember being shown.

Limbering Up with Milligan's Folly: Setting

Once again, carefully reread the news clipping entitled "Miner's Latest Claim Backfires" in Chapter 2.

A. What elements of the setting in this news clipping do you find unique and interesting?

B. What elements of the setting suggest meaning to you? Can you think of any metaphors suggested by the setting?

C. What elements of the setting seem appropriate and/or necessary to the situation for any one of the characters? Can you imagine the setting suggesting metaphor to any of the characters?

D. Is this story inseparable from its setting? If you are not familiar with small mining towns in mountainous regions, are there elements in the setting of this story that could be transferred successfully to a part of the world you know well? Are there appropriate equivalents in a part of the world you know well? What are they? Rewrite the clipping, changing the locations. What other changes should also be made?

E. Write a passage describing the bank as seen by the bank manager looking back from across the street, just before getting aboard the raft unwillingly. Make sure we can tell how she feels about her place of work now.

F. Write a passage describing the surface of the river (or its equivalent in your moved setting) as seen by Milligan just before he crosses it to rob the bank. Write another passage describing the river from Lindstrom's point of view just after she has climbed ashore after that reluctant ride. In each case, try to suggest through indirection whatever meaning this raging river has for you, or for the character.

G. How important do you imagine this setting – mountains, river, raft, small-town street, bank, isolated farm – becoming in your story? A colourful stage set? An opportunity to explore local colour? A contributor to the actions? A powerful metaphor or symbol? A character in the drama? How aware of the setting do you imagine your main character to be? Consider your reasons for all these answers.

RECOMMENDED FURTHER READING ON SETTING
In a Narrow Grave, Larry McMurtry
The Eye of the Story, Eudora Welty
Three Genres, Stephen Minot. Chapter 21
The Story Makers, Rudy Wiebe (ed)

NOVELS AND SHORT STORIES WHOSE HANDLING OF
SETTING REWARDS EXAMINATION
Captivity Captive, Rodney Hall
Tourmaline, Randolph Stow
Amongst Women, John McGahern
Road to the Stilt House, David Adams Richards
The Stone Angel, Margaret Laurence
Oracles and Miracles, Stevan Eldred-Grigg
Potiki, Patricia Grace
Affliction, Russell Banks
The Tree of Man, Patrick White
Cambridge, Caryl Phillips
The Listeners, George McWhirter

The Disinherited, Matt Cohen
A Whole Brass Band, Anne Cameron
Visitors, John Cranna
A Long Time Dying, Olga Masters
The Lost Salt Gift of Blood, Alistair MacLeod
Things as They Are?, Guy Vanderhaeghe
"Kill Day on the Government Wharf," Audrey Thomas
"Ottawa Valley," Alice Munro
"At the Bay," Katherine Mansfield
"Auction Day in Stanley Street," Kylie Tennant
"The Drover's Wife," Henry Lawson
Travelling Ladies, Janice Kulyk Keefer
The Peach Groves, Barbara Hanrahan
Luna, Sharon Butala
Digging Up the Mountains, Neil Bissoondath
Shorelines, Roy MacGregor
Each Man's Son, Hugh MacLennan

Character: "Precious Particles"

ℐ♙

In daily life we never understand each other, neither complete clair-voyance nor complete confessional exists. We know each other approximately, by external signs, and these serve well enough as a basis for society and even for intimacy. But people in a novel can be understood completely by the reader, if the novelist wishes; their inner as well as their outer life can be exposed. And this is why they often seem more definite than characters in history, or even our own friends; we have been told all about them that can be told; even if they are imperfect or unreal they do not contain any secrets, whereas our friends do and must, mutual secrecy being one of the conditions of life upon this globe.

(E.M. Forster, *Aspects of the Novel*)

On Creating Characters

A character, first of all, is the noise of his name, and all the sounds and rhythms that proceed from him. We pass most things in novels as we pass things on a train. The words flow by like the scenery. All is change. But there are some points in a narrative which remain relatively fixed; we may depart from them, but soon we return, as music returns to its theme. Characters are those primary substances to which everything else is attached.

(William Gass, *Fiction and the Figures of Life*)

I suppose the fact is that to be interested in writing novels, you have to have a passion for reading people and their behaviour and their lives. You are sort of an everlasting observer, and it's not really a conscious decision. From as far back as I can remember, I have spent my time watching and listening, and wondering about what I watched and listened to.

(Janet Frame, in *In the Same Room*)

Those "people" who began as scraps of paper, or as bits and pieces of memory, or as voices heard, and who talked and strutted and fought their way through your first draft, may or may not have taken on full-blown life. Sooner or later you want them to sit up and start to breathe on their own.

The right name helps. A character's history must be explored, whether or not this is given to the reader. Physical appearance, clothing, tastes in cuisine, facial expression, driving habits – all must be considered, perhaps on the page, perhaps only in thought. Accumulated information that is merely gathered data rarely brings a character to life, however, though description and background and explanation can help get us started. In the fiction I admire, it seems that the most vivid character takes on life not so much from an accumulation of information as from the experience of watching this person in action over a number of scenes. And even then, the most memorable characters will sometimes leap to life in a single moment that reveals a unique and peculiar detail of manner, or a unique and peculiar turn of phrase in dialogue. Something, in other words, that causes a sharp flash of recognition: "I know this person." It may be that there is someone in real life I'm reminded of; more likely it is that the telling detail or revealing speech pattern is so sharp and fresh and singular that it automatically contains within it all the rest I need to know about the character. Somehow the writer has found a detail so precise and suggestive that it hints, in a way that perhaps even the writer may not fully understand, at an entire unique soul.

New Zealand novelist Maurice Shadbolt refers to that "precious particle" that must be sought out to define a character. Milan Kundera insists, in his *Art of the Novel,* that nothing is necessary except to capture the "essence" of a character.

The narrator of William Goyen's story "Bridge of Music, River of Sand" takes on life with his opening words:

> Do you remember the bridge that we crossed over the river to get to Riverside? And if you looked over yonder you saw the railroad trestle? High and narrow? Well that's what he jumped off of. Into a nothing river. "River"! I could laugh. I can spit more than runs in that dry bed.

In Elizabeth Bowen's *Eva Trout,* the narrator tells us: "Anyway here was Eva, right back on top of one. Eva, as ever, extra heavily breathing, about to twitch the ignition key." In both cases, the rhythm of the sentences conveys as much as the words. (Seeing Eva throw her ocelot coat over her shoulders and heave herself into her Jaguar helps too!) I imagine I would recognize either of these "characters" on the street or in a theatre foyer in a way I would never recognize someone I'd read about in the newspaper. If this is my experience as a reader, it makes sense that as a writer I try to cause this sort of thing to happen to *my* readers. To look for the unique spark – whether mannerism or habit of speech or personality quirk – and let it ride at the very centre of all the accumulating experiences and reactions that make up the story.

Finding Characters

> *Characters pre-exist. They are* found. *They reveal themselves slowly.*
> (Elizabeth Bowen, "Notes on Writing a Novel")

> *I always start with the main character or, as it may be, characters. Usually there are a number of people who have been inhabiting my head for a number of years before I begin on a novel, and their dilemmas grow out of what they are, where they come from.*
> (Margaret Laurence, in *Eleven Canadian Novelists*)

If Elizabeth Bowen insists that characters pre-exist and must be found, where are they hiding? Where did those characters come from who populated Margaret Laurence's head for years before they found life on paper?

Some writers insist that they find all their characters within themselves – that each character is one fragment of the writer's own complex personality. Some claim to be keen observers, building characters out of this person's walk, that person's smile, another person's habit of grabbing your arm while he talks. Some insist that characters arrive already full-blown, just waiting to be translated into words. Very few claim to have lifted real people from life and put them in a story intact. In fact, some writers caution against attempting such a thing.

I think it can be deadly for writers to import characters from real life. They must begin life in the imagination, exert their pull from there, and once they begin doing that, then they require detailing that only experience can supply. The detail can snap a characterisation into focus as much for the writer as the reader. I remember in 1915 a character who lived for me as soon as I saw she had a white "knuckle" on the tip of her sharp nose. With Olga in Slipstream *I had her coming to the door one day with silver frosted nail polish on her toenails, and Claude McKechnie, in a contrast of texture, offering her a gift of onions. Page by page the details must never be relinquished. Logic and intellect play no part in these selections: they're the warming-up into existence of the emotional wave that is the real manifestation of living character.*

(Roger McDonald, in *Yacker 2*)

If characters are not to be lifted from life in their entirety, Jessica Anderson suggests they can be fanned into life with the aid of real-life props.

For me, they don't work until I have a visual image of them. I had one character, and I couldn't get her right, this was in my first novel. She was a plumpish blonde, and suddenly one day I saw her as tall and dark, and from then on she worked. Again, I might have had some actual person in mind, even someone half-forgotten, who gave me a starting point for that fictional character. It must work like that. You must draw on buried memory.

(Jessica Anderson, in *Yacker 2*)

William Trevor suggests that characters are created out of details accumulated over years of observing the world with a writer's eye.

Well, I think it does seem to me that the only way you can create a character is through observation. I don't think there is any other route. And what you observe is not quite like just meeting someone on a train, having a conversation, and then going away. I mean, really, a kind of adding up of people you notice. I think there's something in writers of fiction that makes them notice things and store them away all the time. . . . Fiction writers remember tiny little details, some of them almost malicious, but very telling.

(William Trevor, in *The Writer's Chapbook*)

Memories of others, fragments found in oneself, people observed, emotions projected, ideas personified . . . it seems that characters can have their beginnings in any number of ways, but if they are to be fully realized, complex, and convincing, they will have to be more than creatures manufactured out of consciously collected data. Eventually – as you watch them, as you describe them, as you put them through scenes in which they are required to react with other characters – it is to be hoped that something not anticipated will happen; you will stumble upon some physical detail like that knuckle on the nose of the character in 1915, or some surprising revelation from the character's own mouth, or some unconscious gesture that reveals more than you suspected, something that starts the character breathing on her own. That moment, I suspect, is not likely to happen until the writer has progressed beyond the act of "creating characters" and has made some emotional link with the emerging figure, which allows the writer to relax a little and allow the figure considerable autonomy.

What interests me is people, that is, characters – creating them, finding out about them, revealing them through showing how they think and feel, what they say and do. I like to explore relationships – family and extended family relationships, spiritual relationships, relationships with land and the environment, inter-cultural relationships.

(Patricia Grace, in *In the Same Room*)

Student writers struggling with characters who resist all attempts to force life upon them have sometimes found it useful to do some serious thinking about the people who most affected them as children, those people who became the archetypes that haunt their lives.

Think about your first bus driver, your first nun, your first bully, your first scandalous adult, your first drunk, your first spineless adult, your first terrifying old person. Find out what those people have to offer. Frankly, I sometimes suspect that much of writing is an attempt to get these figures off our backs, or at least to understand them, or to bring them down to human level so we can look them squarely in the eye.

> The characters in my novels – now that I can appraise them after more than twenty years of screening – prove to emerge from abiding preoccupations. Archetypal figures (reasonably clear in a montage of sixteen novels) have the final say as to who will appear as a character in my fiction. They may bear a close resemblance to an actual person (as such persons resemble archetypal humors) or they may be assembled, whole cloth, from my imaginings and the needs of the novel.
> (Wright Morris, in *Afterwords*)

The Goal

> To be convincing . . . the characters must be CONSISTENT in their behaviour. . . . Second, the characters must be clearly MOTIVATED in whatever they do. . . . Third, the characters must be PLAUSIBLE or lifelike.
> (Laurence Perrine, *Story and Structure*)

If we are to care about your characters we must believe in them. That is, we must believe they have enough life of their own to care what happens to themselves. We want to know what motivates them to act as they do. We want to believe they are capable of change. We want to see with our own eyes that their behaviour is consistent, or when it isn't consistent that it is inconsistent in a way that makes sense, allowing us insight into the character.

To understand a character's motivation, we need to know (or sense) the character's goals – long-term and short-term, tangible and intangible. We need to have some knowledge of the reasons that lie behind the goals. This may involve some exploration of the character's life before the story began.

It will also involve some exploration of the character's emotions. Perhaps here is where you have the greatest opportunity to make connections between your character and your reader. Since you may allow us to share the character's thoughts (directly or indirectly) it is possible for you to make us share the character's emotional reactions as well, to the people and events encountered during the journey towards the achievement (or lack of achievement) of the goals.

The journey towards the goals will involve more than motivation and emotion; it will also require some action. Characters who *want* something *do* something – at least they had better if we are to remain interested in them. What they do and how they do it will tell us much about them, including whether we find them plausible.

Introducing the Characters to the Reader

It can be useful to remind yourself of what the how-to books have to say about the creation of character – that you have four basic channels through which you can convey an impression of your characters to a reader:

a) telling it directly yourself
Mr Maurice Smith was something of a snob.

b) allowing the character to tell it

I am much more discerning than I used to be, Smith thought.
Though I suppose I've become a bit of a snob in the process.

c) allowing some other character to express it
"Don't waste your time on him," Jane Roberts said to her younger
sister. "Maury Smith has no time for the likes of us any more."

d) letting the character's actions suggest it
When Smith turned the corner he discovered the source of the
shouting. A demonstration. Labourers in hard hats wielded placards.
One of the men pushed a pamphlet into Smith's hands. He dropped it
as he might have dropped a handful of steaming dung, and hurried
away, glancing to either side in case someone he knew had seen.

The first is easiest, and you might be forgiven for thinking it
ought to be enough. You've told the reader what the reader needs to
know. The trouble is, the reader doesn't necessarily believe you.
And even if he does believe you, such a simple statement without
reinforcement is easily forgotten.

It is the last of the four that readers will most readily believe. They
have seen the evidence with their own eyes, so to speak. Furthermore, you have allowed them to come to their own conclusion –
which is likely to be "Maurice Smith does not want to be seen associ-
ating with mere labourers. What a snob!"

If you examine carefully an admired writer's presentation of a
character, you are likely to see all four methods at work. It is also
likely that the most lasting and convincing impression is the one
that has come about from observing and interpreting the evidence
for yourself.

Sometimes this lasting and convincing impression is conveyed
through a simple but significant gesture.

Body Language

One of the most common features of ineffective writing is the weak verb. Selecting a strong, vital, original, active verb can often help breathe life into limp sentences. "Walk" is a perfectly good verb, and adequately conveys the notion that a character moves one foot in front of the other across the page. Most of the time that is enough. Occasionally, however, a character walks in such a uniquely telling way that a more precise verb seems called for. To say that a character hurls herself across the page is to tell us something about that character's personality, or at least her mood. However, if none of your characters ever walk, and all of them mince, sashay, stomp, march, skip, or hurl themselves across the page, you have tried too hard and spoiled the effect by drawing too much attention to your cleverness. It might be a good idea, where a special sort of walking is called for, to avoid the thesaurus in favour of the metaphor. Perhaps she has the dainty, careful high-rumped gait of a raccoon, or some other creature made for climbing trees.

Observe carefully the people around you; record the body language you observe; take the time to visualize your characters so vividly that you can see what gestures make them unique and knowable. "She never merely entered a house; she flung herself at a door as though it were necessary to break through barriers in order to take possession of the interior. She *dared* you to throw her out."

The novelist Elizabeth Bowen was particularly good at this.

> No sooner was Clare into the large lounge than she hurled herself on to a striped settee placed diagonally to the electric log fire. She puffed and blew, as one is entitled to do after a strain – then turned to eye a near-by table on which magazines were set out in overlapping rows. Seizing upon a top one, she set about staring her way through it.
>
> (Elizabeth Bowen, *The Little Girls*)

Emotions

Clare's behaviour in the Bowen passage very clearly suggests her emotional state. Because readers have experienced or can imagine most emotional responses, you might take advantage of this *connection* to encourage the reader's involvement in your story. The examples below rather obviously demonstrate a few techniques by which you might suggest a character's emotions.

1. Physical evidence: *His heart raced. His palms were damp.*
2. Revealing actions: *Again he dropped the hat. Once he'd picked it up, he squeezed it and twisted it between his hands.*
3. Facial expressions: *He closed his eyes quickly, and turned away. His lips, you could see, were moving.*
4. Stream of consciousness: *I will not let them see, he thought. I will not give them the satisfaction. Let them think I am as courageous as they are.*
5. Dialogue responses: *"Me?" His voice cracked. "Me? But there must be . . . I can't do . . . Excuse me, I'd better sit down."*
6. Projection onto setting: *The room, when he entered, was crammed with people buzzing with contentment at one another's company. All turned, and levelled gazes at him that said: And what right have you to come amongst us?*
7. Metaphor: *Why did he feel, whenever she turned that lion-sized smile on him, that he'd been mistaken for a Christian?*
8. Allusion: *For a moment he felt himself to be a trembling Faustus, about to cry out a plea for a merciful postponement.*
9. Rhythm: *No, he would not. He would not. He would refuse. He would grit his teeth and smile till his lips bled. He would never, never, never let them see.*
10. Diversionary tactics: *"Oh my goodness gracious I'm terrified!" he said, and held up ridiculously shaking hands. For a moment their laughter relaxed him.*

11. Sympathetic language: Perhaps the curtains *flutter nervously,* or the walls *sweat condensation;* perhaps the people *bray* when they laugh, *growl* when they suggest, *bully* when they persuade, or *rear back, as though about to charge him.*

My examples illustrate the danger in using these techniques – where they are noticed at all, they can be embarrassingly clumsy. Perhaps this is why T.S. Eliot has suggested that the *only* effective manner of portraying emotions in art is the use of what he called an objective correlative – that is, a symbolic object that has become associated with a character. This will be discussed in Chapter 9.

Dialogue

Much more exciting to me is the intricacy, the plot form, of dialogue. The speaker is making up his drama as he goes along, and he doesn't know how good he is or how bad he is. It's natural, so therefore dialogue gets me out of any chip I have about not being able to think of a good plot. Dialogue is one of the things which I seem to be able to do, hit upon doing, and like. Dialogue is my form of poetry.
(V.S. Pritchett, in *The Writer's Chapbook*)

Much of what we learn about characters in fiction comes to us as we listen to them talk to one another. What they say, how they say it, what they avoid saying – these provide us with impressions we interpret, and store for later use.

1. TASKS DIALOGUE CAN DO
a) Advance the plot
"So it's agreed, then. We plant the bomb tomorrow at eight."

b) Reveal and express character traits and emotions
"I insist on doing this myself. Don't argue. I won't allow you to take risks. You know what I'm like."

c) Crystallize relationships and situations

"We all know what you're like. Do you have any idea how patronizing you've become?"

"Don't pretend. You know very well you're relieved that you won't be called upon to be brave."

d) Allow characters to confront one another

"Are you suggesting that I'm a coward?"

"I'm suggesting that you consider yourself too valuable to the world to risk going on a venture like this. Did you bring the schedule?"

e) Reveal by concealing (What is *not* said? Why?)

"My mother worries about me."

"The schedule. You did bring it? It is the only thing that was asked of you."

"She thinks I'm seeing someone she wouldn't approve of."

"We can't do this without a schedule. But we can get a schedule from someone else. We can do this thing without you."

f) Deliver a punch or deciding blow in a conflict (new information that changes things)

"Have you forgotten? I am the only one here with a key to the building."

g) Comment on setting, weather, surroundings, and so forth, in a manner that suggests interpretation

"This room seems to grow smaller and hotter every time we meet. Perhaps someone commands more than his share of the space, or considers the air to be for his breathing alone."

h) Introduce or reinforce an allusion, symbol, or repeated motif

"You are playing with your watch strap again. One of these days you will break it."

i) Offer a cue for transition to new scene or narrative summary

"I will be visiting everyone on this list, then, before we meet tomorrow for a final decision."

2. SOME CHARACTERISTICS OF MUCH SUCCESSFUL DIALOGUE

a) It adds new information for the reader.

b) It usually avoids the largely meaningless routine exchanges in conversation: "Hello, how are you?" "Oh, not too bad."

c) It avoids, except where useful for character development, the sort of repetitions many people exhibit in their everyday conversations.

d) It suggests the way each speaker feels about the other, and about himself or herself.

e) It reflects the individual vocabulary and speech patterns of the individuals.

f) If it suggests dialect, or ungrammatical speech, or individual pronunciations, it does so with a minimum of phonetic spellings, and achieves its effect through rhythm and word choice.

3. WHAT TO NOTICE WHILE LISTENING IN ON CONVERSATIONS

a) level, type, and breadth of the person's vocabulary (education)

b) diction level (slang? colloquial? precisely scientific?)

c) characteristics with a national or racial origin

d) sentence lengths

e) rhythms

f) favourite expressions

g) implied emotional states; present circumstances

h) accompanying gestures, facial expressions

i) the extent to which the person allows speech to say what is really meant

4. DIALOGUE AS A POWER STRUGGLE

In key scenes we often witness people having a conversation in which each tries to get something out of the other, each tries to come out the winner in a competition. Here is the *beginning* of a list of the dozens of ways people try to get what they want. Continue the list until you have fifty or more. Keep the list nearby when you're writing. Turning to these can help you move your plot forward while developing a scene through strong dialogue.

demand	use physical force
whine	use logic
blackmail	appeal to sentiment
pout	use bluster
coax	hold out hope
promise	diminish importance of
plead	call up precedent
exchange	
charm	
weep	
refuse	
withdraw	
cheat	
lie	
flatter	
threaten	

Quick Characterizations

Often a character can be sparked into life with a single stroke – a unique revealing detail, a metaphor, a gesture, a mannerism, a line of dialogue, or a glimpse at his or her room.

> You could walk through the entire market and look at every stall, but never would you see calabashes and earthen pots any better than

those sold by Mammii Ama. She was honest – true as God, she really was. You might claim that there were as many honest traders here as there were elephants, and Mammii Ama would understand your meaning, and laugh, and agree with you. But she would let you know she was the one old cow-elephant that never yet died off.

(Margaret Laurence, "A Gourdful of Glory")

I never knew her real name and it is quite likely that she did have one, though I never heard her called anything but Gold Teeth. She did, indeed, have gold teeth. She had sixteen of them. She had married early and she had married well, and shortly after her marriage she exchanged her perfectly sound teeth for gold ones, to announce to the world that her husband was a man of substance.

(V.S. Naipaul, "My Aunt Gold Teeth")

I am the only person I know whose father was a dandy, a man who failed at almost everything except keeping his shoes polished to perfection, and at a kind of kidding all the time that he was more melancholy than anyone understood. He loved standing on the back porch with his jacket off but his white sleeves rolled down, the cuffs held with slender jade cufflinks, his waistcoat buttoned and his watch-chain shining across his lean stomach. He would stand with a book open and resting on one palm and in the sunlight (it is never winter when I remember him), from the distance, he was lithe and solitary, a kind of figure from a western who held a book instead of a gun. But he would take books up and lay them down as though there were something in them which roughness would spill.

(Vincent O'Sullivan, "Palms and Minarets")

But when his mother twirled, she kept her right foot in one spot, using it as a pivot, and used the left foot as if she were on a scooter, pushing herself around and around, her arms held out at shoulder level, and she threw back her head and laughed. William could see under her dress when she twirled, her slip and the tops of her stockings, whose seams were always straight. He was both excited that she could be so carefree and competent at twirling and also uneasy that she was capable of such abandon. Only after many, many revolutions did she flop onto the lounge, almost flying into it, so that there was a moment when her whole body was completely in the air, after her feet had left the floor, as she flung herself at the brown couch, and before her body touched the cushions.

"I'm really the passionate European type," she called to him as he sat with his legs crossed on the carpet, gazing up at her. "I'm not really English at all." She fanned herself with both hands, still laughing, shaking her head so that her yellow hair danced off her neck. "I have to keep it secret."

(Glenda Adams, *Longleg*)

"That cheeky one will get a hiding before the day is out," said Father sitting down.

Fred, Letty and Grace laughed because it was wise to laugh when Father joked and the idea of Father's favourite, beautiful innocent four year old Rosie being belted with the leather strap was quite laughable.

Mother sent a small smile Father's way thanking him for his good humour. Tom was opposite Father and Father fixed his brown eyes suddenly gone hard on him, because Tom, lifting a shoulder again and rubbing it around his ear, hadn't laughed.

(Olga Masters, "The Snake and Bad Tom")

Harris arrived. He was dressed in a policeman's uniform. "Evening," he said. He took the helmet from his sweating head and looked round the office. He did not approve of the jungle of potted ferns and palms cluttering the room. They were unprofessional, he maintained. The tropical pot-plants turned Niall and himself into a pair of sweating monkeys peeping at clients between the greenery. Niall had let his wife do the decorating. "I like it. They're creative," Niall had said. Harris wanted to get rid of them: "It's a rainforest," he had argued. Harris wanted to wash the walls, too, but Niall would not allow it. A foot from the ceiling was the high-water mark of last year's floods. Below that the walls were stained in brownish streaks. "If we wash them we invite another flood," Niall had said. The logic of it escaped Harris: "By that reasoning," he had replied, "the city should not rebuild the Victoria Bridge."

(Nigel Krauth, *Matilda, My Darling*)

Mabel was in a bad state all right. She said the operation hadn't done her any good, but she was afraid to go back to the doctor and tell him. It was her third operation.

"Why are you afraid?"

"Leave me alone."

"Why are you afraid —"

"Leave me alone — my stomach hurts."

She sat in her grey winter coat with her stockings rolled down about her ankles. The coat came down to her calves, and thread and lining brushed her legs. The coat still had a Christmas decoration on the lapel, as if she would be going to midnight mass.

She'd got the coat six years ago. Arnold once thought she'd looked pretty good in it, and she still wore it in the winter, though its life had been sucked out of it; and in the winter she put on a skittish pink scarf to dress it up.

"I'm afraid the doctor will blame me for not getting better," she said.

Arnold said nothing.

"I'm afraid to bother him all the time."

Tears came. She sniffed. Her coat pockets were filled with bingo markers, which jiggled when she made a move.

(David Adams Richards, *Road to the Stilt House*)

Sam Pickles grew up on that racetrack, hanging around the stables or by the final turn where the Patterson's Curse grew knee high and the ground vibrated with all that passing flesh. Old Merv had Sam down as a rider. He was small and there was something about it in his blood, but when Merv died the dream went with him. A gambler's wife has ideas of her own. Fools breed a hardness in others they can't know. Sam Pickles tried to knuckle down to his mother's way. He came to love labour the way his father never did, but there was always that nose for chance he'd inherited, an excitement in random shifts, the sudden leaping out of the unforeseen. He did badly at school and was apprenticed to a butcher. Then one day, with the shifty shadow upon him, he shot through, leaving his mother without a son, the butcher without an arse to kick, and a footy team without a snappy rover for whom the ball always fell the right way. A lot of things had happened since that day. His luck had waxed and waned. Like a gambler he thought the equation was about even, though any plant, animal or mineral could have told him he was on a lifelong losing streak.

(Tim Winton, *Cloudstreet*)

Writing Characters

1. Invent a situation where two characters come together and each wants something out of the other (e.g., he's just locked his shop door and she wants in?). Write a page of dialogue in which each of these uses a number of techniques to try to get what she or he wants out of the other.

2. A. For one of the characters in your passage, list the following information: age, height, weight, shape, career, present state of career, clothing, one significant element of clothing, hands, feet, throat, education, vocabulary, speech patterns, home, living conditions, marital/sexual status, general ambition in life, immediate goals, attitude to people, transportation, favourite music, favourite writers, favourite food, favourite sport, dominant personality trait, name.

B. So far you have only a catalogue of information, rather than a character. Choose two or three of these pieces of information that strike you as unique and significant. Analyze what they imply.

C. Now you can *begin* to create a character:

a) Rewrite your character's side of a conversation with the other person.

b) Write a sentence or two showing your character entering a room in such a way that we immediately sense all of the above. Pay close attention to your verbs.

3. Dig deeply into your childhood. Perhaps go back and read the passages you wrote on your earliest house. Recall those people who most affected you in your pre-school years. Which attracted you most? Which frightened you most? Which puzzled you most? Of them all, which took on the shape of archetype in your imagination (e.g., "typical neighbourhood bully" or "typical cranky old man")? Which of them interest or puzzle you even today, or at least come back in occasional memories? Which would you most like to bring back or find for an interview? Whose "story" holds the most interest or mystery?

For any one of these people you've recalled, begin to write down for a reader what you remember. Keep writing until you find yourself beginning to invent or guess in order to fill in gaps. If you're interested, keep on going!

4. For each of the characters in the story you are now writing, create a "fact sheet" in which you list as much as you know. Begin with obvious facts like sex and age, then go on to include such matters as favourite TV program, attitude to self, and long-range goals. Find out how far you can go before you begin to discover aspects of the characters that remain unknown to you. Search through the known facts for clues to the unknown.

Limbering Up with Milligan's Folly: Character

Reread the news clipping entitled "Miner's Latest Claim Backfires" in Chapter 2.

A. Of the three active characters in this drama, which two interest you most? Which one interests you most? Why?

B. For each of the three characters, how much can you supply of physical appearance? Make a list. Begin with height and end with the scuff mark on one toe.

C. Imagine the ways in which Milligan and Cates have different attitudes towards that cabin he wants to fix up for her. Imagine her private reasons for putting off the marriage. For each character, write a passage in which you watch the character respond to a chimney fire in that cabin. Follow each with a paragraph that captures the way that person is privately feeling while experiencing the moment you've chosen.

D. Consider the careers of each character. A lone miner working his claim. A bank manager. A clerk in an assayer's office. For each, jot down what this person does in the course of his or her work. For each, jot down some of the special language that might be associated with his or her job. For each, consider which activities associated with the work are of most interest and significance to him or her. When you look over your notes, does anything suggest itself to you as a metaphor – that is, does the person's work have metaphorical implications in the way that a road mender's work might be thought of as "making the journey smoother for others" or a fence builder might be thought of as "keeping the border clear between where you are welcome and where you are not"? Consider whether these characters are likely to have thought of their careers in these terms. Record this information and save it for later.

E. You may have discovered, while doing exercise D, that you wish these two characters had careers you knew more about or were more interested in. Now is your opportunity to rewrite the clipping once more, changing their careers (which will also mean changing their reasons for being where they are). While you're at it, you may wish to change their ages and relationship as well. (Subsequent exercises will continue to refer to the original clipping but you can make the appropriate adjustments at each stage. It is a good idea to settle now on the characters' careers and reasons for being where they are, before starting to imagine plots.)

F. Whoever may become your protagonist, it is clear that the witness Marsden has her opinion of all three. Fill out the front-page information of an income-tax form for her – name, age, address, career. Write a paragraph in which you allow us to discover, indirectly, what she does for a living and how she thinks of her career.

G. For the character who interests you most, the person you imagine becoming the main character in this story, sketch a brief biography that includes the main events and places of this person's life up to the day of the robbery. Sketch a biography for the person you consider the second most important person in this story.

H. Write the letter Milligan might send to his fiancée from jail.

I. Write the thoughts going through the head of the bank manager when she realizes that Milligan is serious when he says she has to accompany him out of the bank.

J. Imagine yourself to be a newspaper reporter in the small town where the incident took place. Interview a few townsfolk who have an opinion of Milligan from having seen him in town before. Write the results. Write what two eye-witnesses report noticing inside the bank at the time of the robbery, keeping in mind that each would likely notice some different aspects – appearance, gestures, actions, clothing, overheard conversations, accents, facial expressions, etc.

K. Write a passage of dialogue in which your three characters are all in the same room – a restaurant, say – and talking together, some weeks before Milligan even thought of the robbery. Make it your task to capture the differences in their speech so sharply that it will be unnecessary to identify who is speaking. Pay attention to level of diction, sentence structure, rhythm, idiom of the place, signature phrases, present mood, and purpose.

L. In the passages you've written, can you find instances where you have made use of the four following techniques to reveal your character to the reader?

1. what *you* tell the reader directly.

2. what *he* tells about himself, or thinks.

3. what *others* in the story say about her.

4. what *actions and reactions* you supply so readers can come to their own conclusions.

NOTE: If you begin to feel too restricted by the news clipping you are working with, don't abandon the exercises or make frivolous changes. Stare at the given material looking for areas where it might be expanded naturally. For instance, you may already have decided that the witness, Marsden, has hired Milligan to pull this whole thing off so that she can go behind the counter and make changes to important papers. Or, if you've moved the setting to the Australian bush, you may also have changed the motorbike to a horse and decided to set this story in the nineteenth century. Or, if you've moved the setting to the Smoky Mountains, you may discover that Lily Cates is not the farmer's daughter at all but his niece, a Nashville singing star trying to lead a quiet life here in order to recover from the pressures of a rocky career. Or, you have decided that Milligan is a lonely sheep farmer in a New Zealand valley. Or perhaps that he is a Vietnam deserter who's grown restless with his isolated quiet life in Canada. Whatever changes you make, be certain that they seem natural extensions of the original and that you then make other changes necessary to keep the story believable. It will be up to you to interpret the exercises that follow in a manner that allows for your changes.

RECOMMENDED FURTHER READING
ON CHARACTER DEVELOPMENT

Writing Fiction, R.V. Cassill. Chapter 7
Three Genres, Stephen Minot. Chapter 19
Literature: Structure, Sound, and Sense, Laurence Perrine. Chapter 3
Living by Fiction, Annie Dillard. Part I, Chapter 2
Starting from Scratch, R.M. Brown. Part III
Playwriting, B. Grebanier. Chapters VII & IX
Text Book, Scholes, Comley & Ulmer. Part I
The Company We Keep, Wayne Booth. Part II, Chapters 8 & 9
Fiction and the Figures of Life, William H. Gass. Part I, Chapter 3
The Writer's Time, K. Atchity. Chapter 5
Aspects of the Novel, E.M. Forster. Chapters III & IV
The Art of the Novel, Milan Kundera
The Writer's Craft, John Hersey (ed). Part 2
The Writing Book, Kate Grenville. Chapter 3
Writing in General and the Short Story in Particular, Rust Hills
The Story Makers, Rudy Wiebe

RECOMMENDED NOVELS AND SHORT STORIES THAT REWARD
CLOSE EXAMINATION FOR CHARACTER DEVELOPMENT

Eva Trout, Elizabeth Bowen
The English Patient, Michael Ondaatje

The Great World, David Malouf
The Burning Boy, Maurice Gee
The Book of Evidence, John Banville
The Moviegoer, Walker Percy
Waiting for Childhood, Sumner Locke Eliot
The Transit of Venus, Shirley Hazzard
The Stone Angel, Margaret Laurence
Lillian's Story, Kate Grenville
Cloudstreet, Tim Winton
The Sweet Second Summer of Kitty Malone, Matt Cohen
Healing the Dead, D.F. Bailey
The Matriarch, Witi Ihimaera
Strangers and Brothers, Maurice Shadbolt
The Apprenticeship of Duddy Kravitz, Mordecai Richler
Such a Long Journey, Rohinton Mistry
Beloved, Toni Morrison
A Thousand Acres, Jane Smiley
1915, Roger McDonald
Cutting Stone, Janet Burroway
The Stories of William Trevor
The Moons of Jupiter, Alice Munro
The Home Girls, Olga Masters
Collected Stories of Katherine Mansfield
The Collected Stories of John McGahern
Blue Husbands, Don Dickinson
Marine Life, Linda Svendsen
The Hanged Man in the Garden, Marion Halligan
Jump, Nadine Gordimer
Foreign Affairs, Keath Fraser
Limbo River, Rick Hillis

Plot: A Causal Chain

༄

There are three necessary elements in a story – exposition, development, and drama. Exposition we may illustrate as "John Fortescue was a solicitor in the little town of X"; development as "One day Mrs Fortescue told him she was about to leave him for another man"; and drama as " 'You will do nothing of the kind,' he said."

(Frank O'Connor, *The Lonely Voice*)

Some Observations on Plot

Plot can be most easily seen in those genre novels and stories whose sole aim is to keep the reader entertained or thrilled or terrified, eagerly turning the pages to see what happens next, anxious to discover whether the protagonist achieves what she wants, or gets what he deserves. In these stories (and in movies or television dramas equally dependent upon plot) our interest depends upon (a) a protagonist we care about, or at least are interested in, (b) our knowledge that the protagonist has a goal and a strong reason for achieving it, (c) obstacles that arise, often at the instigation of an antagonist, to prevent our protagonist from achieving that goal, (d) the sense that each event is somehow the cause of the event that follows, (e) conflicts that intensify to the point where something has got to break, causing the protagonist's life to turn a corner, and (f) a resolution that allows us to close the book with a sense that the story has indeed come to a satisfying end. We can, then, think of the traditional plot as a series of causally related events, involving some sort of conflict (or tension), leading (probably) to a climax and (possibly) to a resolution.

If our protagonist wants to be vice president of her company on page one and is made vice president on page two, you may not have a plot. You may not have any readers either. If things are that easy for her, why should we stay around? Why, in fact, should we care? If, however, she discovers on page two that three of the company's vice presidents are determined that she not join them, our interest may pick up. She's run into an obstacle. We want to see how she handles it. Once she's overcome that first obstacle (if she does) we expect she will probably run into a second, even more challenging one.

Of course, this approach to plot can apply to more complex character-driven stories as well, though not so baldly. Here we are as interested in why the protagonist is in pursuit of a goal as in the question of whether she will achieve it. Janet Burroway reminds us that "the human desire to know why is as powerful as the desire to know what happened next, and it is a desire of a higher order" (*Writing Fiction*).

Australian novelist Kate Grenville writes, "The great danger of the conventional plot is that it becomes so contrived and unlifelike that it becomes dead: a pale, shallow imitation of the richness of real life." Lest this be taken as encouragement to throw out the whole idea of plot, she adds that, on the other hand, the "great danger of the plotless narrative is that there isn't enough forward movement for the reader to stay interested" (*The Writing Book*).

To avoid the contrived and unlifelike plot and at the same time maintain forward movement, the writer should probably put aside all preconceived notions of the demands of plot, at least temporarily, and put more effort into understanding and exploring the characters. If the main character or protagonist has struggled to achieve a life of her own, she is likely to suggest a situation that will challenge her to use all her resources. By responding to these challenges, she is already suggesting to you a direction of action that resembles something like a plot.

Letting the characters take care of the plot, so to speak, may be less risky a matter if, as E.M. Forster suggests, the writer has a strong sense from the beginning of where the story needs to go:

The novelist should, I think, always settle when he starts what is going to happen, what his major event is to be. He may alter this event as he approaches it, indeed he probably will, indeed he probably had better, or the novel becomes tied up and tight. But the sense of a solid mass ahead, a mountain round or over or through which the story must somehow go, is most valuable and, for the novels I've tried to write, essential. There must be something, some major object towards which one is to approach.

(E.M. Forster, in *The Writer's Chapbook*)

The truth is, of all the aspects of fiction writing, it is in discussing plot that I feel the least confidence. If written or spoken about with too much authority, plot begins to look like a formula or a blueprint. Discussions of plot can seem to suggest that a writer should distort events, alter the personalities of characters, and forget about meaning, all in order to make the story fit a pattern that has been proved to have the widest appeal. A too-confident discussion of plot begins to sound like those books out of Hollywood on writing successful screenplays: "Plot Point #1 must occur within the first half hour and put a complete spin on the protagonist's direction." Plot, there, seems to be a matter of nailing all the required parts in the required places.

Consider the differences in approach taken by the following writers to the matter of plot construction.

I think it is important to make a detailed plan before you write the first sentence. Some people think one should write – "George woke up and knew that something terrible had happened yesterday" – and then see what happens. I plan the whole thing in detail before I begin. I have a general scheme and lots of notes. Every chapter is planned. Every conversation is planned. . . . The second stage is that one should sit quietly and let the thing invent itself. One piece of imagination leads to another. You think about a certain situation and then some quite extraordinary aspect of it suddenly appears. The deep things that the work is about declare themselves and connect. Somehow things fly together and generate other things, and characters invent other characters, as if they were all doing it themselves. One should be patient and extend this period as far as possible.

(Iris Murdoch, in *The Writer's Chapbook*)

I do know the story when I begin, but I don't know how it's going to end. I know about two-thirds of it, and then the end emerges as I go on. . . . I hear the story, I am told the story, I record the story. I don't pretend that some remarkable person somewhere else is whispering in my ear, or that a beautiful lady in a diaphanous garment is telling me what I should write. It is just part of my own creative process which I am not immediately in touch with and certainly not in full control of. And so the story emerges.

(Robertson Davies, in *The Writer's Chapbook*)

Well, I usually have one firm character, perhaps two, and an underlying theme – certainly a situation. And from then on, if it works at all, the characters shape the plot rather than the other way round.

(Jessica Anderson, in *Yacker 2*)

It may be that these three writers are talking about different stages of the same process, but we may take them as representing the variety of approaches to plot – from the writer who designs a plot before doing anything else to the writer who allows his characters to work out their own plot. Fine fiction has resulted from all these approaches.

Many writers approach plot as though it were a kind of war, creating stories of heroes, battles, intrigues, quests, and romances. Recent challenges to this traditional approach should not be ignored – in fact, they offer exciting new possibilities. Ursula Le Guin, in "The Carrier Bag Theory of Fiction," wishes to think of a novel not as a hero's bloody quest but as a carrier bag, or "a medicine bundle, holding things in a particular, powerful relation to one another," where conflict is only one element amongst many. In *Spaces Like Stairs*, Carol Scott expresses a desire to escape servitude to the conflict-dominated plot, and contemplates Julio Cortázar's comment that a short story is shaped like a sphere. Some writers prefer to approach plot in terms of a birth metaphor, rather than in terms of conflict:

> *Seeing the world in terms of enemies and warring factions not only limits the possibilities of literature, [critics] argue, but also promulgates an aggressive and antagonistic view of our own lives. Further, the notion of resolution is untrue to life, and holds up perfection, unity, and singularity as goals at the expense of acceptance, nuance, and variety. . . . Birth presents us with an alternative model in which there is a desired result, drama, struggle, and outcome. But it also represents a process in which the struggle, one toward life and growth, is natural. There is no enemy. The "resolution" suggests continuance rather than finality. It is persuasively argued that the story as power struggle offers a patriarchal view of the world, and that it would improve both stories and world if we would envision human beings as engaged in a struggle toward light.*
>
> (Janet Burroway, *Writing Fiction*)

Burroway suggests that the "plot as war" model has been most eagerly abandoned by many contemporary women writers. Instead of heroic quests and individual triumphs, we journey inward, gathering and connecting and sharing and healing. Stories move sideways, in circles, in parallel lines – creating networks instead of confrontations, solving problems through compromise and consensus rather than force or triumph. Although women writers have most dramatically demonstrated both the appeal and the power of these patterns, we should not consider them the exclusive property of women writers. Notice how like the birth process – "a struggle toward the light" – are the stage and movie plots of Horton Foote and the novels and short stories of Wright Morris.

The movement of my novels is always towards knowledge – self-knowl-
edge in the characters, and they get there, they have their victories, all of
them, and a vast amount of entertainment is had along the way. It
entertains me.
     (Maurice Gee, in *In the Same Room*)

Rather than present plot as though it were a set of blueprints to
follow in the construction of a story, I will try to explore the role plot
has traditionally played in attempting to satisfy readers' needs or
expectations. Having considered these expectations, you may wish
to adhere strictly to a traditional form or you may prefer to find (or
invent) other means to satisfy the same needs – as, say, Italo Calvino
and Angela Carter have done. You might wish to discover how
Owen Marshall fashioned a story out of a list of all the people the
narrator has known ("Off by Heart"), how Keath Fraser fashioned a
story filled with specific instructions to consult a thesaurus
("Roget's Thesaurus"), or how Donald Harington fashioned an
epic novel out of what appears to be a textbook, complete with illus-
trations (*The Architecture of the Arkansas Ozarks*).

What, then, does a plot do for the reader?

1. *A plot concentrates on a character (or a group of characters) whom*
the writer believes to be of considerable interest to the reader.
     As a fiction writer, of course you may feel that all human beings
are interesting enough to become the central figure in a story. Your
task is to choose a character you find immeasurably interesting
yourself, and to present that character in such a way that the reader
cannot resist the invitation to spend some time in this character's
company.

2. *A plot becomes more than a character sketch when a character*
is selected who is of interest to the reader for having motives or

personality traits capable of precipitating events, and for having some
goal or need the reader can be encouraged to care about.

A character filled with resentment is sooner or later likely to act. A character who desperately wants to wield power over others is one day going to take the first step towards achieving that power. If a character doesn't care what happens to her, why should we? If the character is determined not to pursue any goals, he may be interesting to us only so long as we're curious about his reasons; he can become interesting enough for a story only when he has to fight to maintain his position of apathy – and thus has become a person with a goal. We become involved in other people's lives when we care about them, and we begin to care about them when we understand what it is they hope for. Then we are put in the position of cheering them on, tensing on their behalf, getting impatient to discover whether they succeed. We can be made to feel that we too have something invested in their pursuits.

3. *A plot concentrates on only that portion of a character's life that the reader will discover to have the most significance.*

If a novel begins with a character's birth and proceeds to his death, we can assume the writer feels that the entire lifetime is of intense interest and importance (though parts will be selected for inclusion, parts left out). More often, a writer finds that a certain portion of a character's life is of the most interest because that is where something with *meaning* happened, something that may have changed the world for that character or thrown light on the significance of that character's actions. Even so, a writer may decide that the significance lies in one segment of the important portion rather than another. Short stories sometimes concentrate on a single event.

Imagine for a moment a story of a country and western singer whose meteoric rise to fame is followed by a descent into alcoholism, a marriage failure, and a diminishing of his talents to the point where he is a washed-up has-been brawling drunkenly in a back-roads motel. Imagine, too, that this motel is run by a widow with a small boy, and that she offers the once-famous singer work as a maintenance man around the place, and that they fall in love, and that the singer becomes a father replacement to the boy, and that the ex-singer fights hard to stop drinking, and helps a local group of young singers get a start with some of his songs. One writer may feel the entire story must be told, since all aspects of it seem of equal interest and significance. Another may see the main appeal and sole significance in the story of the terrible damage fame can do an artistic person, and may begin the plot when, at a moment of greatest success, the singer's wife first draws his attention to the fact that he's been drinking too much lately; this plot might end with a tragic portrait of a wasted talent, reduced to working as a labourer in some godforsaken roadside motel. Another writer, however, could look at the same sequence of events and decide that its main appeal and sole significance lie in the story of the ex-singer's rehabilitation (as Horton Foote must have done, when he wrote *Tender Mercies*) – the power of love and determination and decency and imagination to bring a person back from the brink of tragedy and find not just new interest in life but a richer involvement in life than he'd had before. The writer chooses that part of the story that offers an opportunity to explore meanings that he or she considers to be the most important.

4. A plot causes the reader to feel some confidence that the events are not merely random but connected in some important way – often causally, always thematically.

We are interested in more than things happening. We are interested in "how?" and "why?" and "what does it mean?" The car swerved to miss a pedestrian and went off the road; a flock of birds descended upon the roof of a house; a lone swimmer set out from the shore and kept on swimming beyond her ability to return. We might be interested momentarily in each of these incidents, but our abiding interest would still be in what they may have to do with one another. Where's the connection? Did one cause the other? The simplest plots are constructed of a chain of causal events: A caused B, B caused C, C caused D, etc; if it hadn't been for A, Z might never have happened. The causal chain is most visible in the less sophisticated examples of genre fiction and least visible in the more complex examples of what, for lack of a better term, we'll refer to as "literary" fiction.

5. *After whatever groundwork the writer feels is necessary as an introduction, a plot invites the reader into a story at a moment when the status quo is threatened.*

We sense a story beginning to happen when the protagonist takes her first step towards her goal. Will she succeed, or will something try to stop her? We know it's worth hanging around to see what happens when a stranger arrives in town with the potential to change everything for our protagonist, who was happy with things just the way they were. The two words that announce most loudly the moment at which a plot really begins are "then" and "but." "Then one day he walked into his supervisor's office with a gun in his hand and demanded a raise." "But a sense of unease settled between her shoulders as she watched a young man step out of his car and walk in her direction with a lumpy garbage bag in one hand."

6. *A plot soon involves the reader in more than an anecdote's easy entertainment by revealing complications and developments that create tension and a need to find out how this series of events will turn out.*

This tension is most often achieved through obstruction and conflict. The character, in moving towards his goal, encounters a person or object or situation that stands in his way. The character struggles to overcome the obstacle. The resulting conflict may involve external actions such as arguments, chases, searches, crimes, or may involve internal struggles such as arguments with himself, decisions to be made, attraction to two mutually exclusive desires at the same time, frustration, fear, and hope. Whatever the nature of the conflict, the difficulties experienced by the character in pursuit of his goal will create a suspense that is shared by the reader.

7. As a journey causes us to anticipate its destination even while we enjoy the passing scenery, a plot causes the reader to maintain interest in the central character's desired goal even while feeling involved emotionally in the events that occur along the way.

The protagonist's goal has probably been suggested in quite tangible terms (to marry the rich widow of his former tormentor), which we understand to represent an intangible goal (to boost his own self-esteem by "showing" his dead tormentor he's his equal). A good plot manages to keep the reader's eyes on that goal even while engaging her in the entertaining individual matters most closely at hand – the struggle to get the rich widow even to notice his existence, perhaps, or the effort involved in convincing her to be his guest at a Christmas party. If we are reading *only* to find out if he gets what he wants, why shouldn't we skip over the middle and just read the end?

8. A plot causes the reader to maintain and even increase interest in the period between a good opening and a satisfying ending.

If you find you can describe a story's plot by telling about the beginning and then saying, "Then one thing led to another until such-and-such happened," you're probably talking about a story whose middle sags. Similarly you should not be able to explain the end of a story without having to explain the middle. Reminders of the goal's importance can keep the middle from sagging; so can smaller conflicts related to the larger battle; and so, too, can serious setbacks or reversals in the protagonist's journey. Cartoons may simply repeat a pattern of conflict, with variations, but we expect serious fiction to make better use of "middles" than simply to keep things going. We expect change, development, complication, reversals, the introduction of new elements, increasingly compelling reasons to keep on reading. If there needs to be something at stake for the character before the reader commits her interest in the first place – that is, something of importance to be lost if the goal is not achieved – the reader's continuing interest may depend upon events, decisions, or discoveries *raising* the stakes. Somehow the man who risked failing to marry the wealthy widow and get his revenge upon his former tormentor has got himself into a position – through his reactions to the obstacles he encountered – where failing to marry the widow could now mean a lengthy time in prison, say, for his inability to pay an enormous amount promised to the man he hired to murder the woman's son. While some short story writers may have shorter middles to worry about, the novelist is aware from the outset that the very nature of the form demands a constant restrengthening of the tension, a repeated raising of the stakes; thus the introduction of new characters, the working out of subplots, the major setbacks, and the chapter-by-chapter imitation of the short story's general rise to a crisis or turning point, with each chapter rising a little higher than the chapter that preceded it.

9. *A plot eventually brings the reader to a moment that promises to relieve the increased tension, where conflicting forces are brought face-to-face in an ultimate contest which will cause everything to change, or at least look different afterwards.*

Climax. Turning point. Point of no return. This is the moment towards which, the reader feels, everything has been leading. It is also the moment after which nothing will ever be quite the same again. Whether our protagonist's battle has been with herself, with another person, with society, or with the forces of nature, everything else has led the reader to expect an eventual showdown that will determine how matters will go afterwards. In stories where the conflict has been physical, the climax is likely to involve some sort of physical confrontation; in quieter stories of internal conflict, the climax is likely to be a moment of increased discomfort that brings urgency to a need for a decision, for a discovery, or for a recognition. When this moment has been reached, it seems as though every word of the preceding story has been a preparation for it. Whatever tension the reader earlier felt now becomes a pressing need for things to be resolved.

10. *A plot releases the reader from involvement when some moment of significance has been achieved – a moment of self-understanding, perhaps, or a moment that signals a final success or failure, or a moment that demonstrates that everything will go on more or less like this forever without much change.*

An inevitable result of all that went before, that turning point is not simply a device to release the reader from tension, but an experience that gives the reader some insight into what all this struggle has been about – what meaning the preceding sequence of events has had for the character, and what significance it has had for the writer.

11. *A plot does not expect the reader to go on reading past #10, though the writer hopes to have provoked the reader into continuing to think about the protagonist's past and future.*

Some writers are less willing than others to admit the importance of these elements. To scorn such an approach to plot may be an attempt to distance themselves, quite understandably, from any suggestion that they write to a formula, or even that they allow reader expectations or traditions to have a serious effect upon what happens in their stories. Yet it is interesting to discover the extent to which the elements I've isolated above are present even in the stories of the writer who has made the following comments about plot:

I don't work with plots. I work with intuition, apprehension, dreams, concepts. Characters and events come simultaneously to me. Plot . . . is a calculated attempt to hold the reader's interest at the sacrifice of moral conviction. Of course, one doesn't want to be boring . . . one needs an element of suspense. But a good narrative is a rudimentary structure, rather like a kidney.

(John Cheever, in *The Writer's Chapbook*)

Middles

Beginning writers who find satisfaction and success in creating beginnings and endings for their stories sometimes have less interest in getting from one to the other. Often the "one thing led to another" approach is the most tempting. To keep a plot not simply moving along but *developing,* Jerome Stern's approach to plot construction is worth some attention, as he explains it in *Making Shapely Fiction.*

In Stern's approach to plot, your protagonist begins with what he calls a "position," determined by both external and internal factors. Our ambitious businesswoman who wanted to be vice president at the beginning of this chapter, for instance, may be a highly successful member of her firm, the most brilliant executive they've ever employed, whose brusque personality has made her unpopular with her colleagues. These are external factors. At the same time, she may be privately eager for what she considers a well-deserved promotion, a step she hopes will be particularly distasteful to a father who tried to talk her out of pursuing a career. So long as she moves in a straight line towards that goal, meeting and overcoming each obstacle that rises to meet her, her "position" does not change. She remains an ambitious and talented woman after a promotion to throw in her father's face.

If, on the other hand, her reaction to the first obstacle (the vice presidents' move to oppose her promotion) is to attempt to blackmail each of them with tapes of private conversations they've had with clients or secretaries, then her "position" has changed. She has become an ambitious and talented woman who is violating an ethical code in order to pursue her goal. Our interest, now, is not only in whether she will achieve her goal but in whether she will succeed in her unsavoury scheme or find herself in trouble with the law. This makes a more complex and more interesting plot.

To illustrate more fully with another simple example: say we have a man whose beloved wife has left him for another man (his external "position") and who is devastated about it (internal "position"). If his goal is to get his wife back, the simplest plot may be that he (a) discovers she doesn't want to come back, then (b) loses a fight with the other man, then (c) loses a battle in the divorce court, then (d) fails in an abduction attempt. Throughout this plot, the man's "position" hasn't changed. He is always "a devastated man who wants his wife back." In fact, this pattern is common to many successful plots.

The plot would be much more interesting and engaging if the man's "position" were to keep changing. That is, if he begins as "a devastated man who wants his wife back" but, because of his reaction to the first obstacle (his wife's refusal to listen to his plea, say), changes his "position" to that of "a devastated man who has assaulted his runaway wife when she refuses to return." His goal will not have changed, necessarily, but it will now have to include something like "to save himself from a jail sentence resulting from an uncharacteristically violent act of desperation." If he escapes the charge somehow, but angry women picket his house with placards, his general goal could remain the same but his "position" would now be that of "a confused and guilt-ridden man who wants his wife back but has driven her further away from him, behind a barrier of offended women." The stakes have been raised, the plot has thickened, the reader has waded deeper and deeper into the story.

Types of Plot

The writer can sometimes learn from those teachers of literature who are struggling for ways to help their students become more successful readers. Although the teacher and students may be looking at stories from seats in the audience, so to speak, and you may be watching from backstage in order to see how the show is produced, much can be learned about a performance from listening to the audience's response. In an article published in the *Journal of General Education* (VIII, 1955) and reprinted in Philip Stevick's *The Theory of the Novel*, Norman Friedman searches for ways to encourage students to think of plot as much more than a series of "events." Plots, he suggests, are made of change. And the change may be primarily in *fortune*, in *character*, or in *thought*. In an individual story, one of the three will be dominant, but the other two will contribute or be affected. The change may be for the better or for the worse. He suggests the following as the most common patterns of plot.

Plots of Fortune include *The Action Plot*, where our main interest is in "what happens next"; *The Pathetic Plot*, where a sympathetic protagonist undergoes misfortune through no fault of his own; *The Tragic Plot*, where a sympathetic protagonist who has strength of will and ability to change his thought "suffers from a misfortune, part or all of which he is responsible for . . . and subsequently discovers his error only too late"; *The Punitive Plot*, where a protagonist who is essentially unsympathetic, in that his goals and purposes are repugnant, suffers well-deserved misfortune; *The Sentimental Plot*, where a sympathetic protagonist "survives the threat of misfortune and comes out all right at the end"; and *The Admiration Plot*, where our "final response is respect and admiration for man outdoing himself and the expectations of others concerning what man is normally capable of."

Plots of Character include *The Maturing Plot*, where a sympathetic but apparently purposeless protagonist achieves strength and direction; *The Reform Plot*, where "we feel impatience and irritation when we begin seeing through [a sympathetic protagonist's] mask, and then indignation and outrage when he continues to deceive others, and, finally, a sense of confirmed and righteous satisfaction when he makes the proper choice at last"; *The Testing Plot*, where "a sympathetic, strong and purposeful character is pressured . . . to compromise or surrender his noble ends and habits"; *The Degenerative Plot*, in which a sympathetic and ambitious protagonist is subject to "some crucial loss which results in his utter disillusionment."

Plots of Thought include *The Education Plot*, where "a sympathetic person undergoes a threat of some sort and emerges into a new and better kind of wholeness at the end"; *The Revelation Plot*, where the protagonist "must discover the truth [of his situation] before he can come to a decision"; *The Affective Plot*, where the protagonist comes to see some other person in a truer light than before; and *The Disillusionment Plot*, where a sympathetic and idealistic protagonist, "after being subjected to some kind of loss, threat, or trial, loses that faith entirely."

Professor Friedman's plot categories are presented here, not so that you may choose one and shape your material to its expectations, but so that you may notice the variety of possibilities all growing out of the simplest notions of plot discussed earlier in this chapter.

A strongly motivated need or desire sets in motion actions and revelations that return to dramatically affect a character, resulting in the final cry from Henry James's The Wings of the Dove: *"We will never again be as we were!" The plot has worked from disorder to order, from an unstable situation to one of at least temporary rest, to success or renunciation.*

(Oakley Hall, *The Art and Craft of Novel Writing*)

Rather than think of plot as a prescribed formula (or choice of formulae) to which you must make your material "fit," I suggest that you think of it as a general pattern floating somewhere in the back of your consciousness as you write, ready to come to the rescue when you are looking for the reasons a story doesn't satisfy, refuses to move forward, seems to have gone off some invisible tracks, or simply bores you. Let the combination of your material and your hopes for it, rather than anyone's list of characteristics, guide your story's progress. Wright Morris begins with a character in a situation and lets the character lead him. He thinks of his writing as an "organic" process – stories grow quite naturally to take on their own right shape. If you read his stories and novels you will see that where his characters lead him is through difficulties and setbacks in pursuit of a goal more often felt than known. Meanwhile, the writer and the reader are pursuing a goal of their own: a search for whatever *meaning* might be revealed by characters, situations, actions, responses, and results.

Asking Questions About Your Plot

Even in stories where plot is less important than other elements it is necessary at least to consider its demands. If you have set yourself the goal of doing away with plot, you are not likely to succeed unless you first examine carefully what it is that plot has satisfied in the reader and then consider inventing something new that satisfies the same (or a similar) need – as several fine contemporary writers have done. For the plot of a story where you have reached at least the first-draft stage, some questions to ask:

1. Whose story is it? Whom do you most care about? Why?

2. Does your main character have a purpose or a goal that is specific enough or immediate enough for us to care?

3. Once the character sets out after this goal, are there obstacles that get in the way, causing a struggle? Is there conflict (internal or external) as the result of this opposition? Does this conflict create tension? (Do you care which way it works out?)

4. What's at stake here? If "nothing much" is the answer, the reader is likely to be much less interested than you hope.

5. Is there some kind of causal relationship between each event and the next? (If not, is it clear that the character is in the grip of indifferent meaningless "fate," or a victim of someone or something else's deeds?)

6. When the story reaches the point where it has to work out one way or the other, have you paused and looked back over the whole story to see what in the character and in the events seem to be the strongest forces? Does the way it works out seem almost inevitable,

once you look back and see all that's led to it? (It probably should.) Yet has it avoided being totally predictable? If it is predictable have you treated it in a fresh way? Has the story encouraged the reader to be involved in this most important scene?

7. Once you've passed the "point of no return" how fast can you end the story without losing something of importance?

8. When you consider this character you know so well, and the experiences he or she has been through, do you know what it *means* – to the character? to you?

9. Has every step of the plot also contributed something to the development of character, setting, mood?

10. If your story does not conform to any of the above expectations, are you confident your scheme will make readers care about your protagonist, carry readers on the story's emotional journey, and reward readers with insight, pleasure, and satisfaction?

Limbering Up with Milligan's Folly: Plot

A. Trace a cause-effect chain of events in Milligan's life leading from the last meeting between Cates and Milligan and this day of the robbery. Now trace a separate cause-effect chain of events for the same period of time in Cates's life.

B. For either Milligan or Cates, trace a series of possible cause-effect events to follow this day of the robbery. Which of the two characters suggests the more interesting story after the robbery?

C. Imagine yourself to be a police investigator who does not believe the story as reported in the paper. Write a passage of internal monologue in which you are mulling over your suspicions.

D. Choose the character you find most interesting, and imagine a goal for that character – a goal that character is pursuing on the day of the robbery (whether this information did or did not get into the news clipping). Then imagine an obstacle that has temporarily deterred the character from achieving the goal.

E. If you think the story might be more interesting *after* the day of the robbery, choose one of the characters and imagine a new goal to be pursued in the days following the robbery. Then, imagine an obstacle that temporarily deters the character from achieving the goal. Now, on paper, trace a series of goal-obstacle-reaction-complication events that follow the day of the robbery.

F. For any moment of confrontation between character-pursuing-goal and character-or-thing-blocking-pursuit in one of your answers above, write a scene in which each of the two "actors" tries to use the other to achieve his or her own goal (for example, a scene in a town café in which Cates announces that she may not want to marry Milligan after all and he tries to convince her not to desert him, or a scene in which Milligan tries to talk Lindstrom into giving him a home-improvement loan a day or so before the robbery, or a scene in which the investigating officer or detective discovers some information that suggests the bank manager has lied to him and to reporters about what went on that day and tries to get the truth out of her).

G. Choose one protagonist and one plot line from the exercises you've just completed. Within that pattern, answer the following questions:

1. Who is the primary antagonist trying to stop the protagonist from achieving his or her goals?

2. Does the sequence of deterrents increase in difficulty, causing not only delays but complications?

3. Does the protagonist respond to obstacles in ways that reveal something about his or her character? Are the responses always similar, or does each obstacle cause a different sort of response?

4. Once you know what the protagonist's goal is, and have encountered the first of the serious deterrents, do you know what is at stake for the protagonist?

5. Do the stakes get higher?

6. Is it possible to think of this protagonist's struggle to achieve a goal as an internal struggle? Could you, in other words, achieve the same amount of tension and interest without relying on dramatic external events?

7. Is there within the plot as you've imagined it so far a character, a place, or an institution that voices or represents the central values and goals of the protagonist? If not, is there someone or something with this potential? What role might that person or thing play?

8. Is there within the plot as you've imagined it so far a character, a place, or an institution that voices or represents the central values and goals of the antagonist? Who, or what? What role might this

person or place or institution play? (Questions 7 and 8 might seem superfluous and confusing at this point, but if you have at least considered them you may discover later that you are glad to have them standing by for purposes that have come to the surface during the writing of the story.)

H. Look back over your decisions made while considering the questions on plot. Of the various sequences you explored, choose the one that interests you most. Be certain that you are not allowing the "plot" of the news clipping to restrict your choices where your ideas would take you in other directions. Consider the various points at which the reader might enter the story. For any two of these, write an effective opening paragraph or passage.

I. Considering the material available and your own interest in it, do you think your plot would be more suitable for a short-short of just a few pages, a short story of ten to twenty-five pages, a long story of more than twenty-five pages, a novella, or a novel? What are your reasons? (Of course you don't need to decide before starting a first draft, but it may be of use to have an awareness of the differences. This may influence other decisions you make.)

RECOMMENDED FURTHER READING ON PLOT
Aspects of the Novel, E.M. Forster. Chapter V
The Art of Fiction, John Gardner. Part 2, Chapter 7
Three Genres, Stephen Minot. Chapter 15
The Art and Craft of Novel Writing, Oakley Hall. Part One
The Writing Book, Kate Grenville. Chapter 8
The Craft of Writing a Novel, Phyllis Reynolds Naylor. Chapter 4
Revising Fiction, David Madden. Part IV
Writing Fiction, Janet Burroway. Chapter 2

SHORT STORIES AND NOVELS WHOSE
PLOTS REWARD EXAMINATION

Vanishing Points, Thea Astley
Matilda, My Darling, Nigel Krauth
Strangers and Brothers, Maurice Shadbolt
Wildlife, Richard Ford
A Life, Wright Morris
Fifth Business, Robertson Davies
A Jest of God, Margaret Laurence
The Good Terrorist, Doris Lessing
The Age of Innocence, Edith Wharton
Outerbridge Reach, Robert Stone
Famous Last Words, Timothy Findley
To All Appearances a Lady, Marilyn Bowering
The Book of Secrets, Fiona Kidman
Ellen Foster, Kaye Gibbons
Lies of Silence, Brian Moore
A Burnt-Out Case, Graham Greene
The Silence in the Garden, William Trevor
The Knife in My Hand, Keith Maillard
Woman of the Inner Sea, Thomas Keneally
"A Good Man is Hard to Find," Flannery O'Connor
"The Drunkard," Frank O'Connor
"Man Descending," Guy Vanderhaeghe
"Friend of My Youth," Alice Munro
"Initram," Audrey Thomas
"The Grave of the Famous Poet," Margaret Atwood
"The Mask of the Bear," Margaret Laurence
"One's a Heifer," Sinclair Ross
"Tea with Mrs Bittell," V.S. Pritchett
"The Drover's Wife," Henry Lawson
"The Drover's Wife," Murray Bail

"The Drover's Wife," Frank Moorhouse
"Palms and Minarets," Vincent O'Sullivan
"Along Rideout Road that Summer," Maurice Duggan
"Mrs Pratt Goes to China," Shonagh Koea
"Bliss," Katherine Mansfield

Structure: The Architecture of Fiction

ℱℚ

You're not born knowing structure or how to do it. You learn as you do it, and while you can say that novels must have a structure and certain other given things, you have to discover it all for yourself – even though thousands of other writers before you have already discovered it. In my first book of stories I can see how I was discovering structures to fit the subject matter. Structure is a tremendously emotional part of a story. It's not just a framework that you hang your subject matter on, like washing on the line; it is integral to the emotion of the story, so if you find the right *shape* for your story, whatever it is, it will add to it.

(Glenda Adams, in *Yacker 3*)

Contemplating Form

The difference between content, or experience, and achieved content, or art, is technique.
(Mark Schorer, *The World We Imagine*)

SHORT STORY OR NOVEL?

When Edgar Allan Poe defined the short story in the nineteenth century, he stated that it should be short enough to be read in a single sitting, its separate elements combining to bring about a single effect. Apparently he wished to make it clear how the short story was different from the novel, a slightly older and more familiar form that required a considerable investment in time and could leave you feeling a variety of emotions about a number of different matters.

To Frank O'Connor, the difference between short story and novel was clearly the difference "between characters regarded as representative figures and characters regarded as outcasts, lonely individuals" (*The Lonely Voice*). Novels were about people who fit into society, short stories were about people who didn't. He observed this in other fiction of his time; he reinforced it in his own. Length had little to do with the matter; the choice of protagonist did. Short stories, then, were to be more focused than novels, and more exclusive.

Although successive generations have recorded what they considered to be the differences between the novel and the short story, writers have gone on experimenting with both forms, their successes contributing to a continuing evolution. If we recognize that the length of time covered in a story has little to do with the difference between the contemporary short story and the contemporary novel (we can think of short stories that last a lifetime and novels that confine themselves to a day), and that the choice of protagonist has little to do with it (we can think of novels about outcasts and short stories about pillars of the community), and that the size of the cast hasn't very much to do with it (some novels have only one or two characters and some short stories include a whole village), and that even the number of pages has little to do with it (Chekhov's story "The Duel" is unusually long, while Nina Bawden's novel *The Afternoon of a Good Woman* is unusually short) – and if we agree that the good novelist takes as much care with every word as a good short story writer does (none of this "novelists can afford to be sloppy" business) – then what is there left to distinguish between the forms?

Complexity, perhaps. The successful short story tends to be so finely tuned that every word, every nuance of every word, is contributing to a single final impression. To strike one sentence from a fine short story is to do as much damage as to toss away a line of a good poem. A short story's power lies in its density.

The novel may also build its final effect upon a single obsession, but it will be an obsession large enough to include within it the strands of more than one plot, perhaps, or several conflicting ways of looking at the single theme, or a complex multiplicity of symbols reaching out to other stories. A novel's power lies in its scope.

And just to complicate matters further, there is the novella. This is neither a long short story nor a short novel, though it is some-times published within story collections and sometimes put between covers and sold as a novel. In fact it has its own history, its own traditions, and its own shape. Writing in *Canadian Fiction Magazine*, Robert Harlow draws our attention to a study done in 1934 by the British scholar E.K. Bennett, who saw the novella as a basically epic form that "deals with events rather than actions. . . . It restricts itself to single situations or conflicts" and concentrates on a main event that shows "the effect of this event upon a person or group of persons." This single event tends to be presented at first as chance, but usually turns out to be actually Fate. In a novella, which concentrates on a small group of people, the plot will make a major turn and lead to a conclusion that is both surprising and logical. Most novellas deal with a "striking subject," often associated with a concrete object that takes on symbolic significance.

Popular genre fiction such as the western and detective story have grown out of the novella tradition. At the same time, a number of remarkable literary successes have been novellas: Joseph Conrad's *Heart of Darkness*, Henry James's *The Turn of the Screw*, Thomas Mann's *Death in Venice*, Alexander Solzhenitzen's *One Day in the Life of Ivan Denisovich*, Marian Engel's *Bear*, and Thea Astley's *Vanishing Points*.

Believing that the material held within itself a suitability for a specific form, Edith Wharton urged the writer to choose carefully.

Every "subject" (in the novelist's sense of the term) must necessarily contain within itself its own dimensions; and one of the fiction-writer's essential gifts is that of discerning whether the subject which presents itself to him, asking for incarnation, is suited to the proportions of a short story or of a novel. If it appears to be adapted to both the chances are that it is inadequate to either.

(Edith Wharton, *The Writing of Fiction*)

In deciding whether a story idea is best suited for a short story, a novella, or a novel, it is wise to keep in mind Frank O'Connor's caution against trying to force your story into any prescribed or selected shape. Stories can be damaged by forcing them into established or expected forms. Thinking about the "best" form for a story must include the possibility of a form that has not been used before.

The Story as Journey

The more you write, the more you will realize that the form is organic, that it is something that grows out of the material, that the form of each story is unique.

(Flannery O'Connor, "Writing Short Stories," in *Mystery and Manners*)

Even when you feel confident that what you are writing is meant for a particular form, there are other factors that will govern that narrative's shape. Just because you wrote your first draft from what you thought was the beginning to what you thought was the end does not mean the reader must experience it that way. Some writers have suggested that a story is like a house: it doesn't matter which door you enter so long as you visit all the rooms before you leave. Yet choosing this door instead of that door, visiting this room before that room, can make a difference. By the time you step out of the house and stand back far enough to get some perspective, your experience of the building will have been affected by the order in which you visited the rooms as much as by the contents of the rooms themselves. Imagine visiting Manhattan immediately after spending some time in the tiny mining village of Elsa in the Yukon Territory. Imagine visiting the same two places in the reverse order.

The people who design the interiors of department stores know the importance of organizing your journey. Remember when you could walk into a department store and make a beeline straight to the back wall where you knew you could buy that record you'd been saving for? Not any more. People have been paid big money to find ways of making that impossible. They make sure you're forced to take a circuitous route, so that you have to visit as many departments as possible before you get to where you wanted to go (which won't be there any more anyway). Around a semicircle you go, looking for an opportunity to take a shortcut – no shortcuts are possible any more, without getting entangled in lingerie and skis – exposed at every step to a rapid succession of merchandise set out to trigger your buying lust. The journey from the door to the record department has become a series of emotional encounters.

Like it or not, if the reader's experience of your story is to be an emotional journey, you are the floor-designer who gets to decide what kind of journey it will be. If you push your readers through the smells of the fishmarket on their way to cosmetics they'll come out with quite a different impression than if you'd taken them to cosmetics by way of the toy department. This is not to suggest a story's structure should be determined with the T-squares and compasses of a cold-blooded retailer plotting to separate people from their money. But it is a reminder that you have choices. If you are told who the murderer is right at the beginning of the story, you read about the detective's search with quite a different feeling than if you are stumbling along from clue to clue as confused and ignorant as the detective.

"Must" reading for every fiction writer is Mark Schorer's essay "Technique as Discovery," which is included in his book *The World We Imagine*. His premise is that the meaning of your fiction is suggested by the techniques you employ. The fiction writer must take responsibility for choosing how the reader will experience the story, because the choices the writer makes will, according to Schorer, be the story's meaning. The way you write – the choices you make in matters of language and structure – tells your reader how you see the world.

Rudy Wiebe's short story "The Naming of Albert Johnson" is about a fugitive pursued by the police across the frozen north. But Wiebe tells the story backwards, from capture and shooting through different stages of the chase to the crime that caused the chase in the first place. He doesn't want us to read simply to discover "what happens next" as we might if he'd ordered the story chronologically. Because we know what happens next, we're interested in other matters. We come upon the story's ending with a full understanding of all that would happen to the protagonist afterwards.

Elizabeth Jane Howard's novel *The Long View* is also structured in a series of chapters moving backwards through time. An entire marriage is examined, from the moment of its dissolution in middle age to the moment when the two protagonists meet. As a result we are forced to keep re-evaluating the impressions we'd been given in the previous chapters. In the end, presumably the writer wanted us to come away with a sense of the story's inevitability: "Naturally that marriage would eventually fail!"

William Faulkner invented or adapted a new structure for every novel. *As I Lay Dying* is narrated in fifty-nine first-person segments, by members of a backwoods family and their neighbours, creating a kind of cubistic dance around the central shared narrative of a journey with a coffin through fire and flood. In *Light in August,* a story of several characters whose lives converge in a single act of violence, each character's story has its own unique structure. Because *Absalom, Absalom!* is a novel that asks questions about the nature of fiction, it is structured as a series of overlapping tellings of selected moments in a grand narrative, returning again and again to important moments, with one narrator taking the material supplied by a previous narrator and reforming it to tell yet another listener. *The*

Hamlet, which contains several rewritten versions of previously published short stories now woven into a larger narrative, comprises several quite distinct sections, each appropriate in tone and style to its subject matter: a comical and largely "oral" account of the arrival of Flem Snopes to the village of Frenchman's Bend; a highly embroidered and flamboyant epic on the effect of Eula Varner's beauty upon the men who meet her; a mock-epic account of a love affair between an idiot and a cow; a murder story; and finally a comic sequence with qualities reminiscent of the tall tale.

Some novels are modelled after other literary or subliterary forms. Milorad Pavic's novel *Dictionary of the Khazars* is structured, as its title suggests, like a dictionary. Georges Perec's *Life: A User's Manual* is a jigsaw puzzle. Gesualdo Bufalino's *Lies of the Night* is a series of stories told by a group of prisoners to one another on the night before their execution. Sinclair Ross's *As For Me and My House* is a diary. Leon Rooke's short story "Biographical Notes" is presented as a series of brief biographies of "people called to give evidence for or against me." Edna O'Brien's "Mary" is a letter. Laura Esquirel's *Like Water for Chocolate* begins each chapter with another of its heroine's favourite recipes and incorporates the instructions into the narrative. Kate Grenville's *Joan Makes History* records the adventures of a woman who was present in various disguises at important historical events throughout Australia's history. Max Frisch's *I'm Not Stiller* is a series of prison journals and a Postscript by the Public Prosecutor. Each of the four novels in Ford Madox Ford's *Parade's End* has a structure quite different from the others but appropriate to its own content. John Gardner's *October Light* contains a "trashy paperback" novel that one of its characters is reading.

It is unlikely that these unusual structures were chosen for novelty alone. By way of emphasizing the importance of allowing your material rather than your interest in geometry to suggest a structure, let me confess that I once wasted five years working on a novel with disastrous results because I'd fallen in love with what I thought was a brilliant and original structure and then foolishly tried to invent a story to "fit" it. On the other hand, while working on a more recent novel I was uncertain about an appropriate structure until I had written several chapters – enough to notice an important similarity between character and place. Several of my main characters were people who kept their pasts well hidden from others, giving themselves false names and invented histories; similarly, the town in which the story was unfolding had a pattern of periodically applying new false faces to its buildings (over previous false faces) in order to imitate the architecture of various foreign cities. I decided to apply the architectural principle to the novel's structure and ordered the story so that readers would be required to alter their notion of what was "true" every time a chapter had been put behind, or stripped away like a false front, and a new one revealed, each successive "face" a little closer to the original and presumably most truthful version.

Of course many writers have looked to a metaphor within the story for an appropriate form. David Malouf's novel *Harland's Half Acre*, about a painter who keeps discarding his past and moving on, is structured as a series of separate novellas.

The structure of *Harland's Half Acre* gave its author reason to discover that not all readers are especially appreciative of the link between content and form:

> *The English have a lot of trouble about form. They like things to be well-shaped, or what they think of as well-shaped. Even my original editor there . . . was worried about [Harland's Half Acre] because characters kept turning up and disappearing. But that seems to me to be what life is like as well. The English like books which have a plot-shape, whereas my books tend to have a poetic shape. That is what holds them together.*

Not the continuing plot but the working out of the metaphor, the working out of a set of correspondences or affinities. . . . Mind you, none of that worried the Americans at all. It was quite heartening to see the way they just took the book as having whatever shape it presented itself in. Instead of starting with the notion of how a book should be done and saying, "Why couldn't he do that?", they tried to work out why a writer would give it that shape.

(David Malouf, in *Yacker*)

Some Common Short Story Shapes

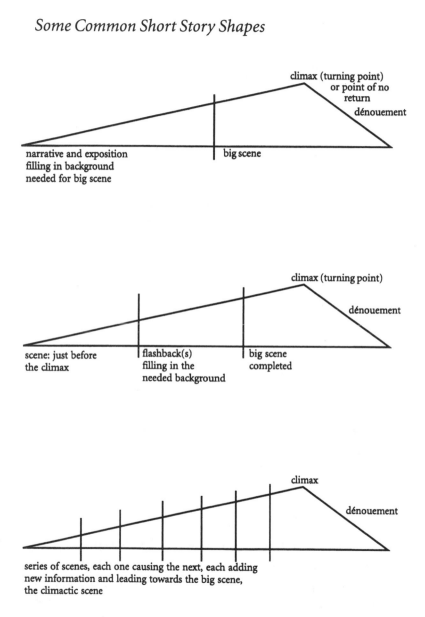

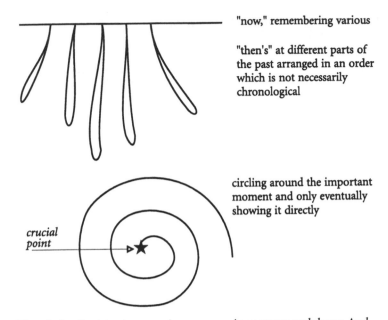

"now," remembering various

"then's" at different parts of the past arranged in an order which is not necessarily chronological

circling around the important moment and only eventually showing it directly

crucial point

The whole of writing is expressing an emerging pattern and shape. And the satisfaction is when the shape is concluded, although there is the frustration of knowing it may not be quite right or something is amiss. It's something that emerges, and this is for me the real joy of writing. I mean it's not publication or anything else, it's just as one is writing a pattern grows and everything seems to fall into place – very exciting, very exciting just to see it.

(Janet Frame, in *In the Same Room*)

Some Common Novel Shapes

1. The horizontal novel, such as Charles Dickens's *David Copperfield*, follows events chronologically. The events of Chapter 1 lead to the events in Chapter 2. This is most suited to the autobiographical novel or the plot-driven novel, and of course will sometimes include flashbacks that briefly interrupt the forward movement.

2. The converging novel, such as Thornton Wilder's *The Bridge of San Luis Rey*, follows a number of separate sequences, perhaps a number of separate characters, until events and characters finally coincide at one place and time. William Faulkner's *Light in August* explores, quite separately, the stories of a half-black orphan trying to find out who he is, a pregnant peasant woman in search of her father's runaway father, a preacher who has lost his faith, an unmarried woman who is a Northern reformer living in the American South, and others – all stories converging upon a burning house in Mississippi and leading to a horrendous murder.

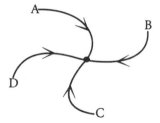

3. The vertical novel, such as Margaret Laurence's *The Diviners*, sinks a series of narrative shafts down into memory according to some order *other* than chronological, working towards an understanding that comes about the total experience. A present-time narrative may be going on simultaneously, as it is in *The Diviners*, though it needn't – and does not in *The Good Soldier*, except to the extent that we are made aware of the narrating character sitting by the fire relating the story.

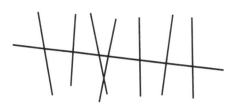

(These three categories were suggested by critic Clifton Fadiman.)

The Flashback

> *The summonings of memory can have only one purpose – to illuminate and influence the present. They should never, either through garrulity or their own fascinations, overwhelm the intentions of the present story.*
>   (Robie Macauley and George Lanning, *Technique in Fiction*)

It has been suggested that the short story should start as close as possible to its end. If you throw away the first page and discover that nothing of importance is missed, you may try throwing the second page away too. How far can you go with this before something begins to hurt? (I can think of many student writers who have found their stories' true beginnings on page 3 or 4!) The closer you start to what your first draft discovered to be your ending, the more tension you are likely to achieve.

Occasionally, of course, there are events in the character's past that have an influence upon the action in the story. Do you move the story's beginning back in order to include that earlier event, or do you pause in your story to remember it? Writers have done both.

Sometimes the flashback is set up as though the protagonist is remembering it; at other times the narrator abandons the protagonist and takes the reader into the past to witness the events directly. In the first situation, some part of the reader's attention remains with the main story while revisiting the past with the character; in the second, the reader is asked to leave the main story in suspension, turn back the clock, and journey through the events of the past before returning to the present.

Remember, though, that the flashback material must be there to *serve* the main story, not compete with it. I have read countless short stories in which the flashback went on for so long that I forgot what the main story was about, countless short stories in which the flashback was far more interesting than the main story, and countless short stories in which an introductory frame leads us into a flashback that goes on for too long and then is followed by the rest of the frame *in which nothing happens that depended upon that flashback*. Sometimes this suggests that the writer should have started the story earlier, sometimes that the flashback is all the story the writer wanted to tell, and sometimes that the writer was too rushed to remember that a flashback must be an experience through which a reader goes in order to understand better what follows and precedes it.

Beginnings

> With the beginning of a book, I will often re-write first paragraphs, and the first few pages, thirty and forty times, because another belief I have is that in that moment, in that fix, in those first crucial pages, all the reader's decisions are made. To trust or not to trust? And all stylistic decisions are really made at that point, especially nowadays.
>
> (Brian Moore, in *Conversations with Canadian Novelists 2*)

Gabriel García Márquez also emphasizes the importance and the difficulty of a story's opening, claiming that "[one] of the most difficult things is the first paragraph."

> I have spent many months on a first paragraph and once I get it, the rest just comes out very easily. In the first paragraph you solve most of the

problems with your book. The theme is defined, the style, the tone. At least in my case, the first paragraph is a kind of sample of what the rest of the book is going to be.
(Gabriel García Márquez, in A Writer's Chapbook)

"In the stories I admire," Clark Blaise writes, "there is a sense of a continuum disrupted, then re-established, and both the disruption and the re-ordering are part of the *beginning* of a story."

The first paragraph tells us, in effect, that "this is how things have always been," or at least, how they have been until the arrival of the story. It may summarize, as Faulkner does in "That Evening Sun":
Monday is no different from any other weekday in Jefferson now. The streets are paved now, and the telephone and electric companies are cutting down more and more of the shade trees. . . .
or it may envelop a life in a single sentence, as Bernard Malamud's often do:
Manischevitz, a tailor, in his fifty-first year suffered many reverses and indignities.
Whereupon Malamud embellishes the history, a few sentences more of indignities, aches, curses, until the fateful word that occurs in almost all stories, the simple terrifying adverb:
Then,
Then, *which means to the reader: "I am ready." The moment of change is at hand, the story shifts gears and for the first time,* plot *intrudes on poetry. . . .*
Suddenly there appeared . . .
Then one morning . . .
Then one evening she wasn't home to greet him . . .
. . . The rest of the story will be an attempt to draw out the inferences of that earlier upheaval. What is often meant by "climax" in the conventional short story is merely the moment that the character realizes the true, the devastating, meaning of "then." He will try to ignore it, he will try to start again . . .; he can't of course.

... *"Then" is the moment of the slightest tremor, the moment when the author is satisfied that all the forces are deployed, the unruffled surface perfectly cast, and the insertion, gross or delicate, can now take place. It is the cracking of the perfect, smug egg of possibility.*

(Clark Blaise, "To Begin, To Begin")

In the best fiction, there is a sense that the entire story, including its ending, somehow grows out of the first sentence, that everything is organically related to the first cluster of words the reader encounters. Below, you will find some opening sentences from successful short stories and novels. For those that make you wish to read on, can you identify the qualities you respond to? Notice that some make us feel something is wrong. Some raise questions. Some imply an uneasy position in time. Some establish a strong sense of a narrator's voice. All of the best ones make us in some way curious.

Many years later, as he faced the firing squad, Colonel Aureliano Buendia was to remember that distant afternoon when his father took him to discover ice.

(Gabriel García Márquez, *One Hundred Years of Solitude*, trans by Gregory Rabassa)

Laforgue felt his body tremble. What can be keeping them? Has the Commandant refused? Why has he not sent for me? Is this God's punishment for my lie about my hearing? But it wasn't a lie; my intention was honorable. Or is that a sophistry? Am I now so mired in my ambition that I can no longer tell truth from falsehood?

(Brian Moore, *Black Robe*)

Cripples, one-eyed people, pregnant women: we are all the children of eggs, Miss Miller, we are all the children of eggs. Consider Isobel, leaning over the railing on the promenade deck of the HMS Pylades, watching a workman, a spanner sticking out of the back pocket of his overall, run lightly and self-consciously down the gangway on the balls of his feet.

(Audrey Thomas, *Blown Figures*)

Once upon a time – if we counted time not by calendars but by assimilated history and scientific change I'd be tempted to say four or five thousand years ago: before total war and all-out war, before death camps, Nagasaki, before fusion and fission, jets, moon shots, cosmonauts, Luniks in orbit, before antibiotics, polio vaccine, open-heart surgery, before TB, carburetors and other wonders of automation, before dead-faced hoods on motor cycles, dead-faced beatniks on maldecycles – once upon *that* kind of time lived a boy and his horse.

The year was 1939. This is no pastoral tale. The boy and the horse are both dead.

(Jack Ludwig, "Requiem for Bibul")

Suddenly – dreadfully – she wakes up. What has happened? Something dreadful has happened. No – nothing has happened. It is only the wind shaking the house, rattling the windows, banging a piece of iron on the roof and making her bed tremble.

(Katherine Mansfield, "The Wind Blows")

As he weakened, Moran became afraid of his daughters.

(John McGahern, *Amongst Women*)

I'm not Stiller.

(Max Frisch, *I'm Not Stiller,* trans by Michael Bullock)

Nothing as appalling had happened before at Drimaghleen; its people had never been as shocked.

(William Trevor, "Events at Drimaghleen")

There are times even now, when I awake at four o'clock in the morning with the terrible fear that I have overslept; when I imagine that my father is waiting for me in the room below the darkened stairs or

that the shorebound men are tossing pebbles against my window
while blowing their hands and stomping their feet impatiently on
the frozen steadfast earth.

(Alistair MacLeod, "The Boat")

This morning I got a note from my aunt asking me to come for
lunch. I know what this means. Since I go there every Sunday for
dinner and today is Wednesday, it can mean only one thing: she
wants to have one of her serious talks.

(Walker Percy, *The Moviegoer*)

And then he understood that he was going to die. The thought came
to him in the middle of a sentence, as he was looking for the right
words, unsatisfied with the ones he had found.

(Victor-Lévy Beaulieu, *Don Quixote in Nighttown*, trans by
Sheila Fischman)

The

train

was

leaving

town.

Lying back with his head against his mother's
shoulder, Patrice followed the dappled countryside with a melancholy expression. Behind his forehead everything grew confused,
like a billowing stormcloud on a screen. He watched in silence and
did not understand, but his idiot face was so dazzling that it made
one think of genius.

(Marie-Claire Blais, *Mad Shadows*, trans by Merloyd Lawrence)

I was never so amazed in my life as when the Sniffer drew his con-
cealed weapon from its case and struck me to the ground, stone
dead.

How did I know that I was dead?

(Robertson Davies, *Murther & Walking Spirits*)

Endings

*The good ending dismisses us with a touch of ceremony, and throws a
backward light of significance over the story just read. It makes it, as
they say, or unmakes it – a weak beginning is forgettable, but the end of
a story bulks in the reader's mind like the giant foot in a foreshortened
photograph.*

(John Updike, Introduction to *Best American Short Stories 1984*)

Sometimes a writer will have a story's ending in mind from the start,
and will see the writing of the story as a way of working towards it.
At other times, a story's ending will remain unseen until several
drafts have brought the writer to its brink. It is one thing to know
that in general stories should end as soon as possible after the climax, but it is another to write that precisely perfect ending for a particular story.

I suspect the best endings do not have to be invented at all, but
recognized. Even those that have existed from the beginning in the
writer's plans may have to be abandoned when characters insist on
having their say. A good ending may not reveal itself until after
many, many drafts have run up to the climax and stalled. I tend to
think of a story's ending as something waiting for me, unseen,
behind the hill of the story's climax. When I get to that pinnacle, so
to speak, I ought to be able to see the end quite clearly. If I can't,
maybe there's something wrong with the peak I've climbed, or
maybe the ending has been underfoot and travelling with me all
along. Sometimes I discover that it was hiding all the while in the
opening paragraph – the subtlest hint.

It is not a good idea to give a story a merely adequate ending "just
for the time being" – you may be fooled into thinking you have finished the story and have only to work a little harder on the ending
itself. Until the right ending comes along it is the whole story and
not just the ending that must be worked on. A story should not be

ended at all until an ending presents itself that leaves you breathless with its "rightness," its surprise, and its inevitability. Reread the final paragraphs of "Miss Brill," of *The Old Man and the Sea,* of *The Tree of Man,* and of the stories in Alice Munro's *Friend of My Youth*– good endings leave us with a sense that they could not possibly have been anything but what they are.

Reprise: What Difference Does Your Choice of Structure Make?

1. The structure of a story – or a novel – controls the *order* in which the reader receives information, thus affecting how the reader reacts to events and people, depending upon what is told, what is withheld, and even how events are juxtaposed to *create* a relationship in the reader's mind.

2. The structure *suggests* something of how you, the writer, see the world – at least at the time of writing (for example, order or chaos, logical or random, surface or depth, tidy endings or open endings, complex or simple, etc). You are *creating* a world in the reader's mind, and the world you create will likely reflect how you see the events of your time and the actions of your fellow humans.

3. The structure contributes indirectly to the story's "theme" or total meaning. For example, the structure could suggest that the process of poking around in the past could help make sense of the present, in your story, OR that the past could be full of booby traps waiting to ruin everything; your structure could reflect your private belief that life is an endless repetition of the same type of mistake, OR that surviving mistakes teaches us how to avoid them next time they come round; your structure could suggest that things which happen to people are the direct or indirect result of their character and their earlier actions, OR that people have no control over their own destinies. Sometimes you discover these things yourself even as you are discovering the structure that most satisfies you – I'm certainly not suggesting that all of this must be intellectually plotted and planned. For the good storyteller, much of this seems to have become a matter of good instincts for "the best way to get the effect I want."

4. The structure controls the extent of reader *involvement*. In the purely horizontal story the reader might do little more than go along for the ride – each event leads on to the next event, which it caused – hence this structure is the most popular with the "lazy" reader, though of course it can also offer a challenge to the writer who wants to work against this tendency. More complex structures require the reader to *remember* and *make connections* – this will appeal more to the reader who likes to be involved in the process, to notice "clues," to be surprised, and to be aware of subtexts and symbolic counterpoint, than to the reader who just wants to find out what happens next. For the given material, is it more desirable that the reader sit back and let the story roll by in a chronological, logical, and causally related sequence of unfolding events, or is it more desirable to demand that the reader roll up sleeves and participate? (If so, why? Will you put the reader through a psychological exercise that will approximate the more physical experience of the character perhaps?) This is not to suggest that horizontal fiction is simple-minded; the very complex novel *One Hundred Years of Solitude* follows this pattern, as do most epics. And Robert Louis Stevenson's *Treasure Island* is an example of a horizontal novel in which the alternating triumphs of the protagonist and antagonists are, in successive chapters, so perfectly calibrated that a diagram would look like a saw edge, with each reversal of fortune unpredictable to the first-time reader.

> *If you use only the craft and the form you are going to get an arid architecture, and if you depend only on the psychic energy and the passion, well then you might end up with a blancmange.*
>
> (Thomas Shapcott, in *Yacker*)

Considering Structure: An Exercise

1. In simple point form, outline a plot for a short story based on the news clipping below. Choose one of the two conflicting men as your protagonist.

2. Again, using a point form outline, design three different structures for this story. In one, start with the shooting. In a second, start with entering the theatre and proceed chronologically. In the third, start in a hospital room two hours after the shooting.

3. For each of the three structures, examine the effects created upon the reader's experience. Consider the reader's attitude to your chosen main character, to the narrator's values, and to the story's general tone. Compare the three "emotional journeys" for the reader. Is it possible to conclude which structure would be more effective for a "thriller" version, for a "comical satire," or for a deep psychological study?

ARGUMENT OVER POPCORN ENDS IN THEATRE SLAYING

NEW YORK (AP) – An argument between two men over who was first in a popcorn line before the start of the movie *Batman* ended with one man being shot dead Monday in a crowded theatre, police said.

"The concession stand was running out of popcorn," said Det. Christopher Horn.

While they argued, one man threatened to get a gun from his car. "The victim says, 'Go ahead,' gets his popcorn and goes into the movie theatre," Horn said.

The gunman soon returned to the theatre and found a seat. Then "he spotted the guy across the aisle, three or four rows down," Horn said.

While the movie credits were rolling, "the suspect yells something like, 'Hey, are you the guy with the popcorn?'

"Then they both stand up and the guns come out," Horn said.

The victim fired one shot from a .38-calibre handgun. His assailant fired two shots, one of which struck the victim in the head. No one else was hurt.

The gunman ran away. The victim, described as a man in his 20s, was pronounced dead at the scene, Horn said.

Limbering Up with Milligan's Folly: Structure

A. Read through the writing you did for the exercises in "Limbering Up With Milligan's Folly" for Chapter 6. After consulting your decisions for exercises G and H, list the main sequence of causally related events. Moving from the first event down to the last, stop at each event to imagine that you will start the story here. How much of what you've left behind is necessary? How much of it could be satisfyingly done in flashback? How much in exposition? How far can you go down this sequence before you feel you're leaving out important events and subordinating essential events to flashbacks or exposition? Is there anything about the plot or the central imagery that suggests an unusual structure? (Converging separate plot sequences, for instance. Or working from the end back to the beginning. Or circling around the crucial confrontation.) What difference would it make if this was a short story that kept moving from person to person and was done completely within that one farmhouse scene, culminating in the violence, or if it was a novel that began last year when Milligan and Cates first met, concentrated on one protagonist, and went on beyond the robbery to the day that, say, Milligan is released from prison and – to our surprise – Lindstrom is charged with the robbery?

B. Reconsider the choices you made of places to enter the story (above). Either choose one of those opening passages and continue it onto a second page, or else write a new passage that brings us into the story at a more desirable point.

C. Go back to exercise D in "Limbering Up" in Chapter 5, in which you considered the metaphorical implications of the careers of the main characters. In creating the various plot possibilities, did you consider how the nature of any of these careers might affect events, or affect the way your protagonist responded to events, or contributed to the direction in which the plot moved? Choose any significant plot point (where your protagonist is making a decision about his or her next action as a result of encountering an obstacle or deterrent) and write a passage that demonstrates how the protagonist's career, or habits formed in the protagonist's career, affect the decision.

D. The preceding exercises will have encouraged you to discover conflicts and other sources of tension in the story. Consider the various ways in which the central conflict might be manifested. If you were to concentrate on one character's internal struggle, which character would you choose? Why? If you were to add to that internal struggle a conflict between individuals, which of the conflicts interests you most? Why? If you wished to expand the individual's internal struggle and the conflict between individuals to the extent of examining a struggle between groups of people, where do you find the potential for this in the original news item? Townies versus eccentric loners? One side of the river versus the other? Champions of law and order versus champions of rugged individualism? Having extended the conflict this far, is there a way in which you can see the struggle as a struggle between forces – opposing ideals, opposing values, opposing ideologies? There is no necessity for extending the conflict thus far, understand. A good story could be created out of no more than the private thoughts of Milligan when he realizes how far his misguided plan has carried him. By considering these possibilities you are not committing yourself to a wider story, but simply exploring the material's potential.

RECOMMENDED FURTHER READING ON STRUCTURE
Three Genres, Stephen Minot. Chapter 15
Norton Introduction to Literature: Fiction, Section I
The Eye of the Story, Eudora Welty
The Writer's Craft, John Hersey (ed). Part 2
Writing in General and the Short Story in Particular, Rust Hills
The World We Imagine, Mark Schorer
The Chapter in Fiction, Philip Stevick
Understanding Fiction, Cleanth Brooks & Robert Penn Warren

NOVELS AND SHORT STORIES OF INTEREST
FOR THEIR STRUCTURE
The Good Soldier, Ford Madox Ford
I'm Not Stiller, Max Frisch
The Long View, Elizabeth Jane Howard
See Under: Love, David Grossman
The Sorrow of Belgium, Hugo Claus
A Summons to Memphis, Peter Taylor
Strangers and Brothers, Maurice Shadbolt
Symme's Hole, Ian Wedde
The Last Magician, Janette Turner Hospital
Spidercup, Marion Halligan
Riders in the Chariot, Patrick White
Lady Oracle, Margaret Atwood
In the Shadow of the Wind, Anne Hébert
The Leavetaking, John McGahern
Light in August, William Faulkner
Autumn of the Patriarch, Gabriel García Márquez
The Blue Mountains of China, Ruby Wiebe
Scann, Robert Harlow
Famous Last Words, Timothy Findley
Possession, A.S. Byatt

Waterland, Graham Swift
The Sweet Hereafter, Russell Banks
Burning Water, George Bowering
If On a Winter's Night a Traveller, Italo Calvino
Tay John, Howard O'Hagan
Children of Light, Robert Stone
The New Ancestors, Dave Godfrey
The Lord Nelson Tavern, Ray Smith
"The Rat River Trapper," Ruby Wiebe
"First Confession," Frank O'Connor
"The Garden of Forking Paths," Jorge Luis Borges
"The Count of Monte Cristo," Italo Calvino
"The Owl Creek Incident," Ambrose Bierce
Friend of My Youth and *The Progress of Love,* Alice Munro
It's Raining in Mango, Thea Astley
The Bay of Contented Men, Robert Drewe
The Wild Blue Yonder, Audrey Thomas
Stories, Elizabeth Jolley
Rock Springs, Richard Ford
A Sleep Full of Dreams, Edna Alford
You Are Now Entering the Human Heart, Janet Frame
The Stories of Frank Sargeson

Point of View and Voice:
"Where I'm Calling From"

ﾞＱ

It is not surprising to hear practising novelists report that they have never had help from critics about point-of-view. In dealing with point-of-view the novelist must always deal with the individual work: which particular character shall tell this particular story, or part of a story, with what precise degree of reliability, privilege, freedom to comment, and so on.

(Wayne C. Booth, "Distance and Point-of-View")

Choosing a Point of View

Whose story is it? Who will tell it? How much time has gone by between the events and the telling? Should the story be told by the main character himself? If so, what has happened to him since the story took place and how does he feel about the experience now? Should it be told by a witness? Why? Should it be told in the third person? If so, who is this third person, and how much is she capable of knowing? Is she omniscient, objective, or limited in her knowledge to the thoughts and motives of only the main character?

This can be a killer. It's important to know what the choices are; it's important to know the limitations and possibilities of each; it's also important to know the responsibilities that go along with each choice. But how to choose? Any story could be written from any point of view. Perhaps the thing is to try them all, or at least to imagine how different the effect would be in each case before trying the ones you think might be the most satisfying. Chances are you will choose the point of view you "feel like" writing, but who knows what mysterious factors lie behind that urge?

It may be true that pre-school girls most often tell stories in the first person and boys in the third, as some educational studies have shown, but what matters to the adult writer of either sex is the difference that can be made to the reader's experience through the selection of a point of view. What matters is that you give some thought to the effect you want to have, the effect the material needs to have. Perhaps by the time all other aspects of the story have been thought about, and experimented with, there may, if you're fortunate, be only one choice that can help you carry out all the other things you want to do.

Occasionally, even when you are content that you've chosen the best point of view for a story, you may find it useful to convert the entire work to another, quite different point of view. Fresh discoveries can sometimes be taken back with you to the original.

Choices

A story written from the first person point of view can be told by the *protagonist* ("I" tells his or her own story), by a *witness* ("I" tells the story of someone observed, a story in which the witness may or may not have played a secondary role), or by a *reteller* ("I" narrates a story first told by someone else).

In a story written from the third person point of view, the narrator may choose from three possibilities: to be *omniscient* (where the author knows everything about everyone – including the thoughts of the characters and motivations, which they don't even necessarily know themselves), to be *objective* (where the author knows nothing but what is heard and seen, pretending to be a fly on the wall, or a combination of camera and tape recorder), or to be *"omniscient" in a limited manner* (where the author knows and tells all about one character, and can even enter this character's head, but knows nothing more about the rest of the cast than the chosen character does).

In the rare story successfully written from the second person point of view – "You cross the room and raise the blinds" – the unspecified narrator seems to be talking to an earlier self. Occasionally, one half of a divided consciousness is talking to the other.

Attempts at the second person point of view can be noticeably unsuccessful, however, if it seems that the reader is intended to be the protagonist but refuses to cooperate. During a class discussion about a story written in the second person, one student said, "I went along with you when you told me I entered the room. I didn't mind when you told me I accepted the drink. But when you told me that I put my hand on your thigh, I went 'No way, pal. I'm outa this story right now!'"

Examples

1. FIRST PERSON PROTAGONIST

In "The Persimmon Tree," it is clear from the first paragraph that the narrator is setting out to tell us about an event that has occurred to herself.

> I saw the spring come once and I won't forget it. Only once. I had been ill all the winter and I was recovering. There was no more pain, no more treatments or visits to the doctor. The face that looked back at me from my old silver mirror was the face of a woman who had escaped. I had only to build up my strength. For that I wanted to be alone, an old and natural impulse. I had been out of things for quite a long time and the effort of returning was still too great. My mind was transparent and as tender as new skin. Everything that happened, even the commonest things, seemed to be happening for the first time, and had a delicate hollow ring like music played in an empty auditorium.
>
> (Marjorie Barnard, "The Persimmon Tree")

2. FIRST PERSON WITNESS

From this first paragraph of a novel about a failed school teacher and masseur who becomes a famous healing mystic, we are aware that a character ("I") is narrating a story about a second character ("him") whom we suspect will become the protagonist.

Later he was to be famous and honoured throughout the South Caribbean; he was to be a hero of the people and, after that, a British representative at Lake Success. But when I first met him he was still a struggling masseur, at a time when masseurs were ten a penny in Trinidad.

This was just at the beginning of the war, when I was still at school. I had been bullied into playing football, and in my first game I had been kicked hard on the shin and laid up for weeks afterwards.

(V.S. Naipaul, *The Mystic Masseur*)

3. THIRD PERSON OMNISCIENT

Notice the authoritative tone in the voice of this narrator, whose story depends upon your trusting his wisdom and judgement.

On the second evening an upright spiral of smoke (it could only have been from their camp-fire) was seen for the first time within memory of man standing up faintly upon the sky above a razor-backed ridge on the stony head. The crew of a coasting schooner, lying becalmed three miles off the shore, stared at it with amazement till dark. A negro fisherman, living in a lonely hut in a little bay near by, had seen the start and was on the look-out for some sign. He called to his wife just as the sun was about to set. They had watched the strange portent with envy, incredulity, and awe.

The impious adventurers gave no other sign. The sailors, the Indian, and the stolen burro were never seen again. As to the mozo, a Sulaco man – his wife paid for some masses, and the poor four-footed beast, being without sin, had been probably permitted to die; but the two gringos, spectral and alive, are believed to be dwelling to this day amongst the rocks under the fatal spell of their success.

(Joseph Conrad, *Nostromo*)

4. THIRD PERSON OBJECTIVE

For this famous Australian short story, Henry Lawson presents us with the setting, the people, the actions, and the dialogue – all fairly dispassionately – as a way of emphasizing the inescapable and unremitting harshness of the life of this stoic woman.

> The two-roomed house is built of round timber, slabs, and stringy-bark, and floored with split slabs. A big bark kitchen standing at one end is larger than the house itself, verandah included.
>
> Bush all round – bush with no horizon, for the country is flat. No ranges in the distance. The bush consists of stunted rotten native apple-trees. No undergrowth. Nothing to relieve the eye save the darker green of a few she-oaks which are sighing above the narrow, almost waterless creek. Nineteen miles to the nearest sign of civilization – a shanty on the main road.
>
> The drover, an ex-squatter, is away with sheep. His wife and children are left here alone.
>
> Four ragged, dried-up-looking children are playing about the house. Suddenly one of them yells: "Snake! Mother, here's a snake!"
>
> The gaunt, sun-browned bushwoman dashes from the kitchen, snatches her baby from the ground, holds it on her left hip, and reaches for a stick.
>
> (Henry Lawson, "The Drover's Wife")

5. THIRD PERSON LIMITED OMNISCIENT

Notice below that the narrating voice, though authoritatively relating Mrs Hopewell's attitude towards her daughter, occasionally moves close enough to imitate her interior voice. At the same time, the narrator also allows us to form an impression of what she thinks of Mrs Hopewell – creating the sense that we are seeing the world with two pairs of eyes at the same time.

> The girl had taken the Ph.D. in philosophy and this left Mrs Hopewell at a complete loss. You could say, "My daughter is a nurse,"

or "My daughter is a school teacher," or even, "My daughter is a chemical engineer." You could not say, "My daughter is a philosopher." That was something that had ended with the Greeks and Romans. All day Joy sat on her neck in a deep chair, reading. Sometimes she went for walks but she didn't like dogs or cats or birds or flowers or nature or nice young men. She looked at nice young men as if she could smell their stupidity.

(Flannery O'Connor, "Good Country People")

6. SECOND PERSON

In Edna O'Brien's novel the use of the second person suggests a narrator talking to her former self.

One day your father had a pitchfork raised to your mother and said I'll split the head of you open and your mother said And when you've done it there will be a place for you. And you were sure that he would and you and your sister Emma were onlookers and your sister Emma kept putting twists of paper in her hair, both to curl it and to pass the time. Later when your mother felt your pulse she said it was not normal, nobody's pulse was normal that particular day.

(Edna O'Brien, *A Pagan Place*)

Advantages, Disadvantages, and Responsibilities Associated with Point of View

The advantage a fiction writer has is that right from the beginning he doesn't pretend that his is the only way of looking at it, he doesn't have to pretend that he has the authentic account of what happened. He goes in and shows you, This is the way I see it, as it could have happened. Then he has this fantastic freedom, you see, of shaping that thing according to some kind of world view that he has, some kind of concept of what people are like.

(Rudy Wiebe, in *Conversations with Canadian Novelists 2*)

1. FIRST PERSON

A. In selecting the first person point of view, the writer needs to be aware that the narrator could be telling the story in a variety of ways, some of which are the following:

1. simply thinking it, reliving it in memory, reflecting

2. writing it in a private journal or diary to be read by no one else

3. writing it as a letter or a journal entry intended for a specific or general reader

4. self-consciously creating a literary structure in order to entertain a future reader of whom the narrator is very much aware

5. speaking the story aloud

6. recording the story mentally as it is happening.

The reader isn't necessarily *told* which approach has been chosen but should be able to sense it. Therefore, if you don't know what you're doing, the reader will be confused, irritable, and alienated.

Is every line of your story consistent in vocabulary, tone, and structure with the chosen approach?

B. The writer should be aware of the narrative distance between the *telling* narrator and the *experiencing* narrator.

1. How much time has elapsed?

2. How different is he now? What has happened since?

3. What is her attitude towards her former self?

4. To what extent is he still emotionally involved?

5. To what extent does the story's tension arise out of the character's attitude towards an event as it happens, on the one hand, and the attitude of the remembering narrator on the other?

You can find stories recorded while the events are occurring, stories recorded immediately afterwards, and stories recorded long afterwards. The effect is usually quite different. You need to understand this difference, and you need to be aware of the implications of your choice.

C. At some point you will need to consider the degree to which your narrator is to be trusted. Should the reader believe everything? Does the narrator give away more than she intended? Is his memory trustworthy? What are the narrator's reasons for telling the story?

D. The writer must understand and make clear –

1. how much time has passed between the event and the telling.

2. whether the narrator has changed since the experience.

3. whether the narrator, who already knows the rest of the story (if it happened in the past), is inclined to withhold or foreshadow events still to be revealed.

E. One of the difficulties experienced by many writers using the first person is the monotony of too many "I's" in every paragraph. The paragraphs can suddenly begin to look astonishingly self-centred. The writer can imagine the reader saying "I, I, I! Can't you talk about anything but yourself?" With this in mind, examine some particularly successful examples in order to see how their authors have avoided that problem. You will likely find, for instance, that the most successful first person narrators talk less about themselves than about others. We learn about them indirectly. When talking about themselves they've found grammatical structures that have made it possible to avoid overusing the "I."

2. THIRD PERSON

A. Each of the third person points of view has its own advantages and disadvantages. In the third person omniscient, where the author knows everything about everything and everyone, the writer is able to act as a sort of god, controlling every aspect of his creation. This was a popular choice during the nineteenth century, when readers permitted the writer to assume a position of authority and wisdom and did not even mind being addressed occasionally as "gentle reader." Modern readers are often less willing to approach a piece of fiction with such total trust in a writer's wisdom or authority.

The author who assumes a third person objective point of view, pretending to know nothing but what is heard and seen, does not tell what anyone thinks, and does not explain anyone's motives. The story has to speak for itself. In the hands of the very talented, the details and the dialogue are chosen so cleverly that the writer is in fact causing us to feel we know what is being thought and felt.

The narrator who chooses third person limited omniscient knows and tells all about the main character but knows nothing more about the rest of the characters or the outside world than the main character does. This point of view can be moved in so close to the main character as to be almost first person. We see the world through the character's eyes. But the same voice can also stand back just a little and cause us to see the character from the outside. This is particularly effective if a double vision is desired – that is, if the writer wants us to see that a character's view of things is false or somehow distorted when viewed from a little distance. This can result in irony, sometimes humour. Thus, this point of view has most of the advantages of the first person point of view and some of the advantages of the third person omniscient point of view. Readers' trust again depends upon the authority and dependability that can be detected in that voice.

B. Though the first person point of view is very popular now, and the modern reader has some difficulty accepting the omniscient narrator without question, the third person point of view is still widely used and has been adapted to modern uses.

1. Sometimes the writer chooses a first person narrator and then, having earned the reader's trust (or put the reader off guard) allows the narrator to assume "omniscient" characteristics – knowing that the reader has the option of deciding not to believe this narrator, or not to believe the narrator fully.

2. John Cheever sometimes uses the third person point of view, as though he were an omniscient god-like author, and then disarms his reader by referring to himself – giving the impression that he must be telling about someone down the street he knows extremely well. The reader, then, trusts him because he has proved himself to be a fine person, capable of empathy.

3. The good old-fashioned omniscient point of view can be tempered with irony, humour, and a sense that a real human (though invisible) is in control. Here we allow the narrator to act as though he knows everything because the narrator is seen as capable of sitting back and viewing it all with some distant detachment, or with tongue in cheek, or with the historian's willingness to give all possible explanations a try. This is particularly suitable for the writer who is engaged in turning traditions on their head.

4. The totally objective point of view cannot be separated from the view of the world it implies, and tends to be successful only in the hands of a writer who sees it as a way of making a statement – perhaps about the "lack of meaning in life" or the "impossibility of understanding anything" – or who delights in causing the surface of things to resonate with possible meanings.

5. In metafiction, the writer comes on stage and says: We all know this is a game we're playing, you and I together, and that these people I'm talking about are not real. So most of the fun in reading this story will be in watching me, the artist, at work. And part of the fun will come from both of us pretending we can see inside other people, even if those other people are just words on a piece of paper.

6. Perhaps ironically, the third person point of view can be very useful to the writer who is writing fiction out of a personal experience or memory. Writing directly into the first person can make it difficult to select what is necessary and throw out what is not, even more difficult to invent where invention is necessary for the story. To write even temporarily in the third person gives you some

distance from the material, and helps you feel more willing to alter facts to suit the fiction.

7. Some writers apply the third person "limited omniscient" point of view to a sequence of characters in rotation, enabling the reader to witness events through a variety of consciousnesses while benefitting from the double-vision supplied by a consistent narrator. This has most of the advantages of a series of first-person accounts along with the advantage of a narrator's larger understanding.

> It's become very difficult to use third person well. It leads to an easy kind of characterization. You can step outside and give a summary, instead of dramatizing what the character is. It leads to reader manipulation, where the author tells the reader how to respond without earning the reader's response: and then it leads to an easy use of a borrowed language, a kind of literary third-person voice which is not too hard to pick up.
>
> (Robert Kroetsch, in *Conversations with Canadian Novelists 1*)

Some Thoughts on Voice

> Voice is the presence in the style of what is most personal to the writer. Through voice, the writer is invisibly omnipresent. . . . To perceive the writer in his many disguises is one of the great pleasures of reading. Behind his masks we detect his own ineffable voice.
>
> (Wright Morris, *About Fiction*)

> What you really have about all your material is your own point of view. It should be seen out of your own eyes. Now you don't change your own eyes very much. You take any writer, and that's really what you recognize – you recognize John Steinbeck had a way of looking at things. Hemingway had a way of looking at things, Faulkner had a way of looking at things, Norman Mailer has some kind of a Mailer stance, let's say a Mailer wind-up about things.
>
> (Morley Callaghan, in *Conversations with Canadian Novelists 2*)

The writer's voice, which Wright Morris suggests is inescapably present, is probably not something the writer needs to be much concerned with. Nor is Morley Callaghan's interpretation of point of view (a way of looking at things). This voice-print, style, way of looking at the world will be there, in different degrees, whether it's thought of or not. But it is worth mentioning as a way of reminding you to listen hard for the words and rhythms of your own internal voice, and to beware of falling under the spell of an admired writer's voice to the extent of trying to imitate it.

Behind his masks, says Morris. What may be of interest is the extent to which you may choose to adopt a voice for the purpose of a single story or novel. Despite the giveaway traces of your inescapable voice (for those who carefully read and reread all your works) it is possible to become a different sort of narrator every time. One story may require the formal distance of an historian attempting to be objective while another may require the hurried breathlessness of a village gossip.

If the story is written in the first person, this is a matter of getting the idiom and the rhythms of the narrator "right" in some unique way that brings the narrator to life. If the story is written in the third person, then comes the question of what persona you've adopted to tell it. A few years ago, a student who wrote very successful first person stories told me of his frustration at being unable to write well in the third person. I agreed that his third person stories were flat and uninteresting. When he wrote "as himself" – or at least as he perceived his own "writerly" self to be – he wrote boringly. But once he began to understand that a third person narrator can be an invented character too, though unidentified, he began to write third person stories as vibrant and compelling as his first person stories had been. In a sense, even the third person story is written by an "I," though that "I" never steps out from behind a chosen mask. This voice-mask could be called the narrator's persona.

Narrator's Persona

The voice of the narrator's persona is what you hear when you pick up Wright Morris's *In Orbit* and read, "This boy comes riding with his arms high and wide, his head dipped low, his ass light in the saddle, as if about to be shot into orbit from a forked sling." *This* boy, not *that* boy. *Comes riding,* not *rides.* Word choice. Angle of vision. Cadence. Although an admirer of Morris's work will recognize the writer in this prose, it is also possible to say that *this time* Morris has adopted the voice of someone wound up and ready to let fly, someone who taps you on the shoulder and points out what you're to look at and even makes you feel a little tense about it. *This* particular boy seems a little threatening.

Quite another sort of voice is what you hear when you pick up Saul Bellow's *Mr Sammler's Planet* and read, "Shortly after dawn, or what would have been dawn in a normal sky, Mr Artur Sammler with his bushy eye took in the books and papers of his West Side bedroom and suspected strongly that they were the wrong books, the wrong papers." A different cadence, a different attitude, a different sort of vocabulary. No wound-up spring here. We're hearing the voice of someone calm and sympathetic who knows the power he can give the words he saves for the end of a sentence. Though the last few words make you tense, you don't feel you need to jump out of the way. You may wish to check with other Saul Bellow novels to see whether this is the constant voice of the author or a voice adopted for this particular occasion.

Who will *you* be, for this story you're writing? Will you assume the stance of a wise old grandfather, perhaps, placid and unsurprised? A wise-cracking youth? Will you be emotional about your material, and involved – or will you be cool and distanced?

Much of this will depend upon your attitude to the characters with whom you are obsessed. Do you wish to be an intimate of the characters, or an ironic observer? The voice you adopt informs every line you write, establishes and maintains whatever relationship there is between story and reader. What can be more important?

Voice also assigns the reader a role in the drama: if you've chosen to adopt the voice of an historian (whether or not you are *identified* as an historian) you are asking the reader to be a student of history; if you've chosen to adopt the voice of a rural gossip you've made the reader a rural gossip, too, or party to gossip at least; if you've chosen to adopt the voice of a flashy smartmouth sneering at your characters, you're asking the reader to be the impressed audience and to sneer along with you.

This is not a matter to be taken lightly. Neither is it something to be added afterwards. This may be the most important choice you make – even if your choice is to have none of this "persona" business at all, but to join those many fine writers who write all their stories in the same voice, or in variations of the one voice they consider genuine. You are not really writing the story your readers will read until you've chosen.

Tone

> *I always consciously put the tuning fork up and looked for the tone. . . . If the book isn't going well or the book is to be abandoned – I've abandoned four things half-way through – or if a book has to be rewritten, which it very often has with me, it's often because the tone is wrong.*
> (Brian Moore, in *Conversations with Canadian Novelists 2*)

Whether or not you choose a persona deliberately, you will adopt a tone of voice. This may be thought of as a combination of writer's inescapably consistent voice *plus* the narrator's persona or personality *plus* an attitude towards the subject and the world at large and the matters at hand as well. In *Writing a Novel*, John Braine suggests that finding that tone of voice is the most crucial thing of all. He even suggests that you not begin writing until you've found it. He quotes the autobiography of Norman Podhoretz, who believed that the work of art is already there and that the artist's task in writing is to find the key that "will unlock the floodgates and let the flow begin":

> The key, I believe, is literally a key in that it is musical . . . it is the tone of voice, the only tone of voice, in which this particular piece of writing will permit itself to be written.
> (Norman Podhoretz, *Making It*)

Below are the opening passages from three novels and a short story by Leon Rooke. In each case the writer has adopted a distinct persona for his narration. Listen to the voice and imagine who is telling the story. Imagine the relationship between each narrator and the subject, between each narrator and you. Behind the different masks, can you detect a constant voice that somehow affects them all?

> What she sees first thing as she slows to turn Edward's truck into the driveway is a complete stranger in bulky over-alls perched up there on a ladder and sticking his head plumb through her bedroom window for no reason on God's green earth known to her. Her heart – not reliable anyhow – quickens, and for a second she fears it may stop altogether. One day it will, sure enough: you can't expect a thing to go on pulling what it isn't meant in the first place to be hitched up to. That's what Edward is always telling her, and she knows no better authority than Edward. *Now don't poke out your lips till they get stepped on, you know I wasn't criticizing, that whatever I tell you is for your own good.*
> (*Fat Woman*)

One evening in the autumn nub of the year a girl appeared out of a clump of trees by the side of a gravelly mountain road and steered along the wet mud bank towards the black car that was waiting. The driver removed the cigarette from his lips and spat out of the window, then turned to see would she jump the ditch, to see would she skitter and fall and cry out.

He won't going to come, but here he was, and he wondered about that.

He wondered what would he do with her tonight and whether tonight won't going to be the last night.

(*The Good Baby*)

That spongy, water-licking Wolfsleach was down on the grass doing sport with Marr, and when he saw me romping toward him with choppers flaring, he whirled in gummy panic and gave Marr a great kick in her hind parts that sent her spinning over on all fours, whimpering her sorrows at pleasure abated and leaking drool from her yellow mouth. Agh, you wench, I thought, you thrush-throated, humping dog; oh, the Devil take you. So I tagged her one on the fly, a quick bite that tozed gristle and fur, and kept on going. Blech and blah, woof and roar – oh, you mangy huffers with pig's feet for brains, here humping away to heart's content – and in *my* yard! There goes dignity, as the barrel-eyed Two Foots would say. Well, you'll taste the poison of my fangs, you'll get Hooker's come-upperance and what-for. You'll have my claw studs where dogger was. Woof-woof and arf-arf, damn you all.

(*Shakespeare's Dog*)

He lingered a long time but when the sun was at three o'clock the old man left his place on the park bench and headed for his hotel because by that hour the final mail would have been delivered.

The distance from the park to the hotel was not great but there were some things along the way which the old man took pleasure in watching and today there were some children playing too and because he stood among them until the last one ran home, by the time he reached the Swiss Arms the dinner hour was almost over.

("If Lost Return to the Swiss Arms")

A Sampling of Voices

Record what you think you learn (or only "feel") about each of the narrators in these passages. Try to imagine the personality of the narrator, the narrator's attitude towards the subject, and the tone of voice that has been adopted.

Mrs Golightly was a shy woman. She lived in Vancouver. Her husband, Tommy Golightly, was not shy. He was personable and easy to like. He was a consulting engineer who was consulted a great deal by engineering firms, construction firms, logging firms in particular, any firm that seemed to have problems connected with traction. When he was not being consulted he played golf, tennis, or bridge according to whether the season was spring, summer, autumn, or winter. Any time that was left over he spent with his wife and three small children, of whom he was very fond. When he was with them, it seemed that that was what he liked best. He was a very extroverted sort of man, easy and likable, and his little wife was so shy that it just was not fair. But what can you do?

(Ethel Wilson, "Mrs Golightly and the First Convention")

The day of the angel marks the divide in his life. He was never the same thereafter. Haunted? Hardly. Ghosts haunt. Angels instruct. And Herman Lovelock's part was to construct – well, yes, construct a kind of life in which a measure of grace might enter. Many of us would be similarly shaken, given his almost unimaginable and largely original circumstance. Many of us might likewise look skyward with the traditionally pathetic plea: "Why me, O lord, why me?"

More than a conventional shock to the psyche. Rather, a sword in the soul. With a festering wound thereafter. That is how we might try to see it: if we can swallow his angel, we can inhabit his skin. If not?

(Maurice Shadbolt, *The Lovelock Version*)

Rose came back yesterday, we went down to the bus to meet her. She's just the same as ever Rose. Talks all the time flat out and makes us laugh with her way of talking. On the way home we kept saying, "E Rose, you're just the same as ever." It's good having my sister back and knowing she hasn't changed. Rose is the hard case one in the family, the kamakama one and the one with the brains.

Last night we stayed up talking till all hours, even Dad and Nanny who usually go to bed after tea. Rose made us laugh telling about the people she knows, and taking off professor this and professor that from varsity. Nanny, Mum and I had tears running down from laughing, e ta Rose we laughed all night.

At last Nanny got out of her chair and said, "Time for sleeping. The mouths steal the time of the eyes." That's the lovely way she has of talking, Nanny, when she speaks in English. So we went to bed and Rose and I kept our mouths going for another hour or so before falling asleep.

(Patricia Grace, "A Way of Talking")

I have chosen to call this room Barbados. Ah – I can feel you shrink back already. Oh God am I going to be nagged by another of these madmen who is so confused about reality that he imagines his fireplace is a white sandy beach and that the brown bottle of beer on his table is a character named Nick Tromso?

It is not so. But all day I have been locked in here with myself, searching for a key to that place, Barbados, and all I keep turning up are nails or stones.

(Russell Haley, "Barbados – A Love Story")

In the ensuing days the Pratts called often with that particular brand of persistent inexorability often possessed by the thick-headed. She did not answer the door.

A voracious reader, she gave up her usual diet of novels which for the most part dealt with the implications of life and death, public and private responsibility in satirical but wickedly funny vein. She waded through murder mysteries at the rate of two a day because they presented death, waste, spite, destruction and misery in cheerful guise within bright covers and they warmed her.

(Shonagh Koea, "Mrs Pratt Goes to China")

He did most of his writing at night, rising sleepless and randy in the humidity and stumbling out to the kitchen to find big dappled slugs gliding over his cutlery and dinner scraps. He prised their shrinking, mucilaginous bodies from the Formica and flushed them, shrouded in Kleenex, down the toilet. It took hot water to remove their slime from the fingers. He worked at the kitchen table among their crisscrossed silver trails. The slugs returned every night, sliding out from dark soapy cracks behind the plumbing. One night he stamped one into the seagrass matting, it infuriated him so much. Next night a leopard-printed slug was grazing on the paste of his companion. A night or two later all that remained of the squashed slug was a faint brown outline.

(Robert Drewe, *The Savage Crows*)

Limbering Up with Milligan's Folly: Point of View and Voice

A. Write a paragraph describing the entrance of Milligan into the bank in the first person voice of Lindstrom, the manager. Write a paragraph doing the same thing in the voice of Mrs Marsden. In the voice of one of the other people in the bank. In the voice of the investigator who didn't see it but has interviewed several witnesses. In each case, put some effort into catching the unique qualities of this person's vocabulary, sentence structure, speech rhythm, accent, attitude, mood. It is unlikely that any two paragraphs will include many of the same words.

B. Now write a paragraph describing that same moment in the third person voice of a writer capable of watching all this from an invisible position behind the counter but not capable of knowing what anyone is thinking. Do the same thing in the third person voice of a writer who has had time to think about all this, who has figured out what each person was thinking and feeling, and takes pleasure in introducing us to that moment in all its rich texture and variety. Do the same thing in a third person voice of a writer who is particularly sympathetic to one character, capable of recording that person's feelings and thoughts, but sees the others as that character does. Do the same thing in a third person voice of a writer who views the main character with superior amusement. With disdain. With great pity.

C. Consider the various points of view available to you. Review the various characteristics of each, the advantages, limitations, and responsibilities of each. Decide, for the purpose of this exercise, who will be your protagonist and which of the plot lines you will follow. Write a fresh paragraph or two that might serve as a beginning to the story. Make it your task to establish not only a clear and unconfusing entrance to the story but also a strong sense of the narrator's voice, making it clear what point of view has been chosen. Try this from a variety of points of view, from a variety of voices, until one of them engages your interest enough, or starts your heart racing fast enough, to cause you to keep on going for a page or so.

D. Using the point of view and narrator persona that most appealed to you in exercise B, choose a half dozen key moments from your story and write a few paragraphs. If things are going well you may find you don't want to stop. In that case, just keep going until you run out of steam or material or interest. You will have pages which, however sketchy, may serve as a practice run for a first draft of this story.

RECOMMENDED FURTHER READING ON POINT OF VIEW

Points of View: An Anthology of Short Stories, Moffett & McElheny (eds)

Three Genres, Stephen Minot. Chapter 17

Literature: Structure, Sound, and Sense, Laurence Perrine. Chapter 5

Norton Introduction to Literature: Fiction, Section I

Text Book, Scholes, Comley & Ulmer. Part I

The Rhetoric of Fiction, Wayne Booth. Parts I, II & III

The Writer's Time, K. Atchity. Chapter 5

The Writer's Craft, John Hersey (ed). Part 2

The Writing Book, Kate Grenville. Chapters 4 & 5

The Story Makers, Rudy Wiebe

About Fiction, Wright Morris

Voicelust, Wier and Hendriet (eds)

Writing Fiction, Janet Burroway. Chapters 7 & 8

The Art and Craft of Novel Writing, Oakley Hall. Chapter 2

SOME SUCCESSFUL EXAMPLES OF
THE FIRST PERSON POINT OF VIEW

The Great Gatsby, F. Scott Fitzgerald
The Good Soldier, Ford Madox Ford
As I Lay Dying, William Faulkner
My Son's Story, Nadine Gordimer
The Moviegoer, Walker Percy
I'm Not Stiller, Max Frisch
Lillian's Story, Kate Grenville
Lord Jim, Joseph Conrad
Tirra Lirra by the River, Jessica Anderson
Lives of Girls and Women, Alice Munro
The Stone Angel, Margaret Laurence
The Ogre, Michel Tournier
Visitants, Randolph Stow
The Sportswriter, Richard Ford
Kate Vaiden, Reynolds Price
Love Medicine, Louise Erdrich
Potiki, Patricia Grace
Ever After, Graham Swift
"Meiosis," Italo Calvino
"What We Talk About When We Talk About Love," Raymond
    Carver
"My First Confession," Frank O'Connor
"The Grave of the Famous Poet," Margaret Atwood
"Initram," Audrey Thomas

SOME SUCCESSFUL EXAMPLES OF
THE THIRD PERSON POINT OF VIEW

"Everything that Rises Must Converge" and "A Good Man is Hard
    to Find," Flannery O'Connor
"Night Travellers," Sandra Birdsell
"A Class of New Canadians," Clark Blaise

"The Lady With the Pet Dog," Anton Chekhov
"A Dill Pickle," Katherine Mansfield
One Hundred Years of Solitude, Gabriel García Márquez
The Lovelock Version, Maurice Shadbolt
The Good Baby, Leon Rooke
Amongst Women, John McGahern
Matilda, My Darling, Nigel Krauth
Possession, A.S. Byatt
Oscar and Lucinda, Peter Carey
The English Patient, Michael Ondaatje
Rough Wallaby, Roger McDonald
Longleg, Glenda Adams
Kepler, John Banville
The Burning Boy, Maurice Gee

Making Connections:
Metaphors, Symbols, and Allusions

৭৯

I remember Professor Salter once saying, "Look, a lot of writers will take refuge in obscurity because they know it will be mistaken for artistic restraint, and generally the reason is because they don't know, really, what it is that they want to communicate." I remember Salter saying, "Make damn sure *you* know what it is that you are trying to say with these people and with these events and with this bubble you're building but for God's sake don't let it be said. Let that belong to the creative partner who comes to it. Let him think he's discovered it."

(W.O. Mitchell, in *Conversations with Canadian Novelists 2*)

The Objective Correlative

The only way of expressing emotion in the form of art is by finding an "objective correlative"; in other words, a set of objects, a situation, a chain of events which shall be the formula of that particular emotion; such that when the external facts, which must terminate in sensory experience, are given, the emotion is immediately invoked.

(T.S. Eliot, *The Sacred Wood: Essays on Poetry and Criticism*)

The family dog in Olga Master's short story "A Dog That Squeaked" cannot come inside the house without incurring the wrath of the father. He cowers beneath the food safe, hoping to remain unnoticed, while the small children in this very poor family overhear but do not fully understand a tense revealing conversation between their mother and father. By the end of the conversation, the reader understands that there is serious trouble between the parents and some jealousy over a neighbour couple who seem to be relatively prosperous. "'Lucky Dolly McViety,' the mother said. 'How long since we've had money to spare for a bottle of lemonade?'" In the end, the father spots the dog and explodes. "'Get that mongrel out!' he cried. 'How did it get in? Rump like a wallaby and legs like a blasted bandicoot! Get him out!'" We know from previous

information that the father will now kick the dog, chasing him yelp-
ing and scurrying outside.

In this story, the dog fulfills the role of what T.S. Eliot grandly
calls an "objective correlative," though undoubtedly there would be
little comfort for the dog in knowing this. That is, we know from the
father's reaction to the dog how he feels about the conversation that
has just taken place. While some part of the reader's sympathy is
with the poor dog, the primary emotion experienced at that
moment is a sharp, painful recognition of the father's frustration
with himself and his inability to make his wife happy.

The protagonist of Katherine Mansfield's story "Miss Brill" is a
spinster English teacher in France, who always wears a favourite fur
around her neck when she goes to the park – a fox fur whose mouth
is clasped to its tail. Sitting on the park bench, Miss Brill is happy,
satisfied with herself and her life, enjoying her habit of listening in
on the lives of others. But one day she overhears a pair of youths
speaking of her: "Why does she come here at all – who wants her?
Why doesn't she keep her silly old mug at home?" one of them says.
And the other: "It's her fu-fur which is so funny." The narrator does
not tell us how Miss Brill feels about what she overhears – that is, we
aren't told what she thinks. But we are *shown* that on her way home,
Miss Brill neglects to buy the slice of honeycake she always buys for a
Sunday treat. Back in her "little dark room – her room like a cup-
board" she puts the fur away in its box. "But when she put the lid on
she thought she heard something crying." Only the most inattentive
or insensitive reader would fail to understand what emotions Miss
Brill is experiencing, perhaps better than Miss Brill does herself.

In these two stories, the writers have chosen not to tell us directly
how a character feels at a crucial moment. We don't read: "He felt
terrible that he was not able to make his wife happy," or "Miss Brill
felt as though her whole world were falling apart." This sort of telling would have weakened the stories considerably.

Notice, too, that the writers did not drag dog and fur on at the last minute, assuming they could count on readers to react in a certain way. In each case, the reader was prepared. The dog was there from the start, trembling and hoping not to be noticed. Miss Brill made a great thing of admiring her fur at the beginning of the story. We knew all along what that dog and that fur meant to the father and to Miss Brill. You might say they were symbolic in the eyes of the characters who lived with them. At the moment of crisis, we have been prepared to understand and share the character's emotions.

Janet Burroway warns us against three common errors committed by writers attempting to use the objective correlative – or any symbols, for that matter:

> A symbolic object, situation, or event may err because it is insufficiently integrated into the story, and so seems to exist for its own sake rather than to emanate naturally from the characters' lives. It may err because the objective correlative is inadequate to the emotion it is supposed to evoke. Or it may err because it is too heavy or heavy-handed; that is, the author keeps pushing the symbol at us, nudging us in the ribs to say: Get it?
>
> (Janet Burroway, Writing Fiction)

The Secret Life of the Story

Back to that ploughed field, your first draft. There may be more than originally met the eye. Where did these rocks come from? What does this jawbone mean? How did this old-fashioned bottle get here? Who would ever expect to turn up a toy sailboat in a place like this? Much of this will be hauled away, thrown out – the result of daydreaming, of taking a false turn in your writing, of suffering the aftereffects of a hasty lunch, of brooding about that last remark someone made in this morning's phone call.

Some, however, can be seen to be connected to others: the old bottle has the picture of a sailboat on it? The jawbone, held at a certain angle, has something of the shape of the toy sailboat? Perhaps your character (Old George) is preparing for an ocean voyage but is frightened of going?

It is enough merely to suspect the connections for now. It is enough simply to decide not to throw something out – to let it hang around and grow with the various drafts. Maybe, eventually, it will earn its keep. Maybe it will become indispensable. You may even want to give it a place of honour – in the title, say, or in the final sentence of the story.

If the story is trying to tell you something, listen. If a story has a secret life it isn't enough just to acknowledge that fact. Something is expected of you. Don't be too hasty about this, though. Eventually you may decide that some of those objects should find their way into the language of the piece. In other words, you could help the reader make the connection between the turned-out bottle and Old George. Just having him give it a kick would tell the reader something. Having him pick it up and go all dreamy over it would tell the reader something else. It may be that nothing else is needed. On the other hand, it might be worthwhile setting up camp in Old George's head for a while, until you catch him expressing an opinion about that bottle. When he kicked it, was that because it offended him in a way that he can't quite understand? What *was* it about the bottle that offended him? Its age? The fact that the label reminded him that he is frightened of travel? (How did that bottle get there anyway? How far has *it* travelled?)

If you've gone even this far the bottle has already found a place in your story by way of making a connection with one of your characters. It has already taken on the properties of metaphor. Whether you draw your reader's attention to this is still a matter of choice. Just having Old George kick the thing may be enough. But if you stay camped in his head for long enough, you may discover that it was George who put that bottle in your story because the bottle in your story is really George.

Metaphor to Symbol

It may be that having made a connection between George and the bottle, you may wish to make more of it than metaphor. Something in you will resist this, of course, because you've always had a suspicion that some writers use symbols just to show off how clever they are. And you are almost certain that some writers order up their symbols from a warehouse somewhere (Dr Jung's Symbol Supply) and hammer them into place to give the illusion of more significance than the story had before.

And yet you know that Maurice Gee's *The Burning Boy* would have been a less substantial and satisfying novel if it had been called *Saxton College for Girls*, and had not had at its centre a boy whose permanently scarred face reminds every character of a terrible explosion and a network of community responsibility. And you suspect that Alistair MacLeod's "The Island" would not have had quite the impact if he had not drawn to our attention the way that lighthouse's searchlight revolves and revolves upon an empty sea. You suspect that a symbol, or a network of symbolic images or actions, really can give added depth and significance to a story, can connect it to the world outside itself, and can allow the reader added insight into the story's world – even the reader who has never heard of symbolism or taken an English course.

Before doing anything else with that bottle, though, it might be a good idea to listen to a few writers tell how their stories came to have symbols in them.

> When you write fiction such as mine, fantastic or quasi-realistic fiction,
> it happens inevitably that as you're going over it, thinking about it, you

recognize unconscious symbols bubbling up to the surface, and you
begin to revise to give them room, sort of nudge them into sight. Though
ideally the reader should never catch you shaking a symbol at him.
(Intellect is the chief distractor of the mind.) The process of writing
becomes more and more mysterious as you go over the draft more and
more times; finally everything is symbolic. Even then you keep pushing
it, making sure that it's as coherent and self-contained as a grapefruit.

(John Gardner, in *Writers at Work: The Paris Review Interviews*)

It's nearly always unintentional. I look back at it and think, "Oh, that
relates to that." When you're writing in a certain vein, everything grows
out of the same source. Occasionally it's more deliberate. I was very
much aware when I got to the end of The Ice Age *that it would be nice to*
have another bird. I had put a bird on the first page, it seemed obvious
to put a bird on the last. And there were a lot of dead dogs in that book
but then there were just a lot of dead dogs around that year. It's a natu-
ral associative process, really. It's not exactly symbolism, it's just how
life is. You notice one thing and then you notice the same thing again
tomorrow.

(Margaret Drabble, in *The Writer's Chapbook*)

W.D. Valgardson warns us of how symbols should *not* get into a
story.

I think one of the worst things any writer can do is impose symbols.
That's a dreadful thing, to nail them on. It should be like driftwood. You
don't nail the knots on. The water washes and erodes and what's left are
these hard knobs. That is the way that symbols should be. They should
rise out of the material naturally.

(W.D. Valgardson, in *Strong Voices*)

Like W.O. Mitchell's teacher quoted at the beginning of this
chapter, John Steinbeck cautions against explaining your symbols,
or drawing too much attention to them. He confessed to his editor

that by the time he was writing *East of Eden* he had learned from experience the importance of being subtle.

> *About the nature of the Trasks and about their symbol meanings I leave you to find out for yourself. There is a key and there are many leads. I think you will discover the story rather quickly for all its innocent sound on these pages. Now the innocent sound and the slight concealment are not done as tricks but simply so that a man can take from this book as much as he can bring to it. It would not be well to confuse the illiterate man with the statement of a rather profound philosophy. On the other hand, such a man might take pleasure in the surface story and even understand the other things in his unconscious. On the third hand . . . your literate and understanding man will take joy of finding the secrets hidden in this book almost as though he searched for treasure, but we must never tell anyone they are there. Let them be found by accident. I have made the mistake of telling my readers before and I will never make that mistake again.*
>
> (John Steinbeck, *Journal of a Novel*)

The literary scholars may wish to talk about your symbols. You may wish to do the same yourself. But you will know that you didn't order your symbols like a truckload of plaster elves to be placed in your story's now-landscaped field. (Lit up with neon lights saying "Here is the Story's Meaning!") And you will know that much of this business has to do with instinct and suspicion and perhaps even mischief. And you will know, as well, that those objects or people or actions that are being talked about as "symbols" were there in the unploughed ground of your story from the beginning, and that they had to stay there because something in the story would be hollow without them. Some insight would be missing, some glimpse into character, some hint at a connection between your story and the outside world.

You may not entirely believe that Hemingway really considered the big fish nothing but a big fish, as he claimed, but it's not very hard to believe that he found the big fish already swimming in the ocean of his story, suggesting its connection to the rest of the story's submarine life. Hemingway had to notice it first, and then to be interested in it, and then to see the connections it had to his old man and the old man's plight. And then he had to discover a way of writing about that fish that helped it play its part in the story of how Hemingway saw the world. After that, the big fish was perfectly capable of suggesting all sorts of meaning to the sensitive reader, without any more help from anyone.

George's bottle might do the same, if you saw the potential in it, and if you were as interested in that bottle as Old George seems to be. If it were to go on the trip with George, sit on a shelf in his berth or rest in his hand while he stares at it throughout a rough and lonely evening, and then it were filled with cool drinking water from a mountain stream in Switzerland where George is thirsty after a long climb . . . well, the metaphor is trying to become something else. It is trying to suggest, among other things, that there's more here than meets the eye. Students will write essays entitled "The Functional Significance of Old George's Symbolic Bottle."

It might not be such a good idea after all, to get carried away.

Getting Carried Away

On the other hand, sometimes it *can* be a good idea to get carried away, at least for a while. At least to see where getting carried away might lead.

Suppose your story was about a family moving from one house to another in a far country. And suppose you discovered when you prowled over the ploughed ground of your first draft that after the family had gone, their grandmother was left behind – refusing to be uprooted from her home. She had lived here all her life. She was too old to change. In fact, the day the family announced their decision to move (without consulting her) she discovered it very difficult to lift her feet when she wanted to walk to bed. When she awoke in the morning, she discovered that she had walked in her sleep – she was out in the yard, leaning against a tree, and in order to go inside for breakfast (and another day of arguing) she found it necessary to pull up several little roots that had grown down into the soil from the soles of her feet. She crammed the feet, roots and all, into her favourite slippers and didn't mention a thing, terrified of what was happening to her.

Well, you may want to stop right there, convinced that something has gone wrong. You may want to write a scene in which the grandmother, however much she wants to stay, gets into the car and leaves. Or a scene in which the grandmother, refusing to the end to let herself be moved, stays in the old shack watching her family drive off, convinced that she will come to her senses and follow. (They've left airline tickets in her apron pocket.)

Or, you may have read a few writers who have decided not to stop there, and you may want to see what happens if you allow the metaphor to do what it so obviously wants to do, become literal. There's certainly no law against it. In Michel Tournier's novel *The Ogre,* the protagonist-narrator, Abel Tiffauges, is told on page one (by his wife, Rachel) that he is an ogre. Of course he is only an ordinary garage mechanic, but he lives in France and the Second World War is about to break out, and soon Abel will have become a Nazi collaborator and, by the end of the novel, a real ogre. In Moacyr Scliar's *The Centaur in the Garden,* the narrator is a centaur from the beginning and only later has an operation that turns him into a human (an operation that is later reversed when he decides he'd rather be a centaur after all). Of course we understand at one point that being a centaur in Brazil at a certain time is rather like being a Brazilian Jew. Much of Timothy Findley's *Famous Last Words* is quite literally "the writing on the wall" – that is, a narrative by the murdered Hugh Selwyn Mauberley, in silver pencil, upon the walls of a grand hotel that had been his prison in the Austrian Alps.

If this sort of thing is going on in literature, then why shouldn't your grandmother set down her roots? When she awakes on the second day, she finds that the roots on the soles of her feet have burrowed down so far into the soil that she must dig with a stick for half an hour before she can free them and stuff them into her slippers before breakfast. Who knows where such thinking will end?

Things and people and actions in stories can sometimes suggest meaning and become metaphors. Metaphors may sometimes insist on taking on a larger life to become symbols. And metaphors that have grown into symbols, having more courage from winning all the battles thus far, may just decide that they want to be taken literally. The least you can do is give them a chance to show what they could do.

> One word of warning about symbols, however: If they are too obvious, they can turn a good story into something contrived and artificial. It is very risky (I'm tempted to say disastrous) to start with some symbolic notions and try to make them convincing. Stories which are rooted in the Adam and Eve myth (complete with a junkie named Snake-eyes) are a kind of original sin in writing classes.
>
> (Stephen Minot, *Three Genres*)

Allusions and Echoes

Some writers are adept at making their stories connect to other stories, by allusions, or implied comparisons, or with passages that echo passages we recognize from elsewhere. Characters, images, phrases, patterns may make us think of other stories that have already had their effect upon us. A boy on a raft? How can we not think of Huckleberry Finn? Three women cackle over a steaming pot? We know we're in the presence of evil, thanks to William Shakespeare, even though these three women may live in Winnipeg and ride motorbikes.

It is hardly possible to get far into Jane Smiley's *A Thousand Acres* before recognizing the similarities to Shakespeare's *King Lear* – an ageing father, three daughters, a favourite daughter who is disinherited. George McWhirter's *Cage* is about a Canadian priest working in Mexico, but it encourages us to contemplate a document entitled *A History of Don John of Austria*. The title of Toni Morrison's *Song of Solomon* suggests a biblical allusion, as Victor-Lévy Beaulieu's *Don Quixote in Nighttown* suggests a literary allusion. An Australian reader is certain to suspect that Nigel Krauth's *Matilda, My Darling* assumes a familiarity with "Waltzing Matilda," the unofficial national anthem.

What if Pinocchio, having achieved "real boyhood," grew up and became a distinguished professor in North America? And what if, towards the end of his life, he returned to Italy and found himself gradually turning once again into wood? Robert Coover has undertaken to answer these questions in his novel *Pinocchio in Venice*. All the characters out of the children's story are there. But there is something else as well, echoes of yet another literary source. The ageing professor in Thomas Mann's novella *Death in Venice* visits Venice, succumbs to both the dangerous plague-ridden air and to his own inner weaknesses, and eventually dies.

The critics call it *intertextuality*. You can think of literature as a conversation that covers the globe and spans all time. Maybe your story has relatives living in somebody else's story, and maybe it doesn't.

John Barth's *The Last Voyage of Somebody the Sailor* reminds us of those famous stories told by Scheherazade to save her neck. Indeed, ironically, here the ancient Scheherazade, who has outlived everyone else, tells this story to Death as a way of earning her own demise. The title of Janette Turner Hospital's *Charades* suggests the name Scheherazade as well. Within the novel the title character, not unlike the Persian princess, entertains her professor-lover night after night with tales of her past.

One of the best-known Australian short stories, "The Drover's Wife," was written by Henry Lawson, who was born in the nineteenth century. It portrays the loneliness and courage of a woman alone with her children in the "bush" while her husband is away at work – "droving" sheep. In 1945 Russell Drysdale produced a painting he entitled "The Drover's Wife," picturing a large woman with a suitcase standing before a barren landscape. The painting captured the imagination of viewers and the woman came to be almost an icon, a tribute to the hardy Outback Woman. More recently, Murray Bail published a short story entitled "The Drover's Wife," which begins with a small black-and-white print of the Drysdale painting, and which is narrated by an Adelaide dentist who insists that the woman in the painting is not the drover's wife at all but *his* wife, Hazel, who left a note on the kitchen table and disappeared. Frank Moorehouse then published a short story called "The Drover's Wife," which pretends to be a conference paper written by an Italian student of Australian literature, examining the cultural implications of the Lawson story, the Drysdale painting, and the Bail story – filled with hilarious misunderstandings. Other writers have since produced their own contribution to the strange life of the drover's wife, including stories and poems in the voice – not surprisingly – of the drover's wife herself.

What reason might a writer have for doing this sort of thing? The sense that a story is related to other stories can give added depth and richness to the reading experience. (Humour as well, as the history of "The Drover's Wife" suggests.) An implied relationship with other stories can seem to support the truth suggested by a new narrative by giving it authority. And of course, the writer is attempting to find that place in the reader's consciousness where myth already exists, to set free the ghosts and archetypes that stalk about and haunt.

If the writer is clumsy, however, we find ourselves thinking: "Don't make us read this story about a director of *Hamlet* who is having a hard time getting around to killing his mother's lover. Just send us a note that says: '*Hamlet*'s a great play. Go see it.'" Allusions and echoes can sometimes be clumsy and obvious. Sometimes they can be so subtle as to be unnoticed by even the most discerning reader. Too often they look like showing off. And there is always the chance that a reference to a masterpiece of the previous century might cause that other work to overwhelm and overshadow your own modest story. This is a matter for caution.

Making Connections

Rita Mae Brown bemoans the contemporary determination to remain ignorant of the myths and legends that have so profoundly influenced our culture.

> *Every Western writer – Russian, French, English, Czech, Hungarian, etc – every single one of us everywhere on the globe rides bareback with a foot each on two mighty, conflicting horses: Greco-Roman culture and Hebrew-Christian culture.*
>
> (*Starting from Scratch*)

She might have added, in view of the increasingly multicultural nature of such countries as Canada, New Zealand, the U.S.A., and Australia, that we are poised on the bare galloping backs of the Muslim, Hindu, Buddhist, and aboriginal cultures as well.

Two questions arise. Is it possible to write with depth and understanding without some knowledge of the cultures that have made us? And is there any point in drawing upon the cultural past for our writing when so few amongst today's reading audience are familiar with the sources?

There is no easy answer to either question. When a student submitted a story of sibling rivalry entitled "Cain and Abel" to a workshop, I expected to find us talking about the dangers of the obvious symbol. Instead, when I began the conversation by asking someone to identify the title's reference, fifteen students sat in silence. When my obvious disbelief had turned to obvious alarm, one student reluctantly said, "I know it's got something to do with the Bible but don't ask me what." After further questioning, I suggested (reasonably and calmly) that if they were serious about writing fiction they were cheating themselves and their readers if they did not read the great stories that have imbedded themselves in our literature: the great legends of Europe, the great literature of England, the stories of the Bible, the parables of the aboriginal peoples of North America, the great songs of the Broadway stage. "All these have had their influence on our culture." One young man, a writer of science fiction, sat patiently waiting for me to wind down. Then he said, "Culture has changed. We don't need all that stuff any more."

There are probably best-selling writers who would agree with him. They might suggest that for those readers whose sole purpose in reading a story is to escape the immediate world (through violence, intrigue, erotica, and car chases) a reference to the murder of Abel by Cain, the mapping of the solar system by Copernicus, or the visit of Odysseus to the land of the Lotus Eaters would be superfluous, distracting, and even confusing. This may be intended not as an insult to readers but only as a recognition that "*while they are reading me*" they don't want to be distracted by such matters.

For writers of serious fiction to take such a stance is to limit themselves to writing in a vacuum. Few writers can write well without reading well. To read well any writer from before the Second World War requires some understanding of more than the immediate world. If you believe you need nothing but your own reactions to the immediate material world you may write fiction with less depth than you'd hoped. You may also present the world with something you believe to be startlingly original but which the world knows has already been done much better.

I suspect there is little point in worrying about whether the majority of readers will "get" a reference to some other source. If your story depends entirely upon an understanding of an allusion to some other story, you probably haven't done your work well enough anyway. Perhaps you should try to make the reference in a context that gives it meaning even for those who don't recognize its origins. Or perhaps you should aim for a story whose meaning is clear enough for the innocent reader but enriched for those readers who can bring to it all the emotional impact of that other story you wish to evoke.

> In one way or another, then, all writers are forced to enter into a dialogue or debate with their predecessors, recycling bits and pieces of earlier texts, giving them a fresh application, a nuance of redefinition, a radically new meaning, a different function, an unanticipated elaboration.
>
> (Robert Alter, The Pleasures of Reading in an Ideological Age)

Trying It Anyway (With Mischief in Mind)

But what if you want to use echoes for purposes of irony, for parody, in order to "deconstruct" those stories alluded to? What if you want to take widely acknowledged myths that recur in literature and challenge their assumptions?

Robert Kroetsch's Badlands is set on the Canadian prairies in the early years of the twentieth century. The central figure is a palaeontologist, sailing with his crew on a raft down the Red Deer River in search of dinosaur bones for a museum. As they move down river they sink deeper and deeper into the earth, passing down through the traces of history.

The echoes are loud. The prairies, the river, the journey on the raft reminiscent of Huckleberry Finn suggest stories we have read or heard that have become part of the myths of the American male. That journey deeper and deeper into the earth also suggests the visits made by figures in Greek myths to the underworld, as the protagonist's story may remind us of Ulysses. The palaeontological search could remind us of any number of quest novels and epics we have read. And of course, the accounts of their successes and failures include much of the same material we might find in the field notes, or nonfiction accounts, of scientists and explorers. Indeed the protagonist's name suggests an actual palaeontologist who once explored the prairies. All this is narrated in a voice that is at times Faulknerian in its tone, suggesting the great melodrama of history and mankind's folly.

So many echoes! And yet, and yet. There is something different happening here. These figures are not at all god-like or heroic men in the American mould; they are a collection of grotesques, ridiculous figures (and Canadian). Instead of the holy grail or the golden fleece they are in search of what is, after all, merely old buried bones. Though they are scientists keeping scientific journals, we are more interested in their souls than in their discoveries. Furthermore, the whole thing is being narrated, not by a Faulknerian epic novelist, but by the palaeontologist's daughter – it is a woman's voice, a modern woman's voice. If he is a latter-day Ulysses, his story is told from the point of view of Penelope, the woman who waited at home. Furthermore this daughter, during the telling of the father's story, is making her own questing journey, with an Indian woman as companion, heading not down river into history and dinosaur bones and the scientific journals but up river towards the source.

It is clear that Kroetsch is having fun. But it is equally clear that he is up to something quite serious. He wishes to suggest an attitude towards certain myths that have been accepted by our society without much serious thought. It is possible to see even in this brief summary that he is turning those received myths on their heads in order to raise a few questions.

Thomas King's *Green Grass, Running Water* is set on an Alberta reserve not far from the action of *Badlands*. Along with its five Blackfoot protagonists – relatives gathering at their home town at the time of the annual Sun Dance – are four old Indians who have escaped from a mental institution, and whose names suggest an astonishing variety of literary allusions: Lone Ranger, Ishmael, Hawkeye, and Robinson Crusoe. Trailed by Coyote, the Trickster figure of Indian myth, the four ancients intend to "fix up the world," but bicker with one another throughout the novel as they try to tell the story of how things came about – including a story of creation and their own version of Noah's flood. While most of our attention is on the troubled protagonists, all realistically portrayed, the interspersed passages of the old men's squabbles and narrations connect the central story to the larger world even as it raises (comically) serious questions about the roles of myth in a culture.

These two examples are not particularly unusual. Kate Grenville's *Joan Makes History* forces us to reconsider official histories that exclude the contributions of women. Ian Wedde's *Symme's Hole* somehow weaves Moby Dick, Herman Melville, Katherine Mansfield, Maori and pakeha history, and McDonald's hamburgers into a highly original story. The central character in Aretha Van Herk's *The Tent Peg* is a woman whose name, J.L., reminds us of the biblical Jael, who drove a tent peg through a man's temple and killed him; by living disguised as a man amongst men in the Canadian far north she is able to question – and cause us to question – the way men have, by mapping the world, defined the world in male terms. Timothy Findley's *Not Wanted on the Voyage* gives us a new view of the story of Noah's Ark. In each case, connections have been drawn to other stories, old stories have been retold or recalled in such a way that the reader can learn to question those stories and assumptions that may have been too easily accepted. Although they may seem dreadfully serious in intent, in fact the works themselves are often funny, lively, and richly entertaining.

> Anyone could see that this was a great moment in history, but above the flagpole a crowd of birds was becoming hysterical in a tree,

laughing like lunatics through long beaks. I fancied the idea of a land where the ground repelled flagpoles stuck in it, and where the birds did no feeble tweeting, but gave forth mockery. *This is a land after my own heart,* I decided, and at the risk of a flogging I joined the birds. Mine was not only the first foreign foot to step ashore; mine was also the first foreign laugh to sound out, sharp and rude, across the waters of Botany Bay.

(Kate Grenville, *Joan Makes History*)

Definitely Indians, says one of the rangers, and the live rangers point their guns at First Woman and Ahdamn.

Just a minute, says First Woman, and that one takes some black cloth out of her purse. She cuts some holes in that black cloth. She puts that black cloth around her head.

Look, look, all the live rangers says, and they point their fingers at First Woman. It's the Lone Ranger. Yes, they says, it is the Lone Ranger.

That's me, says First Woman.

Hooray, says those rangers, you are alive.

Boy, says one of the live rangers, that's good news. I'll just shoot this Indian for you.

No, no, says First Woman. That's my Indian friend. He helped save me from the rangers.

You mean the Indians, don't you? says those rangers.

That's right, says First Woman with the mask on. His name is Tonto.

That's a stupid name, says those rangers. Maybe we should call him Little Beaver or Chingachgook or Blue Duck.

(Thomas King, *Green Grass, Running Water*)

Practice in Thinking Double

Reread the flying saucer story in Chapter 2:

1. Consider the metaphorical potential in:

- the car
- the road
- the mountain
- the weather
- the saucer
- any others you wish to add

2. Choose two of the above and for each, tell what it could mean to a certain character, and tell what it could mean to you or the reader.

3. Write a (subtle) paragraph in which one of the characters is shown becoming aware of the metaphoric possibilities in one of these choices above.

4. If you were to choose one metaphor to take on lasting importance, which would it be? Why? From which point of view could this best be handled? How would you avoid making it obvious?

5. Imagine that the choice you made in question 4 is subtly introduced in the first paragraph. Write that paragraph.

6. Imagine that the metaphor in the paragraph of question 5 has grown to take on central symbolic importance by the end of your story. Write a final paragraph to this imaginary story.

7. Push one metaphor even beyond the symbolic to the point where it can be treated literally in a story where the tone is "magic realism" or "surreal" or "symbolist". For instance, it is possible to imagine a

story in which the car becomes, quite literally, a prison – for each character in a different way. What about the falling snow? Write a paragraph in which one of the characters confronts the transformation of a metaphor into metaphor-taken-literally.

Limbering Up with Milligan's Folly: Metaphor and Symbol

A. It's time to go prowling through the ploughed fields looking for surprises and useful discoveries. Read over all the writing you have done for these exercises, keeping your eyes open for repeated images, favourite phrases, suggestive objects, connections and patterns and "accidental" repetitions. Make a list. If you said in one place that Milligan had a scar on his face, and said in another exercise that the surface of the rising river was marked by furrows created by half-submerged trees, and said in yet another that the outside walls of the bank were defaced by graffiti, make a note of the connection. You may be onto something there. Furthermore, make sure you know what that graffiti said. Is there any wall graffiti in Milligan's cabin? In Cates's farmhouse? In Lindstrom's home? At the very least there will be storefront signs "defacing" the walls of the town. What have all these scars got to do with the protagonist of this story? Wade through your materials several times, staring at what you've got, gathering up peculiarities that draw your attention to themselves, putting them aside, gathering them into groups of similar items. People, places, things, actions – all are capable of yielding up these surprises that connect to other people, places, things, actions, and eventually to the protagonist of our story. What does it mean? What does it mean to me? What does it mean to my protagonist, if anything?

B. Having gathered up these peculiar items and segregated them into piles of relatives, pick through them once again and toss out those that seem unrelated to the others, those that point in some direction that is of no interest to you or your story. It is probably possible to walk through your material, borrowing the eyes of your chosen protagonist, and turn almost everything you find into a metaphor of some sort – the river, the river bank, the bank, the town, the street, the people on the street, the motorbike, the mining claim, the mountains, the animals in the farmer's field. That's the easy part. The hard part is, having imagined all those metaphors, deciding whether any of them are worth using. And, having decided on the few worth putting into words for the story's sake, deciding what to *do* with them. Should they just sit there, radiating metaphor fumes? Do they have potential to grow, as the protagonist's story grows? For your purposes here, the useful thing might be to select one metaphor that you suspect promises the most and write a short passage in which it is recorded but not given any metaphorical weight. Then another passage in which someone within the story notices it and has an attitude towards it – still no metaphorical weight, though it is beginning to take on meaning. Then another passage in which your protagonist not only discovers herself (or himself) aware of this thing or person or place you're concentrating your attention upon, but also thinks of it (or speaks of it) in a way that *implies but does not state* a metaphorical connection between that object and either himself (or herself) or the situation that person is currently experiencing.

C. Just out of curiosity, revisit that same object/person/place at a point approaching the end of the story and write a passage in which you try to include it along with the person most associated with it in a way that points to but does not state directly a connection. At this point, only you know whether to stop this business or carry on. It may be that you're manufacturing things the story doesn't need. Or it may be that you've only now stumbled onto the real story, which belongs more to the world of symbol and allegory than to the world of banks and rivers and hunting knives and reluctant fiancées.

Remind yourself (this stuff is dangerous) that all this is only exploration and experimentation. The purpose of the writing assignments is only to provide exercise – limbering up for the task of writing the "real stuff" still down the road. The purpose of these exercises is certainly not to lock you into decisions, or to suggest that stories always arrive in a similar manner, or to imply that you must prepare for your story in a prescribed fashion. You are not writing the story here; you are not even writing a first draft here; you are digging up the raw materials so that you're better equipped for writing a first draft later on, when much may have been forgotten or rejected.

Limbering Up with Milligan's Folly: Echoes, Allusions

Not all writers are interested in creating echoes within their stories or connections to other stories. You may be one of them. However, since one purpose of these exercises is to expand your ability to see all the potential in a story idea, consider the following:

A. Make a list of books and magazines read by your protagonist during her (or his) childhood. What characters in legend, books, movies, history, the news, or television have been the protagonist's "heroes"? Has the protagonist consciously or unconsciously modelled himself (or herself) after someone else? Find out whether it's possible to write a paragraph in which your protagonist sees connections between her (or his) own situation and behaviour and the situation and behaviour of some admired figure.

B. Sort through all the material you wrote as a result of doing the exercises on metaphor and symbol. Are you aware of short stories or novels or movies or plays that use similar metaphors or symbols? Are any of them so well known as to make your choice seem imitative? Are any so well known that you might take advantage of the similarity? How could the story benefit from such a deliberate echo of another story?

C. Consider the pattern of the structure you are most tempted to give your plot. Can you see that this pattern is similar to that you've seen in the novels of a particular genre (thrillers, mysteries, westerns, romances) or in certain myths (quest, rebirth) or in certain dramatic traditions (Shakespearean tragedy, drawing room comedy)? To explore this adequately, you will need to sort through a lengthier list of possibilities than those given as examples. Consider whether there would be any value in introducing this discovered similarity into your story. Consider whether there would be any value in making alterations, or additions, or deletions to your plot in order to make the similarity more complete. Experiment by giving your story (temporarily) a title that makes the connections evident. Does this seem pretentious and artificial? Does it seem a natural extension of the story's specifics? Write a page in which you show your protagonist in behaviour you consider typical (not necessarily within the restricted time of the news clipping) and attempt to suggest as indirectly as possible some connection between this person and some figure outside the story.

D. Write a passage in which you record your attitude towards one of these figures from legend or film or myth or other stories you have thought of in connection to your protagonist. Write a passage in which you record your attitude towards your own protagonist and his or her behaviour. If you have made connections between your story and widely recognized patterns, or widely admired behaviour, do you have an attitude towards the values implied by those stories or heroes or behaviours? Does the plot you have found most interesting seem genuinely consistent with your own attitude towards your fellow humans and the way life is lived around you? What implications does your discovery have for the story?

––––––––––

RECOMMENDED FURTHER READING ON SYMBOLS AND ECHOES

Starting from Scratch, Rita Mae Brown. Part III

The Company We Keep, Wayne Booth. Part II, Chapter 11

Literature: Structure, Sound, and Sense, Laurence Perrine.
   Chapter 6

Playwriting, B. Grebanier. Chapter XII

The Eye of the Story, Eudora Welty

The Writer's Craft, John Hersey (ed). Part 4

The Art of Fiction, John Gardner. Part I, Chapter 4

Writing Without Teachers, P. Elbow. Chapters 2 & 3

NOVELS AND SHORT STORIES WHOSE USE OF
SYMBOLS AND ECHOES REWARDS EXAMINATION

A Night at the Opera, Ray Smith

The Burning Boy, Maurice Gee

Symme's Hole, Ian Wedde

Our Sunshine, Robert Drewe

The Last Magician, Janette Turner Hospital

Badlands, Robert Kroetsch

The Twyborn Affair, Patrick White

The Missing Child, Sandra Birdsell

Green Grass, Running Water, Thomas King

Joan Makes History, Kate Grenville

Famous Last Words, Timothy Findley

Possession, A.S. Byatt

Illywhacker, Peter Carey

Midnight's Children, Salman Rushdie

The Obscene Bird of Night, José Donoso

The Rose Tree, Mary Walkin Keane

The Cards of the Gambler, Benedict Kiely

Cutting Stone, Janet Burroway

Cage, George McWhirter

Burning Water, George Bowering
The Double Hook, Sheila Watson
The Life and Times of Captain N, Douglas Glover
"Island," Alistair MacLeod
"Antigone," Sheila Watson
"Miss Brill," Katherine Mansfield
"The Dog That Squeaked," Olga Masters
"The Reservoir," Janet Frame
"The Empty Lunch Tin," David Malouf
"Roman Fever," Edith Wharton
"The Road from Colonus," E.M. Forster
"Cages," Guy Vanderhaeghe
"The Mask of the Bear," Margaret Laurence
"Sailors Lost at Sea," Carol Shields
"Angels," Joan London

Revising

It might seem dismaying that you should see what your story is about only after you have written it. . . . Nothing is more exhilarating than the discovery that a complex pattern has lain in your mind ready to unfold.

(Janet Burroway, *Writing Fiction*)

Some Thoughts on Revising

READING YOUR OWN WORK OBJECTIVELY

An ability to read your own work as though it had been written by someone else may be the most important skill you can develop. And the most mysterious.

The more you read the writing of good writers, the more sensitive you may become to writing that doesn't measure up. The more familiar you are with the skills a fiction writer must have, the better able you are to recognize your successes and failures – also, the more likely you are to discover your heart racing with excitement and pleasure at those passages that succeed. The more aware you are of the potential in a story you've written – that is, the more you are able to sense what the story is wanting to become, its perfect version that you're travelling towards – the better able you are to discover what steps are necessary to take it closer.

Learn to listen to the story when you read it aloud to yourself. Learn to separate good editorial advice from bad. Learn a little patience, too, for when you think you have finished a story it is wise to set it aside for as long as it takes for you to forget the writing of it, so that you may pick it up as though you'd just opened the covers of a book, and read, with some surprise, what this stranger has written.

"FIXING UP" AND "RE-VISIONING"

Like Jessica Anderson, many writers rework each page or passage before moving on to the next.

> *I always start by revising the preceding day's work. I don't go on until I've got that right. I would like to be able to do a whole rough draft first, but I can't. When I go back to the preceding day's work, I find unexpected things, interesting leads. If I went on and did a whole rough draft I would lose that.*
>
> (Jessica Anderson, in *Yacker 2*)

This approach requires either a strong sense of an already-planned story ahead, or a sturdy faith in the power of the perfected page to generate the most appropriate and satisfying pages to follow. Perhaps the "revise as I go along" writer is one whose imagination is fired by relishing the perfectly chosen word more than by an unrolling sequence of events. Or this preference may reflect, as Margaret Mahy implies, the writer's personality and daily living schedule.

> *In my case the best work is often done in the early morning – I tend to push the cutting edge of the story along at night when what matters is movement forward rather than precision of judgement. To charge forward and then retrace my steps next morning and look at where I've been has developed into a fairly natural pattern for me.*
>
> (Margaret Mahy, in *In the Same Room*)

Many writers, however, prefer to barge right through to the end of a first draft without interruption for changes. The "first draft or bust" writer is likely to be one whose imagination views an interior

motion picture that must be recorded before it escapes. The interest
is in getting it nailed down rather than in getting it right. There'll be
time for improvements later.

Even amongst those who prefer to complete an uninterrupted
first draft before making changes, there are a variety of approaches
to a second draft. Barbara Hanrahan seems to follow the "first draft
or bust" approach with a "revise as I go along" second draft.

> *I don't write an enormous amount because the way I work is to write*
> *something out in longhand – then I'll correct it, then type it, then cor-*
> *rect it again. It's like working on a patchwork quilt, I go very slowly. I*
> *read it aloud to get the sound, I keep cutting out words that aren't*
> *needed. I try to get each page fairly correct before I move on. I re-do my*
> *rough draft, working at little bits, getting them finished as I go along.*
> *Then I might change my mind and think my first version was better.*
> *Though that's no guarantee it's going to stay like that. Because when*
> *I've got what I think is a fairly final version of a chapter done, I'll fit all*
> *sorts of other bits in as well.*
>
> (Barbara Hanrahan, in *Yacker 2*)

Christopher Isherwood, on the other hand, speaks as though his
second and third drafts are written afresh.

> *What I tend to do is not so much pick at a thing but sit down and rewrite*
> *it completely. Both for* A Single Man *and* A Meeting by the River *I*
> *wrote three entire drafts. After making notes on one draft I'd sit down*
> *and rewrite it again from the beginning. I've found that's much better*
> *than patching and amputating things. One has to rethink the thing*
> *completely. They say D.H. Lawrence used to write second drafts and*
> *never look at the first.*
>
> (Christopher Isherwood, in *The Writer's Chapbook*)

Editing and "fixing up" are important, but you probably
shouldn't pretend they're revisions. They can make a story better

but they aren't likely to cause a story to leap into a newer, fresher, richer form of life. Revising requires re-seeing.

In my experience, the best students have been able to take their stories through draft after draft to a point where they could be abandoned with satisfaction and pride. But most "breakthroughs" I've observed amongst student writers, where "good-enough" stories have become "very good" or even "superb" stories, accepted for publication and praise, have come about after the writer has worked through draft after draft, doing everything she knows how to do (editing and fixing up and strengthening the weak areas), and then steps back, abandons the "almost wonderful" story, and begins afresh. That is, after staring at the existing story until she knows it intimately, she sits down at the desk and begins a brand-new "first draft" from scratch. If the story is alive, new insights are more likely to occur while writing this way than while tinkering with a manuscript. In this new draft the writer will be writing from the position of having done all the work, of having no fear of losing the story-so-far, and of relaxing in a way she may not have relaxed before since doing the first "first draft"; this relaxed and joyful retelling of the story is more likely than anything else I can think of to turn up fresh insights, new angles, and original ways of saying things.

If you are lazy about the physical work of writing or typing, and if you are impatient to get to the end to see what sort of new story you've got on your hands, this approach will encourage you to leave out everything that isn't necessary to the story – all those beautiful but irrelevant passages and all those sentences that take too long to say what they need to say. The story may be better off without them. On the other hand, if their absence is felt and you really think they earn their keep, they can still be imported from the earlier story and given a second chance.

Then maybe – if you put it away for a good long time before

taking it out to read, and if you find yourself thinking "Hey, this story is better than anything *I* could have written, I wish it were mine!" – then maybe it's just about ready for other people to read.

When asked if he rewrote, Frank O'Connor replied:

> *Endlessly, endlessly, endlessly. And keep on rewriting, and after it's published, and then after it's published in book form, I usually rewrite it again. I've rewritten versions of most of my early stories and one of these days, God help, I'll publish these as well.*
>
> (Frank O'Connor, in *Writers at Work*)

Perhaps Maurice Gee's comment suggests that a writer's approach may simply reflect his preference for one aspect of writing over another.

> *I like the first shot, the time when you get surprises, when things get on to the page out of nowhere. You start off in the morning with blank paper and by midday something exists that had no existence before. That's the most enjoyable part for me, even when things are not coming easily. As for least enjoyable – there's none really, although final editing is a nervous time, changing this word for that. You don't know whether you're damaging your book or improving it. When to cut off is a problem.*
>
> (Maurice Gee, in *In the Same Room*)

The Importance of Learning the Skills

The following passage deserves careful reading for the very important insights it offers.

> *Early in World War II, a young American soldier happened to be in Oxford, Mississippi. He was an admirer of William Faulkner, so he decided to pay him a visit. . . . Faulkner was rewriting one of the stories [in* Go Down Moses*]. As the revision progressed, he would drop the rejected pages onto the floor beside his chair. The young soldier asked if*

he might have a few as a souvenir of his visit. He was given a handful that otherwise would have gone into the wastebasket. A year or so later, these pages came into the hands of an instructor at the University of Minnesota, and he made a most remarkable discovery. What Faulkner had been doing was changing the story from the first to the third person narration, but in so doing, he had not merely worked automatically, changing the pronoun "I" to "he." He had discovered (or had sensed intuitively) that in making the change, he had shifted the delicate balance of authority in the story from the principal character, a young boy, to the author. In the sample pages that the young soldier had brought away with him, the telling had been extremely vernacular, as it must have been, being told so directly from the character's point of view. In making the change as it appeared in the finished book, the author became the narrator and took on a greater burden of authority, so that the whole tone and the language had to conform more to him than to his character. What happened that we know for sure in this revision was that Faulkner toned down the vernacular, retaining just enough to hint at the kind of language used by the character, not so much that it would run counter to the more refined sensibility of the author, whose language it had now in the third person become.

. . . We might speculate that the early errors were not only failures of skill, but that they were also failures of the imagination. Lack of skill is always a hindrance to the imagination, because having to worry about technical matters destroys the concentration necessary for imagining the whole scene. By the time Faulkner wrote Go Down Moses, *his imagination allowed him to view the scene from the young boy's point of view so completely that all of the attendant qualities of the story took on the tone and manner of the boy himself. In revision, he had to reimagine them from the more complex view of the author, but he had to be careful to avoid disturbing too much the rendering of the boy. The outcome – as we know it in the successful completed story "Was" – exemplifies the imagination freed of restraint by the mastery of skill.*

(Ray B. West, Jr, *The Art of Writing Fiction*)

There are several implications for the young or beginning writer here. One is, of course, that the writer, in order to improve his story, has to be able to recognize the flaws in it. Another, that revising is more successful for the writer who has mastered the skills of narration to the point where the imagination can be free enough from distractions and technical concerns to *re-imagine fully.*

It is worth noting that Faulkner did not write the "he's" over the old "I's," or scribble the other changes in the margin. To be discarding the pages of the earlier draft, he must have been writing it out completely new. He was not "fixing up" a previous draft. He was not "making corrections." He was writing the story all over again from a new point of view, with a new voice – presumably using the earlier draft as a guide.

A writer might be understandably reluctant to write a story out all over again in this manner. And probably most writers scribble all over a manuscript page before breaking down and doing a new one. Still, I believe the reluctance must be overcome. So long as you are working on top of a previous draft, you haven't freed your imagination to re-see the scene completely and with undistracted confidence. You are being an editor rather than a writer.

And this is one reservation I have about writing on the computer. Moving things around, eliminating things, inserting things – all are made so efficient with the word processor that I wouldn't want to do without the machine ever again. But the problem is that moving and inserting and eliminating have become so easy, and result in such an immediate and attractive new draft, that the thought of typing out a new draft in a new file, using a printout of the previous draft as a guide, has little appeal. And yet, I believe it is something that ought to be done. It is not merely typing. It is telling the story again from a position of relaxed confidence – you've done all the work, you can't lose what you've done, you can respond to the words and sentences with all the pleasure of the happy reader, and at the same time allow the imagination to believe it is writing a first draft. You may be surprised to discover what gems the confident and relaxed imagination can come up with when it believes it is writing a first draft. It can, amongst other things, supply some freshly discovered parts of the story that your earlier labouring had not brought to your attention.

Integrity, the Ultimate Goal

Some revisions can be devoted to choosing the perfect word, the most effective phrase, others to strengthening the plot, or creating a more convincing character. Still others can be devoted to finding what other secrets the story might uncover, through exploring the spaces, examining the gaps, looking carefully over the surprises. New material may be added. Everything doesn't have to be done at once.

Some revisions can be devoted to pruning or axing superfluous words, phrases, paragraphs, and even episodes; others to compressing overlong sections into more quickly paced passages.

> It is a struggle when I have to cut. I reduce nine hundred pages to one hundred sixty pages. I also enjoy cutting. I do it with a masochistic pleasure although even when you cut, you don't. Writing is not like painting, where you add. It is not what you put on the canvas that the reader sees. Writing is more like a sculpture where you remove, you eliminate in order to make the work visible. Even those pages you remove somehow remain. There is a difference between a book of two hundred pages from the very beginning, and a book of two hundred pages which is the result of an original eight hundred pages. The six hundred pages are there. Only you don't see them.
>
> (Elie Wiesel, in *The Writer's Chapbook*)

Always, the goal in revising is to achieve a more powerful whole, all of whose parts are dependent upon one another and necessary for the desired effect. The hope is to honour (and preserve) the imagined perfect story's natural integrity. In the works we admire, it is impossible to imagine the actions separate from the characters, the setting and atmosphere separate from the voice and style, the structure anything but what it is, or the theme isolated from any of the elements that are interwoven to create the total form.

The following checklist is intended to help you work towards that state in your stories where every element is not only as effective as it can be but is also related to everything else, where all of it contributes to a strong, unified whole. You should also examine closely those published works that seem so perfect that you can imagine the removal of any small element destroying the work of art – Edith Wharton's *The Age of Innocence,* perhaps, or Anne Hébert's *In the Shadow of the Wind,* or Ford Madox Ford's *The Good Soldier,* or the stories in Alice Munro's *Friend of My Youth,* Raymond Carver's *Where I'm Calling From,* Robert Drewe's *The Bodysurfers,* and Katherine Mansfield's *Collected Stories.*

Preparing to Revise an Early Draft:
Learning to Read Your Own Work

(Do not assume that every question is of equal importance in relation to every story. Do not assume that the questions come from any
sense of certain rules. This is only a guide, these are only suggestions.)

Opening Paragraph: Does it raise questions, cause curiosity, offer
sharp images that arrest the reader? Does it establish the voice of the
narrator?

Prose: Have I taken care in choosing language, aware of its meaning,
sound, and implications? Have I written sentences that achieve the
desired effect? Are the rhythm, pace, and tone appropriate to the
story's intended effect?

Types of Prose: Have I written *expository* prose when I need to give
information directly, *narrative* prose where I want to relate a series
of events to get from one important part of the story to the next, and
full or partial *scenes* when I wish to develop conflict, expose character, work out main plot moves, watch my characters close-up,
involve the readers?

Character: Are the characters seen clearly? Is the main character
felt? Do I have his voice, reveal her appearance, explore his personality? Does the reader know the things about her that are needed in
order to understand her behaviour or reaction at the end? Gestures?
Facial expressions? "Essence"?

Point of View: Do I know what I've chosen? Do I understand why? Is
it consistent throughout? Was it the best choice? How would
another choice change things? Have I taken advantage of this point

of view to do what it can do? Do I understand the narrative persona I've adopted?

Voice: Does the first paragraph clearly establish the voice of the narrative? Is the voice consistent throughout? Is the language always consistent with the narrator's attitude and education? Is the narrator's attitude implied in the language chosen, and in the rhythm of the sentences? Is the voice clearly oral or clearly written, clearly formal or clearly colloquial, etc?

Plot: Does each event happen because it's natural to the character or because I imposed it on him? Has tension been created? Is there a causal relationship amongst events?

Pace: Does my prose move forward or sit on the page? Are the verbs strong? Does the reader feel any sense of speeding up or slowing down according to the needs of the story?

Dialogue: Read it aloud. Does it sound like real people talking? Does each person speak differently? Is each person's speech consistent? Have I used the dialogue to reveal character, move the plot, and give new information all at the same time?

Style: In each paragraph can I see how my sentences control the reader? (Speed her up, slow her down, get him rocking, force him to jump, stop, etc, etc?) Is every word of every sentence the best word available, for meaning, rhythm, sound, connotation? Am I always dealing in the concrete, avoiding the vague, even when I wish to suggest abstractions? Do I show where I ought to show, and tell only when telling is the best way to achieve my purposes?

Theme: Now that I've written the thing, can I see what I'm concerned with here? Now that I can see what it's about, are there parts that don't contribute and should be thrown out? Are there parts that should now be given more attention, importance, and space, in order to illuminate my "theme"? In the process have I uncovered any images, objects, actions, people, that imply symbolic meaning? Should they be emphasized? Do they illuminate the central concerns? Do they help make connections? reveal patterns?

Unity: Does everything here contribute something to the single total impression of the story/chapter? Or could some scene or passage be thrown out without making much difference? Does every scene contribute several things at the same time (character revelation, plot movement, setting, and so on)?

Integrity: Do all of the above elements contribute to one another, depend upon one another, form part of a whole that appears, when you stand back, as though it must have arrived complete, all of a piece, everything in place?

One Way to Prepare for a Revision

For any of the writing exercises you've already done in this book, or for any story you've written, concentrate on the first page in the following manner:

1. For each of the appropriate topics in the preceding checklist for revising, make notes in the margins – questions, challenges, suggestions, doubts. Circle weak sentences, or instances of poor choice of words, and use editorial symbols to indicate faults in punctuation, spelling, grammar, etc.

2. Decide on the best sentence for your first sentence; that is, best for establishing voice, commanding interest, and making the reader

move on to the second sentence. Don't go on! Examine word choice: specific? concrete? fresh? a sentence you'd be proud of even if you didn't continue? Now write (or find) the most natural sentence to follow. What connects them (with regard to grammar, emotion, tone, causality, content)?

3. Using your new beginning, and referring to your margin notes on the previous draft, work your way through a new "page 1" in which you try to address the comments by making improvements to the prose, deleting weaknesses, adding needed new material, and supplying cohesion.

4. Consider that what you've done so far is *not* your next draft but merely preparations to establish the content and intention of your next draft. This is not the story anyone else will read; only the story you've been *discovering* for yourself. Now cut yourself free from it in the following manner. Select two sentences you consider to be "key" important sentences and write them on a separate piece of paper. Now put the rest of the rewritten page aside and firmly establish in your head the rhythm of the narrator's voice. NOW WRITE THE PAGE FROM MEMORY, allowing new material to enter just as though it were a first draft.

5. Compare the new version with the previous. Isolate the elements and sentences in each that you consider to be most successful. What new elements arrived (or surfaced)? Now, referring to both versions, write a brand-new version.

———————

Once You Know the Weaknesses

You've rewritten and revised and corrected your story. You've done everything you know how to do, so you submit it to your favourite critic, your writing group, or your workshop, for a response. (And that is the state any story should be in before you submit it. If you hand a story over prematurely, you'll only be told what you already know and can only be led to make it a little better. If you hand a story over when it's as good as you know how to make it, new insights from new readers can actually show you ways of taking it further.)

The response could take the form of written commentary on separate paper, editorial marginal jottings in pencil, or editorial comments on sticky notes attached to the manuscript. But what do you do with the comments when you get them?

All comments deserve your attention but all comments do not deserve to be acted upon. Consider them all, and then begin to separate them. If you think of your story as on its way to being the perfect version of itself, then you want to find the criticisms and suggestions that will help you get there.

1. Separate out the comments that seem to suggest a misunderstanding of the story, or presume it's trying to be something that you may not have thought of yourself. Have you done something to give this wrong impression, or has the reader read poorly? Put aside those that seem wrong-headed, or that suggest a direction for the story that doesn't appeal to you. Think carefully about those that suggest a direction that is appealing *and* consistent with what you wanted. Make sure that you understand what you want this story to become.

2. Sort through the other comments and separate those that suggest weaknesses that are preventing you from achieving your goal. ("The protagonist is shadowy." "Plot is unconvincing.") Try to

understand why. Search for the omissions, find the misleading moments. Consult all you know about the topics. Consult those books you've found most useful. I would recommend David Madden's *Revising Fiction* here. If you've discovered where your weaknesses are, you'll find that he has several questions you may ask yourself about those weaknesses, and will supply you with examples that demonstrate how successful writers have solved those same problems for themselves.

3. Don't be lazy. Start again as though you intend to write from scratch. New paper, new file. Prop the previous draft up, with your markings on it. Retype it, allowing new words, new ideas, new images to find their way in. Let your imagination believe it is writing a first draft; at the same time let your interior editor relax in the knowledge that none of the earlier work can be lost.

4. Once the new draft is completed, consult your critics' comments on grammar, usage, and style to see how many of them still apply. Make corrections. Compare this new draft with the previous one. You may discover passages that were more effective in the earlier draft. Import them if they will actually help the new draft.

5. Only now, I think, would I suggest working seriously on the hard copy, with pencil or pen. Go through, reading aloud. Then experiment with the sentences to create the effect you want. Consider pace, diction, rhythm, sounds, and all the other aspects of writing good prose discussed in Chapter 3 of this book.

6. It might be necessary to repeat the entire process several times before you've got a story you're proud of. You may want to consult with readers after each draft. Much of what you've done to this point has probably been "putting in" – more character portrayal, more setting, etc. Eventually the time will come when you'll sense

that the story has everything it needs and maybe more. At this point it's time for getting out the hoe and pruning shears. Where it seems to drag, cut out the unnecessary bits to speed it up. Where it repeats itself, or takes too many words to say what could be said more directly, start weeding. Where a whole scene accomplishes only one small task, replace it with a sharp summary narrative.

7. But that's not where it ends. A matter of *focus* is now of interest. There may be images, dialogue, descriptions, scenes, even people, that are not strongly relevant to the central spine of the story, the central interest of the story. You may want to *make* them relevant or you may want to cut them out. The important thing is that you first determine what that idea-spine is, so that you can tell what belongs and what doesn't. When this happens, you're getting close to a finished story – that is, a story that ought to be thrown away as having gone as far as it can go, or a story that ought to be read by an editor.

8. Put it aside for a good while, and forget it. Weeks. Even months. Work on another story. Then dig this one out and read it as though someone else had written it, so far as this is possible. You may decide it's doomed to be no better, you may get wonderful new insights, or you may feel it's just right as it is. Or you may feel that just one more revision could make a "good" story "superb."

Putting the Milligan's Folly Exercises to Some Use

What you have accomplished by doing all the writing exercises related to the news clipping is practise the sort of thinking and note-taking involved in preparing to write a story. Do not assume that these exercises exhaust the possibilities. Don't imagine, either, that doing them has resulted in a short story or a novel. Rather, you probably have an accumulation of related material that could, if you were so inclined, give you the basis for writing a first draft of a story. It is possible that you are tired of this story idea and are impatient to get on with your own. My suggestion is that you now take a story idea that has been awaiting your attention and do this same sort of thinking and writing about it as you prepare to write a first draft. Accumulate notes. Then, of course, sort through the notes for passages worth keeping or referring to. Put everything aside. And write that first draft.

At first glance there may seem to be a contradiction here. On the one hand, I've cautioned you that you shouldn't hinder your imagination by thinking about all these things while writing the first draft of a story – save them for when that draft has been nailed down. On the other hand, I've suggested that working your way through these exercises is a good way of preparing yourself for the first draft. I believe you can have it both ways. If you take the time to do all this sort of thinking and writing – following the suggested exercises – before writing a first draft, you'll have accumulated a familiarity with your story that should make you better prepared to write a successful first draft. Having done the preparation exercises, however, I think it's important that you put them behind you, as you might put finger exercises behind you before tackling a piano sonata, and write that first draft with imagination freed from any restrictions except those that have become second nature, the necessities of the story. New and exciting things should surface during the writing of that first draft. Then, having written that first draft, you are in a position to go back and think about the various skills and techniques discussed in the preceding pages.

There are no "right" ways of writing fiction. In fact, since every story presents new challenges, you need to learn how to write all over again every time. One approach is to begin with the sort of exercises outlined here (discovering what your material has to offer) followed by a first draft that benefits from but does not tie itself to that preliminary work, followed in turn by a more critical examination of the results. Having nailed the prepared-for first draft down, you may do some serious thinking about matters of technique – become your own editor – without fear of paralysing the creative imagination. Using the checklist for revising, you can find your way back into the aspects of narrative technique that are most important for the writing of a second draft.

Limbering Up with Milligan's Folly: Making Your Own

Take an idea you've been considering for a story and create a news clipping you can imagine using for a series of exercises similar to those you've been through. You may wish to imagine preparing them for a friend who wants to do this sort of preparation but doesn't want to use the same news item. Having to bring together the desirable elements for the ideal news item should cause you to stretch (or gather) your material into a shape that better prepares you for writing about it as well. Do you have intriguing characters? Have you placed them in a setting with potential? Is there the possibility of conflict? Does the conflict have potential for varying degrees of experience – one person's internal struggle, a struggle between individuals, a struggle between groups, a conflict of ideas or values? Are there interesting peripheral elements – minor characters and interesting circumstances? The experience of making up good writing and thinking exercises for your friend will probably cause you to discover or create even more interesting possibilities in the material than you first imagined.

———————

RECOMMENDED FURTHER READING ON REVISING
The Writer's Time, K. Atchity. Chapters 2 & 4
The Writer's Craft, John Hersey (ed)
The Writing Book, Kate Grenville. Chapter 9
Revising Fiction, David Madden
Writing Fiction, Janet Burroway
Writer's Revisions, David Madden & Richard Powers
The Fiction Editor, Thomas McCormack

NOVELS AND COLLECTIONS OF STORIES
WHERE ELEMENTS ARE WELL INTEGRATED
Gabriella, Clove and Cinnamon, Jorge Amado
Affliction, Russell Banks
Afternoon of a Good Woman, Nina Bawden
Possession, A.S. Byatt
Collected Stories, Morley Callaghan
The Awakening, Kate Chopin
The Shooting Party, Isabel Colgate
Light in August, William Faulkner
Famous Last Words, Timothy Findley
The Great Gatsby, F. Scott Fitzgerald
Rock Springs, Richard Ford
Love in the Time of Cholera, Gabriel García Márquez
Ellen Foster, Kaye Gibbons
My Son's Story, Nadine Gordimer
The Choiring of the Trees, Donald Harington
In the Shadow of the Wind, Anne Hébert

Dubliners, James Joyce
The Big Chapel, Thomas Kilroy
All the Pretty Horses, Cormac McCarthy
1915, Roger McDonald
Amongst Women, John McGahern
The Lost Salt Gift of Blood, Alistair MacLeod
Death in Venice, Thomas Mann
Girl in Gingham, John Metcalf
The Field of Vision, Wright Morris
Beloved, Toni Morrison
Friend of My Youth, Alice Munro
American Appetites, Joyce Carol Oates
Collected Stories of Frank O'Connor
The Second Coming, Walker Percy
The Source of Light, Reynolds Price
Collected Stories of V.S. Pritchett
Midnight's Children, Salman Rushdie
Of Heroes and Tombs, Ernesto Sabato
Perfume, Patrick Süskind
Crossing to Safety, Wallace Stegner
Waterland, Graham Swift
Marine Life, Linda Svendsen
Collected Stories, Peter Taylor
Collected Stories by Eudora Welty
Ethan Frome, Edith Wharton
The Tree of Man, Patrick White
Swamp Angel, Ethel Wilson

Breathing from Some Other World:
The Story of a Story

၅၁

If I'd known I'd get a letter from her a day later with this piece of paper in it, one of these mixed-up unreadable modern poems called "The Man Without Legs," she wouldn't have got inside my pickup for even a minute. You can't trust people who write things on paper, they think they own all the world and people too, to do what they want with.

(Spit Delaney, in *Spit Delaney's Island*)

About a year after the 1976 publication of my first book, *Spit Dela-ney's Island*, an ad appeared in the Classified section of a Victoria newspaper. "LOST, a small black spaniel, male, answering to the name Spit Delaney." I began to wonder even then if in writing fic-tion you might be setting loose much more into the world than you think.

Just *how* much more, I had yet to learn. Years later, the two short stories about Spit Delaney were adapted for both radio and the stage. During the intermission of the stage production's preview, I was approached by a fellow who'd grown up in the same rural com-munity as I had, eager now to talk about the recognitions and memories provoked by the play. He was sure he knew who Spit was, he said, giving me a sideways sort of look that said "you cheeky bugger." He recalled several incidents out of his own past as a child-hood friend of "Spit's" – incidents I hadn't known before but which I mentally filed away as material for a future story. "Old Spit! Old Number One!" He laughed, and shook his head. "By golly, that's just the way it was!" After the final curtain, however, someone else cornered me to express quite a different reaction. That was certainly not the way *she'd* thought of Spit! She was, in fact, insulted. That the performance had not reinforced precisely her own impression of the character was a personal affront. "Spit Delaney is us!" she said, indicating members of the departing audience. "How *dare* they do this thing?"

Driving home down the long dark Island highway that night, I had plenty of time to wonder at what I'd witnessed. What did it mean, that others had taken possession of a character I had released to the world? Were people fooling themselves when they insisted that Spit Delaney spoke, or felt, for them? I didn't know, but I found myself recalling how Spit had come into being – fifteen years before.

Like many of my stories, this one (or rather, these two) began as the result of a conversation with my parents. Their down-Island visits have always included a round-up of the latest developments in the lives of relatives and friends and acquaintances in the Comox Valley. This time they had news about a certain uncle who worked in a pulp mill, where he operated the company's steam locomotive, hauling railcars of pulp and newsprint on and off the barges. "I guess you haven't heard what's happened to Fred," my mother suggested, knowing very well that I hadn't.

Her face told me this would be worth pursuing.

"Well," she said, "they've sold his locomotive! Just like that. One of the museums in Ottawa bought it. Took it away."

I knew immediately what a blow this must have been. "That train was the centre of his life. How's he taking this?"

"Well *yes!* We always teased him about it. The mill would have to shut down if he wasn't up there every morning at four, getting up his head of steam. Now they're giving him a diesel!"

My father said, "He's had one of these here painters go into the mill and paint it for him. Old Number One – before they take it away."

"An oil painting?"

"They've got it hanging over the fireplace," my mother said. She didn't need to say: "Can't you just *imagine*?"

"And he's got the number off the front hanging on the rec-room wall."

"And made a tape of the loci before they took it. *Hours* of it! He sits and listens."

He did more than sit and listen to his tape. He took it with him wherever he went. He especially liked to take it into the mountains when he and my aunt went on fishing trips in their truck and camper. "He waits until all the other people have gone to sleep around the lake – in their tents and campers and RVs – and then he puts the tape on and turns it up full blast! Watches them come running out, wondering how in hell a train got up where they were!"

"Really," my mother said, "it's something that ought to be put in a book."

It wasn't the first time she'd said these words. In fact she'd said them often over the years – still does. If someone ought to put Uncle Fred in a book, obviously she intended it to be me. I started to work the next day.

It seemed that little needed to be invented. At least at first. I gave my uncle a new name (as I've done again here) and simply recorded what had happened to him in a manner that combined a rapid narrative exposition with brief scenes that included dialogue. But then, when I came to where I was about to set a scene in a lakeside campsite in the Vancouver Island mountains, I found myself thinking: What if he didn't stop there? What if he carried this obsession farther afield? What if he took his tape to some other continent? Europe! I'd been to Ireland recently, and thought I could imagine the sort of uproar he might create in a foreign country. Part of the fun was watching his poor family's exasperation.

As I wrote this sequence, though, I began to see that somewhere along the way his wife had lost my aunt's sense of humour about the situation. This wasn't the least bit funny to Stella Delaney. I wasn't sure what to do next. Back up and *give* her a sense of humour, let her become his partner in this eccentric performance? Or see how far she could be pushed, see what might happen when she reached the limit of her endurance?

Should I alter a character who seemed to have a mind of her own, in other words, so that she wouldn't spoil a good anecdote? Or should I listen to her (and to him) and follow wherever they might take me? I was stalled. I'd written quite a good tale, I thought. It was humorous. It was about an appealing character. It included an entertaining sequence of events. But it was not, I felt, a story. Or at least it was not a story that satisfied me. Something important was missing.

The something important that was missing was something that I'd come to recognize in the fiction I most admired: a richness, a complexity which suggested that the experience, however entertaining, was beginning to catch some small illuminating glimpse of meaning beyond itself. Good writing should be something that scares the writer a little – the reader too – the way a bolt of lightning can do. It startles, frightens, but it also illuminates for a moment, perhaps even shows us our way in the dark. I wanted something like that.

Excitement died. The original urge to record the anecdote had been satisfied. The part of me that is a lover of good literary fiction had come along and spoiled everything. I put the draft away.

(Of course I might have chosen *not* to put it away. I wonder now what difference that might have made. I was once an avid reader of Erskine Caldwell after all! If I'd believed I had written a satisfying story and found someone to publish it, would I, by now, be happily and successfully publishing humorous anecdotes about eccentric characters, repeating a happy formula in book after book? Volume twenty-three of the shenanigans of Spit Delaney and his eccentric relatives! Instead of still trying with only modest success to write fiction that at least *attempts* to track down and corner and secure a glimpse of some small patch of truth, I might be – what? But there is no use thinking about this sort of thing now. However entertaining a well-told anecdote might be, the repetition of any winning for-mula becomes, I suspect, an accumulating lie. Good fiction, though based on made-up things, endeavours to tell the truth. And the writers I admired most – Faulkner and Chaucer and Steinbeck amongst others – had managed to do that "something more" with-out altogether jettisoning their love of the eccentric tale. Better to risk failure in trying to join the writers I've admired. I thought this then – I still do.)

Spit Delaney lay dormant for a year while life (mine) went on without him. I did some revisions to a collection of stories that had been accepted for publication – my first book, still untitled. I worked on a novel, which looked so unlike any novel I'd ever seen that I practically feared for my life. I taught high-school English by day, taught night-school English by night, directed a television play for students, finished a couple more rooms in the house, fixed bro-ken toys, attended family reunions, read novels and collections of short stories, and dreamed (ludicrously) of one day selling enough fiction to make it possible to quit teaching.

Then, one day, I found the Spit Delaney piece and reread it. It was, just as I'd remembered, a good anecdote. But during its time in the drawer it hadn't become what I was pretty sure it was capable of becoming. No lightning flashed.

At least not at first. Then all at once it was as though an assort-ment of ideas and images that had been sitting idly by in their vari-ous corners (twiddling their thumbs) had come rushing in from every direction to collide in a moment, setting off an explosion. It seemed that during that year of Spit Delaney's dormancy I had been preoccupied (on and off) with a number of topics that almost cer-tainly related to Spit and his predicament.

I had, for instance, watched a number of friends go through the anguish of ending a marriage – separation from a companion and from a lifestyle that had been central to their lives for several years.

In particular, I was given plenty of opportunity to see what a separation could mean to a man in his forties who had taken his marriage's stability for granted. More than one friend confided his feelings of having been devastated by the experience – nothing remained solid, everything had to be re-evaluated, life had taken on a brand-new colour. In more than one case it had happened all at once, a surprise. I imagined how I might react to such a thing myself. If all these people were genuinely surprised by the collapse of their marriages, who would be next?

I had visited the west coast of Vancouver Island during this year, fascinated with its wild spectacular beauty, and more than once had wondered to what extent living on the western edge of a continent affected a people. (Any place that interests me must be stared at until I can glimpse what it must mean to those who live there. Even then, I find myself poking at it until it suggests a metaphor. Where was the metaphor in living at the ragged green edge of the world?) A magazine article drew my attention to the attitude of native Indians to the coastal dividing line between land and sea – stories of Kanikuluk, the monster who came up out of the sea and changed people into fish, fish into people. I read of the fissure that lies beneath the sea not far from here, the crack in the ocean floor that oozes molten stuff from the underworld, pushing the continents apart.

Separation, separation. Land and sea, human and fish, husband and wife, man and family, adult and plaything, man and work . . .

During this year I had also, not incidentally, been able to observe how my uncle had recovered from the blow of the lost locomotive. In fact he was doing quite well. While holidaying in California he'd received a call from Ottawa. To his delight, the officials hadn't been able to put Old Number One together again. They needed him. They flew him directly to Ottawa and paid expenses while he lent his expertise. His wife, though almost as exasperated as Stella Delaney by the constantly listened-to tapes, did not show any signs of letting this affect their marriage. She seemed to delight in accepting – as all members of my family seem to accept quite joyfully – that a person's obsession, however eccentric, is what defines him best.

Perhaps this was what I needed. Spit and my uncle had parted company. By reacting so differently from the original, my character had freed himself (in my mind) to take charge of his own life in his own way. I was ready to try a new draft. Remaining as faithful as I knew how to the language and personality of the Spit of the anecdote (that is, by falling into the remembered idiom of my growing-up place), I allowed those various other related matters to join the story and help nudge Spit Delaney through his rapidly collapsing world.

Of course there was more to be done than mere "nudging." If Spit and his experiences were not to be mere entertainments any more, to be observed with amused smiles, I was faced with the need to build something else. He and his story – his life – were to be constructed in such a way that a reader travelling past (or through) the words would be taken on a journey of the emotions that might approximate Spit's own journey, or might at least allow the reader to empathize with this imaginary person. And I had nothing at all from which to build this man but words.

He had, of course, a name. A gangly name, with the rise and fall of his own long step. The first a rude, rustic nickname with some explosion in its sound. (No passive kindly Trevor, no fancy Roderick, not even an ordinary solid Pete. His was a name you could put in your hands and *expect things from*.) An Irish surname, a peasant name, but of the sort that originated elsewhere in the misty past. French aristocracy well and truly hidden? More than the eye might see, though the eye might be accustomed to stretching things a little.

Being first a name, he then became an image. "People driving by don't notice Spit Delaney." Why not? If people driving by didn't notice him was he worth looking at? Perhaps the reader would like to be someone who didn't just drive by. (An invitation to read.) If that was the case, then what was there to see? An old gas station, some second-growth firs, a scalloped row of half-tires planted instead of a fence, a figure seated on a big rock, scratching his narrow chest. A man on a rock. Watching the world go by. Watching the world go by that had no time for watching him sit still. A few words flung at the page in such a way that they assembled themselves into something resembling a sketch of a sitting man.

Muttering. He was also a sound. A complaint. An unhappy long-necked man in engineer cap, giving a side-tilted look. Muttering. An attitude: he despised those who noticed him – hitch-hikers – as much as he was fascinated by them. "Stupid old fool." Yet he grinned at the grizzled old man with the yellowed beard.

And thinking: I am a wifeless man. Spit Delaney was nobody's uncle now, nor was he the full-blown hologram result of some magician spell. He began to take life, if he took life at all, from the words: a name, a collection of images, a sound, an attitude, a thought, a sentence spoken aloud (though not by him). "There's enough in the fridge to last you a week." His wife Stella thus pronounced his doom – which would last, presumably, for quite a bit longer than a week.

Then a hitch-hiker's gaze caught Spit's gaze and something changed. Spit might be made up of words, but the words included an assumption. He had assumed that he was a survivor – until now – a man in his forties who thought his marriage was safe. It seemed that it wasn't as safe as he thought. This man-made-of-words had been thrown for a loop, just before we met him, by this shocking discovery. Nothing in life was quite as safe as he'd thought.

Thus the process of revising the story was a matter of quite literally re-visioning it – that is, not trying to "fix up" the earlier draft but seeing it again from a new perspective and starting all over again. This time the impulse was not a tale heard and a desire to retell it – or at least not *only* that – but the explosion that occurred somehow in my imagination when those various elements collided.

New life – its own – had begun there. My job was to find it, and keep it breathing, and help it seek out its end. Building it line by line out of words.

Hitch-hikers helped me get started. Because here was something else that had happened during that year. Suddenly you couldn't drive a mile along the highway without feeling you were part of a parade. All along the gravel shoulder, hitch-hikers in violently coloured clothing (or in almost no clothing at all) sat or lay or occasionally stood with thumbs upraised, heading for the west coast – nude beaches, makeshift driftwood communities, "plenty of good grass, man, and friends from all over the planet." (Earth had ceased being a world about that time and become a planet instead, making us feel as if we'd just stepped off a space ship and didn't know whether we ought to stay.) If these hitch-hikers had been brought up on Vancouver Island they would know that the idea was to keep on walking when you weren't thumbing cars – to show you intended to get where you were going with or without the help of someone else's gas. These people took an all-or-nothing approach, not knowing this would offend the native view of things. "If you don't pick me up, I'll lie here spoiling the view until someone does." I did not drive over any of them myself. Nor did I especially feel a need to. But I knew many who would, heard many who planned to, saw many come as close as anyone dare. Spit Delaney would hate them. Going somewhere (while he went nowhere), they thought the next guy ought to take them. At the same time he would be fascinated: if he was forced to look at them, he could also imagine that they might look at him as well. See someone *suffering*, in fact.

Listening. Listening. That's what it took. Not listening to some voice from the clouds, not listening to the characters themselves as though they could stand up and give me orders. But listening to what the story was trying to tell me as it revealed itself. In words. Its secret life. I wasn't changing all that much in the sequence of events. What I had done was allow a cartoon figure to become a human

being whose pulse I could take; what I was doing now was keeping
that heart beating long enough to let him find out – or not find out –
what was happening to him. Words – the sound and shape and
meaning of words – supplied the blood. Sentence grew from sentence to complete the job.

When poor Spit, beset like Job, opened his mouth and shouted at
me, quite uninvited, from the edge of the sea, I learned very quickly
why his story was one I wanted to pursue, why all those related matters had been preoccupying me. They were all shouting the same
thing at me that much good writing does, all *living* does: how do you
determine where the line is between the real and the unreal, the lasting and the temporal? Spit had simply been unfortunate enough to
run headfirst into a question I thought I'd have my entire lifetime to
answer.

When all this listening and staring and rewriting had finally led
me to the moment that I recognized must be the end of the story,
right where I'd expected to find a resolution there was not much of a
resolution at all. Stripped of his marriage, his family, his job, his
home, and his sense of purpose, he had grown only enough to be
aware that he *had* a problem. I left him crying out in his anguish:
"Okay, you sonofabitch, where is that dividing line?" However hard
I looked I found nothing to suggest any other kind of ending for this
story. It was done. A few attempts at closure simply flapped like torn
gaudy rags off the end. I threw them away and sent the story to my
editor with the suggestion that it be added to the story collection
that still awaited publication, and another taken out to make room.
He agreed. Life – the rest of life, that is – could go on.

It did. So, however, did Spit. That story's end may have been good
enough for literary purposes – it was definitely over – but somehow
it was not good enough for *me*. It took me six months to realize that
I was more than a little worried about the welfare of that man I'd left
howling out his anguish on the edge of the sea. How was he making
out? I found myself thinking: What is Spit Delaney doing at this

moment? Have he and Stella got together again? Has he made some sense of his life? Has he fallen apart altogether?

Occasionally I'd felt something similar after reading other people's stories but I'd never felt an impulse to do anything about it. This was different. It wasn't someone else who'd left Spit howling like that, it was me. Eventually I determined to find out what had happened to him. And the only way I knew of finding out was to write another story about him. Spit Delaney a year later. No one else need know what I found. I needn't publish the results. I'd just do this thing for myself.

I tried several times without success. I planned, mapped out a story. (According to some inherited notion of how a story should take shape, ignoring my own better knowledge.) Tried to employ all the techniques that had gone into the making of the first story. Took up the same narrator's voice, the same language, the same point of view. One paragraph, two paragraphs. It didn't work. Try again. It didn't work. Why? Because I was trying to continue the old story instead of making a new one. Because I was trying to *manufacture* a story. Instead of being the builder who walks onto a piece of land and wonders what it offers that could be used to advantage – how a house could be designed to fit around that beautiful tree, how a garden could make use of that awkward hump of rock, how that creek might run past the living-room window instead of being buried in pipes and culverts beneath the ground – I was trying to be that builder who walks onto the lot with a commercial plan designed in some New York office and published in a magazine. "Cut down those trees. Blast out that rock. We'll put the Cape Cod house right here where it can overlook the Strait of Juan de Fuca." Maybe there was no real reason to write the second story after all.

But: I could not rid myself of the notion that Spit himself wanted me to do this thing. Apparently I was not to know what his reason was until I'd written it.

The solution, it seemed to me, was to abandon my attempts to tell the story of what happened to him and let him tell it himself. This time, instead of being the teller I'd be the listener. Let the bugger surprise me.

He did. I found him in a little seaside motel called the Touch and Go, willing to tell me something he would never tell his friend Marsten or his landlady, Mrs Bested. Something significant had indeed happened to him since I'd seen him last, or had begun to happen. He'd met this woman –

Naturally the woman who would intrigue Spit enough to start his life back on course (or wreck it altogether) would have to be a member of that class of hippie hitch-hikers he despised. Naturally she would lead this discarded man to a secondhand store; naturally she would challenge this man who'd been too attached to a train with a world of cast-off *things*; naturally she would invite this legless man she'd found floundering at the ocean's edge to come climbing with her in the mountains. The rest was entirely up to him.

This second story, quite unlike the first, presented itself in a single writing, once I'd decided to let it be told in Spit's own voice. Very little revising seemed advisable. I'd received the man's report and read it; there was nothing left to do but send it off to join "Separating" in that collection of stories (which *still* awaited publication), where it would replace another story and give the collection the title it had been waiting for. One story would open the collection, the other end it. Bookends, reviewers would say. This latecomer would not only give the collection its name and control its structure, he would – it turned out – give the appearance of having got there first and set the agenda. This first collection of stories chosen from several published over the years in magazines – simply "my best so far" – had altered its character slightly, taking on a frame that gave it the feeling almost of a collection of linked stories. Indeed, in the years since then, I have several times seen the book referred to in print as a novel. This is fine with me. I still have the feeling that, in a sense, Spit *deserved* a book of his own.

There is no lesson in any of this. Some stories arrive as gifts to be copied down and passed on, most to be tossed away. Others require planning and sweating and long periods of gestating while waiting for the fortuitous collision of related elements – to be followed by draft after draft of revising, rethinking, reworking.

In subsequent years, stories (and indeed novels) have continued to arrive in one or the other of these two different ways: the collision of separate and apparently disparate elements (some of which were clumsy earlier attempts that failed and some of which were thin and unsatisfying anecdotes and some of which were obsessions and preoccupations I thought quite outside the world of my writing) or the excited journey spent chasing along after the voice of a character who has something he feels compelled to tell me. Something, I hope, to surprise me.

And that is the one element common to all stories that begin to satisfy me – surprise. The long hard work of rewriting drafts is as much a search for the unexpected and unexplained as it is an attempt to make things better and clearer. I consider any story of little interest if all that it ultimately accomplishes is what I'd intended. I even want to be a little unsure that I fully understand it. The only stories that give me sufficient pleasure that I can bear to send them out into the world for other eyes to see are those that, when I read them, make me wonder where on earth they came from.

I want to discover myself putting down a story and thinking, "I wish I'd written that!" for a split second of wonder and envy before realizing, with joy, "Hey, I *did* write that!" It doesn't happen often, but it's something I aim for every time.

And all these years later, when I discover the number of people who feel possessive enough about the character of Spit Delaney and his problems to express vehement opinions about the manner in which he is interpreted on the stage, or in the radio adaptation, I realize I do not have the capacity or the tools to explain satisfactorily to myself or to anyone else how it was that this man and his story came into being and got loose in the world. Sometimes I am playing with fire, sometimes with magic, sometimes merely with little black figures on a page. Always, always, though, I am indulging in the marvellous business of constructing a *story*, of building a structure out of words, of spinning out a yarn, of listening to the heavy breathing from that other world.

A Postscript: And Now What?

There have always been creative schools in various forms. Like in Moscow or St Petersburg or Vienna at the turn of the century where people sat around and shared their ideas. That's all we do. I share my experience with young people. Now universities have finally recognized the value of that kind of learning environment and they're sponsoring it.

(Robert Harlow, in *For Openers*)

Avoiding Paralysis

Having worked your way through this book, you may be overwhelmed by the feeling that you ought to know and understand and remember all of it before you begin to write. It would be better for your fiction if you decided, for the time being, to relax and forget what you've read.

Well – don't forget it, just push it aside. Who could lift a finger if it were necessary to think about everything required to make that finger move in a natural way? Recently acquired "knowledge," too consciously grasped, can paralyse. The trick is to learn all you can and then somehow, despite it, find a way of writing with all the abandon and energy and joy that was once the product of a happy innocence.

Perhaps that is why I like the idea of doing more than one "first draft." In the first "first draft" you can quite happily be the half-blind explorer stumbling joyfully through a landscape full of surprises. (Or, if I must be consistent and return to my original metaphor, ploughing up an unfamiliar field in a dim light.) In that last "first draft" you are sitting down with the experience of having explored the territory thoroughly before withdrawing from it, and can now take your ideal reader (yourself) on a journey through a landscape where everything is already in place, and where the most important landmarks can be visited with a confidence that everything *not* specifically visited is nevertheless *there*, lending the recorded story its reflected light. Even the thoroughly prepared guide will find new breathing things to surprise and puzzle. In fact, it's the well-prepared guide who is most likely to be aware of the newly uncovered mysteries.

Beware of the story that doesn't leave you just a little puzzled. Perhaps if *you* can thoroughly understand your story, the story can't be doing so very much.

Creating Your Own Workshop

Some writers prefer to work in isolation, and find the notion of talking with a group of other writers about their work to be revolting – not to mention an occasion for terror. I have no trouble understanding this; I approached with doubts and trepidation every session of the only workshop I ever attended, fighting the urge to flee, wondering why I couldn't just *daydream* myself into being a writer. I don't remember precisely what I learned, but I know that the thoughtful and intelligent treatment my stumbling work was given by a skilful instructor and dedicated classmates eventually inspired me to work harder than I had ever done before, to learn from the published work I most admired, and to respect the reader.

A walking paradox in this matter, as in most others, I prefer to work in isolation myself – show nothing to anyone until I think it's truly "ready," and then only to my wife, my editor, and a friend or two – and yet like my colleagues I put a considerable amount of time, energy, and imagination into creating a workshop situation that will succeed for others. I appreciate the value of testing new work on intelligent and focused readers; I understand the need for like-minded company in a life of working alone; I have witnessed dramatic improvements in student writing too often to doubt the value of a well-run workshop at a certain stage in the development of many writers.

But a good workshop aims at eventually making itself unnecessary, since sooner or later every writer must learn to work pretty much alone – to carry on editorial meetings and workshop discussions in isolation.

Occasionally I hear of students who, suffering withdrawal symptoms, make plans to meet once a week or once a month after the end of a term, to keep the workshop process going. Almost without exception, those extended workshops have fizzled and died within a few months. The few that have kept going are groups where someone has taken on the task of giving their meetings some structure. In one case, writers take turns fulfilling the role of the workshop leader – telephoning to remind people, making sure that everyone received copies of the stories to be discussed, and acting as a focal point – or starting point at least – for discussion.

For the reader who is thinking of starting a writers' group or enrolling in an existing workshop, a brief discussion of how some workshops are run might be of interest here.

Each instructor of writing classes develops a method consistent with his or her own personality and approach to writing. Some use the story under discussion as an opportunity to give instructions about needed skills; some take the leading role in discussions, being the most experienced writer and reader in the room; others prefer to let the discussion take its course. Some deal with whatever stories are brought in, and have them read aloud; others expect stories to be submitted and read before the group meets. The teaching style that works best is usually the style the instructor is the most comfortable with – and believes in. Sometimes the teaching style of a specific instructor will be just right for the learning style of a specific student, but there is no reason to expect that should always be the case.

In Windhoek, Namibia, Dorian Haarhoff teaches a writing workshop with the title "Writing the Myths That Make Me." His interest is in encouraging writers to search for new metaphors by connecting themselves to the sources of their inspiration.

Responding to childhood memories and myths, participants will write autobiographical/fictional texts. Then, as a separate process, they will re-vision their work. The course . . . will involve active imagination, free-writing, journaling, drafts, audience and critical voice. Working individually and in groups, participants will explore experientially the sources of inspiration and the roots of meaning. The course will suggest a connection between creativity, dreams and the human birthright – words.

(Dorian Haarhoff, *Creative Writing Workshop* syllabus, University of Namibia)

In New Zealand, Bill Manhire is interested in helping his student writers find their own voices.

I'd hate it if there were a Wellington school . . . where everyone sounded the same, because the one thing I do believe very strongly, and again it's not a fashionable thing, is that each writer has their own voice, and in an important way everyone's task is to find out what that voice is. I try very hard to make sure that the students in the course chase off in a direction that is theirs, and to that extent I keep myself separate from the assessment procedure. . . . So I've devised a useful system where I'm not involved in the assessment programme, and students can go in whatever direction they feel they want to. Though, again, I keep trying to change the direction they came into the course with, because I think there's often a problem with younger writers that they have a very limited sense of their capacity. They think they can do only one thing, and probably they're capable of many others.

(Bill Manhire, in *In the Same Room*)

Like Bill Manhire, I am interested in encouraging all student writers to learn how best to find and write their own stories, how best to write them in their own particular voices – and to experiment with the skills in order to get progressively better at it. The sort of

workshop I run tends to be fairly structured, mainly because experience has taught me that I accomplish more that way. It also
depends upon a certain amount of skill at getting other people to
talk – to express their opinions clearly, to explain the reasons for
their comments, and to respond to one another's contributions.

To succeed, this method depends upon the participating writers'
willingness to submit themselves to a schedule – that is, to agree well
in advance on a date for having a story ready. I realize that this is
fairly rigid, but it encourages writers not to leave the project to the
last minute, or wait for inspiration to strike, and it means that all
stories will get the same amount of attention. It also eliminates a
great deal of confusion. Here are the guidelines I circulate:

Typed manuscripts must be distributed to each member of the
group during the meeting previous to its scheduled treatment. (Two
copies are to be given to me – one to be put in the writer's accumulating portfolio and one to be returned to the student with my comments scribbled all over it.)

Once a story has been through discussion, the student is expected to
work on subsequent drafts, and to submit the rewritten version for
the portfolio (and for discussion if the group can give it the time).

Every participant is expected to read stories by fellow students, to
make notes on these stories, and to contribute to discussions.

Chapters from a novel or novella may be substituted occasionally, so
long as they are put into context. Readers can give little useful
response to Chapter 5 if they haven't read Chapters 1 through 4 (or
read about them, at least). And if the novel is in the first draft stage, it
can be discouraging for readers to discuss a chapter which they
know could very well disappear or alter in some major way in future

drafts. To get the most out of such a discussion, the writer needs to think carefully about what sort of guidance will be useful – and to inform the group.

We will work from the assumption that students in the workshop are here because they

(a) want to be here

(b) want to improve their writing significantly

(c) have some understanding of how a workshop differs from a lecture or seminar

(d) intend to treat the opinions and the writing of fellow writers with respect, however different the points of view may be

(e) understand that while every effort will be made to encourage individual styles and approaches, the bias will be towards fiction of depth, complexity, maturity, and insight, and

(f) accept the responsibility for submitting manuscripts which have been competently typed and carefully proof-read for spelling, punctuation, and sentence structure, and for not submitting manuscripts which are too little advanced to deserve workshop attention.

Each member of the group will be assigned an editor from amongst the group, and will be an editor for another member of the group. The editor's role is to go over the story with the writer before it is submitted to the group, and to make recommendations for changes that should be made before others see it. Although the most obvious benefit of the workshop is the response and guidance the writer gets from others, almost as important is the practice the writer gets in criticizing and editing – practice which should help develop the skills to become one's own best critic and editor. To become a good editor of one's own work is essential, especially now that publishers seem less interested than ever before in considering manuscripts that aren't already nearly ready for publication.

Each member of the group is expected to read the story carefully before the meeting, and to come with notes on the distributed form. This set of notes will be given to the writer at the end of the discussion. [The form simply lists the various topics worth consideration in most fiction, and leaves space for comments. It can be made up from the checklist on revising in Chapter 10.]

During the discussion, my role will be primarily one of discussion leader. That is, I will try to ask the questions and probe the answers in such a way that they will lead to general discussion and allow the writer to hear us struggling with the story. My own comments on the story will be given to the writer at the end of the discussion, in written form.

The writer will be encouraged not to participate in the discussions. However frustrating, it can be useful to hear people struggling with a misunderstanding of your work. Certainly, if the writer is constantly setting the discussion right ("What I intended was . . .") it is possible to go away with a false sense of the story's achievement. People discussing a story can be all too easily persuaded away from an opinion when it becomes necessary to engage in argument with the writer.

The writer will be invited to speak at the end of the discussion – to raise questions that were overlooked, to respond to suggestions, to indicate his or her present relationship with the story.

Most discussions will follow roughly the following pattern:

(a) What do we think this story is trying to become? What are its distinctive features? What seems to be the writer's main interest while writing this?

(b) Where has the story succeeded? What are its strengths? Where can the writer feel a good job has been done?

(c) Where has the story so far failed? What are its weaknesses? Where does the writer need to do some more work? What more has to be done if it is to reach its potential?

(d) What advice do you have for improving the story? (Advice should be given within a specified context: "If the writer *wants* to have a story where the characters are believable, I would suggest that...")

Besides writing their own stories, and preparing for discussion of the stories of others, all members of the group are expected to be reading published short stories and novels by successful writers, and to make reference to the techniques of these writers when it is appropriate to the discussion. It is a mistake to let all of one's reading be of manuscripts written by other beginning writers; it is important always to be reading the best, and to be reminding oneself of the aimed-for standard.

Editing

Critiquing someone else's stories can be excellent training for becoming your own best editor and critic – which you must eventually become.

I like to give students not only my notes on the various areas that need attention in a story but also a copy of the manuscript with a running commentary down the margins. Perhaps the most useful service you can offer as a reader is the recording of your reactions as you're reading. We must learn to calculate the effect of what we do to our readers if we are not to go on blithely assuming that everything we write affects readers just as it affects us, or just as we *want* it to affect readers.

For example, my scribbled comments in the margins of the first page of a story might be something like the following:

Good opening sentence – makes me curious.

Why so many people in the first para? I can't tell one from another.

Sentence fragment deliberate? Why?

I'm confused. Where did this person come from?

Good "telling" details here.

I hope this apparent digression is going to pay off later.

Run-on sentence.

Another run-on sentence and I can't see any good reason for it. Check out the use of the period.

My annoyance over these grammatical problems is distracting me from enjoying the story.

Terrific dialogue exchange. The characters came to life.

But what are they doing? Their disembodied voices float.

Abrupt transition disorients me.

Good image – related to image above.

This sentence might be stronger if order reversed.

This is funny. Did you intend it to be?

I wonder if I'm intended to be so irritated by George. Already I'd like to take a baseball bat to him.

Good word choice here.

Of course, writers have been learning how to be better writers for centuries without institutionalized workshops or even informal discussion groups. Workshops and discussion groups may shorten the apprenticeship but they are not the only way to learn. I would suggest that even for those who do attend workshops with the most talented instructors, the best teachers remain the published works of good writers. These are available to even the most remote and isolated writer, so long as there are postal services, libraries, and bookstores left in the world.

Learning from Those We Admire

This book has never promised to make you a great writer, though presumably even most great writers have had to learn how to do what they do well. It is enough to expect that studying and understanding and practising the techniques discussed here could help to make you a better writer than you now are, and almost certainly will make you a better and more appreciative reader. Nearly as important as practising what you've learned about writing is putting your new reading skills to good use – to reread your favourite writers with the purpose of discovering how they solve the problems of technique discussed here. How did X make her characters leap so unforgettably to life? How did Y manage to guide me through all those transitions without confusing me?

Since I believe the best writing teachers are the well-written stories themselves, I don't hesitate when the occasional student asks for a list of my favourite novels and story collections – those books I have loved and reread and hope to reread again. Many of them are mentioned in this text. All of them, I think, demonstrate wonderfully the successful application of technique – plus a good deal more. I suppose these books are, to me, a literary version of what my story-telling relatives represented on those nights when my brother and I sat listening from the staircase landing – an exchange of voices passionately engaged in narrative.

Notes

༄

Brief Notes on Fiction Writers Quoted or Discussed

Glenda Adams, Australia, *Dancing on Coral.*

Jessica Anderson, Australia, *Tirra Lirra By the River.*

Thea Astley, Australia, *It's Raining in Mango.*

Margaret Atwood, Canada, *Wilderness Tips.*

Jane Austen, England, *Pride and Prejudice.*

Murray Bail, Australia, *Holden's Performance.*

John Banville, Ireland, *The Book of Evidence.*

Marjorie Barnard, Australia, *The Persimmon Tree and Other Stories.*

John Barth, U.S.A., *The Sot-Weed Factor.*

Nina Bawden, U.K., *Circles of Deceit.*

Victor-Lévy Beaulieu, Canada, *Don Quixote in Nighttown.*

Saul Bellow, U.S.A., *Herzog.*

Marie-Claire Blais, Canada, *A Season in the Life of Emmanuel.*

Clark Blaise, U.S.A./Canada, *A North American Education.*

Elizabeth Bowen, U.K./Ireland, *Death of the Heart.*

John Braine, U.K., *Room at the Top.*

Rita Mae Brown, U.S.A., *Rubyfruit Jungle.*

Gesualdo Bufalino, Italy, *Lies of the Night.*

Janet Burroway, U.S.A., *Cutting Stone.*

Morley Callaghan, Canada, *More Joy in Heaven.*

Peter Carey, Australia, *Oscar and Lucinda.*
Roch Carrier, Canada, *La Guerre, Yes Sir.*
John Cheever, U.S.A., *Collected Stories.*
Anton Chekhov, Russia, *The Duel and Other Stories.*
Joseph Conrad, Poland/England, *Lord Jim.*
Robert Coover, U.S.A., *The Public Burning.*
Robertson Davies, Canada, *What's Bred in the Bone.*
Charles Dickens, England, *Bleak House.*
Margaret Drabble, U.K., *The Radiant Way.*
Robert Drewe, Australia, *The Bodysurfers.*
Stevan Eldred-Grigg, New Zealand, *The Siren Celia.*
Marian Engel, Canada, *Bear.*
Laura Esquivel, Mexico, *Like Water for Chocolate.*
William Faulkner, U.S.A., *The Sound and the Fury.*
Ford Madox Ford, U.K., *Parade's End.*
E.M. Forster, U.K., *Passage to India.*
Janet Frame, New Zealand, *The Carpathians.*
Max Frisch, Switzerland, *Homo Faber.*
Mavis Gallant, Canada, *Home Truths.*
Gabriel García Márquez, Colombia, *Chronicle of a Death Foretold.*
John Gardner, U.S.A., *Grendel.*
Helen Garner, Australia, *Cosmo Cosmolino.*
William Gass, U.S.A., *In the Heart of the Heart of the Country.*
Maurice Gee, New Zealand, *Plumb.*
Nadine Gordimer, South Africa, *July's People.*
William Goyen, U.S.A., *House of Breath.*
Patricia Grace, New Zealand, *Waiariki.*
Kate Grenville, Australia, *Bearded Ladies.*
David Grossman, Israel, *See Under: Love.*
Roderick Haig-Brown, Canada, *On the Highest Hill.*
Oakley Hall, U.S.A., *Warlock.*
Rodney Hall, Australia, *Just Relations.*
Marion Halligan, Australia, *Lovers' Knot.*

Barbara Hanrahan, Australia, *The Peach Groves.*
Thomas Hardy, England, *Jude the Obscure.*
Donald Harington, U.S.A., *The Choiring of the Trees.*
Robert Harlow, Canada, *Scann.*
Shirley Hazzard, Australia, *The Transit of Venus.*
Ernest Hemingway, U.S.A., *The Sun Also Rises.*
Janette Turner Hospital, Canada/Australia, *The Last Magician.*
Elizabeth Jane Howard, U.K., *Getting It Right.*
Keri Hulme, New Zealand, *the bone people.*
Christopher Isherwood, U.K., *A Meeting by the River.*
Henry James, U.S.A., *Portrait of a Lady.*
James Joyce, Ireland, *Dubliners.*
Thomas King, Canada, *Medicine River.*
Shonagh Koea, New Zealand, *The Woman Who Never Went Home.*
Nigel Krauth, Australia, *JF Was Here.*
Robert Kroetsch, Canada, *What the Crow Said.*
Milan Kundera, Czechoslovakia, *A Book of Laughter and Forgetting.*
Margaret Laurence, Canada, *A Bird in the House.*
Henry Lawson, Australia, *Joe Wilson's Mates.*
Ursula K. Le Guin, U.S.A., *The Left Hand of Darkness.*
Jack Ludwig, Canada, *Above Ground.*
Roger McDonald, Australia, *Rough Wallaby.*
John McGahern, Ireland, *The Leavetaking.*
Hugh MacLennan, Canada, *Two Solitudes.*
Alistair MacLeod, Canada, *The Lost Salt Gift of Blood.*
Larry McMurtry, U.S.A., *Lonesome Dove.*
George McWhirter, Canada, *The Listeners.*
Margaret Mahy, New Zealand, *The Haunting.*
Bernard Malamud, U.S.A., *The Magic Barrel.*
David Malouf, Australia, *The Great World.*
Bill Manhire, New Zealand, *The New Land.*
Thomas Mann, Germany, *The Magic Mountain.*

Katherine Mansfield, New Zealand, *The Stories of Katherine Mansfield.*

Daphne Marlatt, Canada, *Ana Historic.*

Owen Marshall, New Zealand, *The Day Hemingway Died.*

Olga Masters, Australia, *The Home Girls.*

W.O. Mitchell, Canada, *Who Has Seen the Wind.*

Brian Moore, Canada, *The Lonely Passion of Judith Hearne.*

Frank Moorehouse, Australia, *Futility and Other Animals.*

Wright Morris, U.S.A., *One Day.*

Alice Munro, Canada, *Friend of My Youth.*

Iris Murdoch, U.K., *The Sea, The Sea.*

Vladimir Nabokov, Russia/U.S.A., *Ada.*

V.S. Naipaul, Trinidad/U.K., *A House for Mr Biswas.*

Edna O'Brien, Ireland, *The Country Girls.*

Flannery O'Connor, U.S.A., *Everything that Rises Must Converge.*

Frank O'Connor, Ireland, *Collected Stories.*

Michael Ondaatje, Canada, *Coming Through Slaughter.*

Walker Percy, U.S.A., *The Second Coming.*

Georges Perec, France, *Life: A User's Manual.*

V.S. Pritchett, U.K., *Collected Stories.*

David Adams Richards, Canada, *Nights Below Station Street.*

Mordecai Richler, Canada, *The Apprenticeship of Duddy Kravitz.*

Leon Rooke, Canada, *The Happiness of Others.*

Sinclair Ross, Canada, *As For Me and My House.*

Gabrielle Roy, Canada, *The Tin Flute.*

Frank Sargeson, New Zealand, *The Stories of Frank Sargeson.*

Moacyr Scliar, Brazil, *The Gods of Raquel.*

Carol Scott, Canada, *Heroine.*

Maurice Shadbolt, New Zealand, *Season of the Jew.*

Thomas Shapcott, Australia, *The Search for Galina.*

Jane Smiley, U.S.A., *The Age of Grief.*

Alexander Solzhenitzen, U.S.S.R./U.S.A., *August 1914.*

Wallace Stegner, U.S.A., *The Big Rock Candy Mountain.*
John Steinbeck, U.S.A., *The Long Valley.*
Robert Louis Stevenson, Scotland, *Kidnapped.*
Robert Stone, U.S.A., *Dog Soldiers.*
Randolph Stow, Australia, *The Merry-Go-Round in the Sea.*
Audrey Thomas, Canada, *The Wild Blue Yonder.*
Michel Tournier, France, *The Four Wise Men.*
Michel Tremblay, Canada, *Thérèse and Pierrette and the Little
    Hanging Angel.*
William Trevor, Ireland/England, *Family Sins.*
Mark Twain, U.S.A., *The Adventures of Huckleberry Finn.*
Anne Tyler, U.S.A., *Dinner at the Homesick Restaurant.*
John Updike, U.S.A., *The Poorhouse Fair.*
W.D. Valgardson, Canada, *Gentle Sinners.*
Guy Vanderhaeghe, Canada, *My Present Age.*
Mario Vargas Llosa, Peru, *The Green House.*
Sheila Watson, Canada, *The Double Hook.*
Ian Wedde, New Zealand, *Dick Seddon's Great Dive.*
Eudora Welty, U.S.A., *Collected Stories.*
Edith Wharton, U.S.A., *Ethan Frome.*
Patrick White, Australia, *Riders in the Chariot.*
Rudy Wiebe, Canada, *The Temptation of Big Bear.*
Thornton Wilder, U.S.A., *The Bridge of San Luis Rey.*
Ethel Wilson, Canada, *Mrs Golightly and the First Convention.*
Tim Winton, Australia, *That Eye The Sky.*

Many of these writers are represented by a short story in one of the
following anthologies.

Carmel Bird (ed). *Australian Short Stories.* Houghton Mifflin.
Gary Geddes (ed). *The Art of Short Fiction: An International
    Anthology.* HarperCollins.

Gerald Lynch and David Rampton (eds). *Short Fiction: An Introductory Anthology.* Harcourt Brace Jovanovich.

Bill Manhire (ed). *Six by Six: Short Stories by New Zealand's Best Writers.* Victoria University Press.

John Metcalf (ed). *The New Story Makers.* Quarry Press.

W.H. New and H.J. Rosengarten (eds). *Modern Stories in English.* Copp Clark.

Michael Ondaatje (ed). *From Ink Lake: Canadian Stories.* Lester & Orpen Dennys.

Sources of Quotations

Editions cited are those in my own library. In many cases more recent publications are available.

BOOKS OF INTERVIEWS WITH WRITERS

Alley, Elizabeth, and Mark Williams (eds). *In the Same Room: Conversations with New Zealand Writers.* Auckland University Press, 1992.

Baker, Candida (ed). *Yacker: Australian Writers Talk about Their Work.* Pan Books (Australia), 1986.

————. *Yacker 2: Australian Writers Talk about Their Work.* Pan Books (Australia), 1987.

————. *Yacker 3: Australian Writers Talk about Their Work.* Pan Books (Australia), 1989.

Cameron, Donald (ed). *Conversations with Canadian Novelists 1.* Macmillan of Canada, 1973.

————. *Conversations with Canadian Novelists 2.* Macmillan of Canada, 1973.

Gibson, Graeme (ed). *Eleven Canadian Novelists.* House of Anansi, 1973.

Island, issue 50 (Autumn 1992). Sandy Bay, Tasmania.

Plimpton, George (ed). *The Writer's Chapbook.* Penguin Books, 1992.

——. *Writers at Work: The Paris Review Interviews.* Penguin Books.

Turcotte, Gerry (ed). *Writers in Action: The Writers Choice Evenings.* Currency Press, 1990.

Twigg, Alan (ed). *For Openers: Conversations with 24 Canadian Writers.* Harbour Publishing, 1981.

——. *Strong Voices: Conversations with 50 Canadian Authors.* Harbour Publishing, 1988.

BOOKS ABOUT WRITING AND READING

Alter, Robert. *The Pleasures of Reading in an Ideological Age.* Simon and Schuster, 1989.

Booth, Wayne C. "Distance and Point-of-View." *Essays in Criticism* XI (1961).

Bowen, Elizabeth. "Notes on Writing a Novel," in *The Writer's Craft.* John Hersey, ed. Knopf, 1981.

Braine, John. *Writing a Novel.* McGraw-Hill, 1975.

Brown, Rita Mae. *Starting from Scratch.* Bantam, 1988.

Burroway, Janet. *Writing Fiction: A Guide to Narrative Craft.* 3rd ed. HarperCollins, 1992.

Conrad, Joseph. Preface to *The Nigger of the 'Narcissus'.* J.M. Dent & Sons.

Eliot, T.S. *The Sacred Wood: Essays on Poetry and Criticism.*

Flynn, Christine, and Paul Brennan. *Patrick White Speaks.* Primavera Press, 1989.

Friedman, Norman. "Forms of the Plot," *Journal of General Education* VIII (1955).

Forster, E.M. *Aspects of the Novel.* Harcourt, Brace, 1927.

Gass, William H. *Fiction and the Figures of Life.* David R. Godine, 1989.

Grenville, Kate. *The Writing Book*. Allen & Unwin, 1990.

Hall, Oakley. *The Art and Craft of Novel Writing*. Writer's Digest Books, 1989.

Hersey, John (ed). *The Writer's Craft*. Knopf, 1981.

Keen, Sam, and Anne Valley-Fox. *Your Mythic Journey: Finding Meaning in Your Life Through Writing and Storytelling*. Jeremy P. Tarcher, 1989.

Kroetsch, Robert. *The Lovely Treachery of Words: Essays Selected and New*. Oxford University Press, 1989.

Kundera, Milan. *The Art of the Novel*. Trans by Linda Asher. Grove Press, 1988.

Le Guin, Ursula K. "The Carrier Bag Theory of Fiction," *Dancing at the Edge of the World*. Grove, 1989.

Macauley, Robie, and George Lanning. *Technique in Fiction*. 2nd ed. St Martin's Press, 1987.

MacCormack, Thomas (ed). *Afterwords: Novelists on Their Novels*. St Martin's Press, 1988.

Metcalf, John (ed). *Making it New*. Methuen, 1982.

Minot, Stephen. *Three Genres: The Writing of Poetry, Fiction, and Drama*. 3rd ed. Prentice-Hall, 1982.

Morris, Wright. *About Fiction*. Harper and Row, 1975.

Nabokov, Vladimir. *Lectures on Literature*. Harcourt Brace Jovanovich, 1982.

Naylor, Phyllis Reynolds. *The Craft of Writing a Novel*. The Writer, 1989.

O'Connor, Flannery. *Mystery and Manners*. Farrar, Straus and Giroux, 1969.

O'Connor, Frank. *The Lonely Voice: A Study of the Short Story*. Harper and Row, 1985.

Percy, Walker. *Sign Posts in a Strange Land*. HarperCollins Canada, 1991.

Perrine, Laurence. *Story and Structure*. Academic Press Canada, 1981.

Rico, Gabriele. *Writing the Natural Way.* Jeremy P. Tarcher, 1983.

Schorer. Mark. *The World We Imagine: Selected Essays.* Farrar, Straus and Giroux, 1968.

Stegner, Wallace. *Where the Bluebird Sings to the Lemonade Springs: Living and Writing in the West.* Random House, 1992.

Steinbeck, John. *Journal of a Novel.* Viking, 1969.

Stern, Jerome. *Making Shapely Fiction.* W.W. Norton, 1991.

Thomas, Audrey. "Basmati Rice," in *Canadian Literature.*

Vargas Llosa, Mario. *A Writer's Reality.* Syracuse University Press, 1991.

Welty, Eudora. *The Eye of the Story: Selected Essays and Reviews.* Random House, 1979.

West, Ray B., Jr. *The Art of Writing Fiction.* Crowell, 1968.

Wharton, Edith. *The Writing of Fiction.* C. Scribner's Sons, 1925.

FICTION

Adams, Glenda. *Longleg.* HarperCollins, 1991.

Astley, Thea. *A Boat Load of Home Folk.* Penguin Books, 1983.

Atwood, Margaret (ed). *Best American Short Stories 1989.* Houghton Mifflin, 1989.

Atwood, Margaret. *Cat's Eye.* McClelland and Stewart Inc., 1988.

Banville, John. *Kepler.* Minerva, 1990.

Barnard, Majorie. "The Persimmon Tree," *The Persimmon Tree and Other Stories.* Clarendon, 1943.

Beaulieu, Victor-Lévy. *Don Quixote in Nighttown.* Press Porcépic, 1978.

Bellow, Saul *Mr Sammler's Planet.* Penguin Books, 1982.

Blais, Marie-Claire. *Mad Shadows.* New Canadian Library, McClelland and Stewart Inc., 1971.

Bowen, Elizabeth. *Eva Trout.* Penguin Books, 1987.

———. *The Little Girls.* Penguin Books, 1985.

Carey, Peter. *The Tax Inspector.* Knopf, 1991.

Conrad, Joseph. *Nostromo.* Oxford University Press, 1984.

Crane, Stephen. "The Bride Comes to Yellow Sky," *The Portable Stephen Crane.* Joseph Katz (ed). Penguin Books, 1977.

Davies, Robertson. *Murther & Walking Spirits.* McClelland and Stewart Inc., 1991.

Drewe, Robert. *The Savage Crows.* Fontana Paperbacks, 1986.

Eldred-Grigg, Stevan. "When Bawds and Whores Do Churches Build," *The Oxford Book of New Zealand Writing Since 1945.* Macdonald P. Jackson and Vincent O'Sullivan (eds). Oxford University Press, 1983.

Ford, Ford Madox. *The Good Soldier.* Random House, 1955.

Frisch, Max. *I'm Not Stiller.* Trans by Michael Bullock. Random House, 1958.

Gallant, Mavis. "In Youth Is Pleasure," *Home Truths: Selected Canadian Stories.* Macmillan of Canada, 1981.

García Márquez, Gabriel. *Autumn of the Patriarch.* Trans by Gregory Rabassa. HarperCollins, 1991.

———. *One Hundred Years of Solitude.* Trans by Gregory Rabassa, Harper and Row, 1970.

Gee, Maurice. *Plumb.* Oxford University Press, 1979.

Goyen, William. "Bridge of Music, River of Sand," *The Collected Stories of William Goyen.* Doubleday, 1975.

Grace, Patricia. "A Way of Talking," *Six by Six: Short Stories by New Zealand's Best Writers.* Bill Manhire (ed). Victoria University Press, 1989.

———. *Potiki.* Penguin Books, 1986.

Grenville, Kate. *Joan Makes History.* University of Queensland Press, 1988.

Haley, Russell. "Barbados – A Love Story," *The New Fiction.* Michael Morrissey (ed). Lindon Publishing, 1985.

Hall, Rodney. *Captivity Captive.* Farrar, Straus and Giroux, 1988.

Halligan, Marion. *The Hanged Man in the Garden.* Penguin Books, 1989.

Hardy, Thomas. *The Mayor of Casterbridge.* Penguin Books, 1978.

Hazzard, Shirley. *The Transit of Venus.* Playboy Paperbacks, 1981.

Hemingway, Ernest. "Hills Like White Elephants," *Men Without Women.* Charles Scribner's Sons, 1955.

Hodgins, Jack. *Spit Delaney's Island.* New Canadian Library, McClelland and Stewart Inc., 1992.

Hospital, Janette Turner. *Charades.* McClelland and Stewart Inc., 1989.

King, Thomas. *Green Grass, Running Water.* HarperCollins, 1993.

Koea, Shonagh. "Mrs Pratt Goes to China," *The Woman Who Never Went Home and Other Stories.* Penguin Books, 1987.

Krauth, Nigel. *Matilda, My Darling.* Allen & Unwin, 1983.

Laurence, Margaret. "A Gourdful of Glory," *The Tomorrow Tamers.* Knopf, 1960.

Lawson, Henry. "The Drover's Wife," *Australian Short Stories.* Carmel Bird (ed). Houghton Mifflin, 1991.

Ludwig, Jack. "Requiem for Bibul," *Great Canadian Short Stories.* Alec Lucas (ed). Dell, 1971.

McGahern, John. *Amongst Women.* Penguin Books, 1990.

MacLennan, Hugh. *The Watch That Ends the Night.* Macmillan, 1960.

MacLeod, Alistair. "The Boat," *The Lost Salt Gift of Blood.* McClelland and Stewart Inc., 1976.

Mansfield, Katherine. "Miss Brill" and "The Wind Blows," *The Stories of Katherine Mansfield.* Oxford University Press, 1988.

Marlatt, Daphne. *Ana Historic.* Coach House Press, 1988.

Masters, Olga. "The Dog That Squeaked" and "The Snake and Bad Tom," *The Home Girls.* University of Queensland Press, 1982.

Mitchell, W.O. *Who Has Seen the Wind.* Laurentian Library, Macmillan Canada, 1972.

Moore, Brian. *Black Robe.* Penguin Books, 1985.

Morris, Wright. *In Orbit.* New American Library, 1967.

Munro, Alice. "Thanks for the Ride," *Dance of the Happy Shades.* The Ryerson Press, 1968.

Naipaul, V.S. *The Mystic Masseur.* Penguin Books, 1977.

———. "My Aunt Gold Teeth," *A Flag on the Island.* Andre Deutsch, 1976.

O'Brien, Edna. *A Pagan Place.* Penguin Books, 1971.

O'Connor, Flannery. "Good Country People," *A Good Man is Hard to Find,* 1955, in *Three by Flannery O'Connor,* Signet.

O'Connor, Frank. "First Confession," *Short Fiction: An Introductory Anthology.* Gerald Lynch and David Rampton (eds). Harcourt Brace Jovanovich Canada, 1992.

Ondaatje, Michael. *In the Skin of a Lion.* McClelland and Stewart Inc., 1987.

O'Sullivan, Vincent. "Palms and Minarets," *Some Other Country: New Zealand's Best Short Stories.* Marion McLeod and Bill Manhire (eds). Unwin Paperbacks, 1988.

Percy, Walker. *The Moviegoer.* Knopf, 1961.

Pritchett, V.S. *Collected Stories.* Penguin Books, 1984.

Richards, David Adams. *Road to the Stilt House.* HarperCollins, 1990.

Richler, Mordecai. *The Apprenticeship of Duddy Kravitz.* Paperback Library, 1959.

Rooke, Leon, *Fat Woman.* Oberon, 1980.

———. "If Lost Return to the Swiss Arms," *The Love Parlour.* Oberon Press, 1977.

———. *Shakespeare's Dog.* General Publishing, 1983.

———. *The Good Baby.* McClelland and Stewart Inc., 1989.

Ross, Sinclair. "One's a Heifer," *The Lamp at Noon and Other Stories.* New Canadian Library, McClelland and Stewart Inc., 1968.

Roy, Gabrielle. *The Tin Flute.* Trans. by Hannah Josephson. New Canadian Library, McClelland and Stewart Inc., 1969.

Shadbolt, Maurice. *The Lovelock Version.* Coronet Books, 1982.

Stow, Randolph. *Tourmaline.* Penguin Books, 1984.

Thomas, Audrey. *Blown Figures*. Talonbooks, 1974.

———. "Initram," *Short Fiction: An Introductory Anthology*. Gerald Lynch and David Rampton (eds). Harcourt Brace Jovanovich Canada, 1982.

Trevor, William. "Events at Drimaghleen," *Family Sins and Other Stories*. The Bodley Head, 1990.

Updike, John (ed). *Best American Short Stories 1984*. Houghton Mifflin, 1984.

Valgardson, W.D. "The Man Who Was Always Running Out of Toilet Paper," *What Can't Be Changed Shouldn't Be Mourned*. Douglas and McIntyre, 1990.

Vanderhaeghe, Guy. "The Watcher," *Man Descending*. Macmillan of Canada, 1982.

Watson, Sheila. *The Double Hook*. McClelland and Stewart, 1959.

White, Patrick. *The Tree of Man*. Penguin Books, 1983.

Wilson, Ethel. "Mrs Golightly and the First Convention," *Mrs Golightly and the First Convention*. New Canadian Library, McClelland and Stewart, 1991.

Winton, Tim. *Cloudstreet*. Pan Books, 1992.

Acknowledgements

卵

An earlier version of "Breathing from Some Other World" and several other passages will be published in the anthology *How Stories Mean,* edited by John Metcalf and J.R. (Tim) Struthers.

Hundreds of students over many years have indirectly contributed to the contents of this book, by demanding explanations, examples, clearer direction, and practice exercises. Many have contributed through their participation in classroom discussions. Several of these pages began as handouts that I prepared out of an impatience with my own habit of forgetting too much of what I wanted to say, and a dissatisfaction with words that merely sail out through the air as noise without finding a more lasting home on the page. For opportunity, support, and suggestions in response to early drafts of these pages, I am grateful to students and colleagues at the University of Ottawa, the University of Victoria, and the Saskatchewan Summer School of Writing at "Fort San."

I am particularly grateful to Jay Connolly and Hart Hanson, for numerous conversations and valuable advice; to Gavin Hodgins and Heidi Bugslag, for help in preparing the bibliographies and the excerpts; and to Bill Chalmers, who, as a work-study student employed by the University of Victoria, gave me invaluable assistance in the earliest stages.

I have made an attempt to acknowledge all sources, though I have made so much of what I have read "my own" over the years that it hasn't always been easy to discover origins. Permission to include the longer quotations is appropriately acknowledged on the following page. To the writers of the shorter passages from interviews and works of fiction, I wish to express my admiration and gratitude, not only for the fine examples and illuminating comments but also for the countless hours of reading pleasure they have given me.

Further Acknowledgements

The author gratefully acknowledges the permission of the following publishers to reproduce excerpts from their publications:

Associated Press, for the news stories "Death Encounters Couple Looking for Flying Saucer" ("UFO") and "Argument Over Popcorn Ends in Theatre Slaying" " (Popcorn").

Sheil Land Associates Ltd., London, for the excerpt from *Kepler*, John Banville.

Georges Borcharolt, Inc., for the excerpt from "In Youth Is Pleasure" from *Home Triths*, Mavis Gallant Copyright ©1956

Alfred A. Knopf, Inc., for *The Tax Inspector*, Peter Carey. Copyright © 1991 by Peter Carey.

Currency Press, Sydney, Australia, for the extract by David Malouf from *Writers in Action. The Writer's Choice Evenings*, edited by Gerry Turcotte.

Curtis Brown Ltd., London on behalf of Maurice Shadbolt for the excerpt from *The Lovelock Version*, copyright © 1980 by Maurice Shadbolt.

Clark Blaise for the exerpt from "To Begin, To Begin".

McPhee Gribble, Australia, for *Cloudstreet*, copyright © Tim Winton 1991.

HarperCollins, N.Y. for *Writing Fiction: A Guide to Narrative Craft*, Janet Burroway, and for *Art of Writing Fiction*, Ray B. West.